Waiting for the Cubs

Waiting for the
Cubs

*The 2008 Season,
the Hundred-Year Slump
and One Fan's Lifelong Vigil*

Floyd Sullivan

McFarland & Company, Inc., Publishers
Jefferson, North Carolina, and London

LIBRARY OF CONGRESS CATALOGUING-IN-PUBLICATION DATA

Sullivan, Floyd.
    Waiting for the Cubs : the 2008 season, the hundred-year slump
and one fan's lifelong vigil / Floyd Sullivan.
        p.   cm.
    Includes bibliographical references and index.

    ISBN 978-0-7864-4902-6
    softcover : 50# alkaline paper ∞

    1. Chicago Cubs (Baseball team)—History.   I. Title.
GV875.C6S88   2010
796.357' 640977311—dc22   2010012828

British Library cataloguing data are available

On the cover: Wrigley Field at sunset (Photograph by Chad
Bontrager) ©2010 Shutterstock

Manufactured in the United States of America

McFarland & Company, Inc., Publishers
    Box 611, Jefferson, North Carolina 28640
        www.mcfarlandpub.com

For Trudy

Acknowledgments

This book is largely a memoir, which means that it relies heavily on the often dubious memory of its author. I apologize for any misrepresentation caused by my limited ability to recall events of the past fifty years. Where the accounts are accurate, I had assistance and therefore thank the following for their help not only in verifying the contents of the following work, but also in supporting the effort in a variety of ways. If I leave anyone out, I apologize again and only ask that you forgive my sins of unintentional omission. Thanks to:

Mike Cahill, Bob Cooney, Bob Ficks, Mark Fusello, Charles Lyon and Al Yellon, and to my brother Stephen J. Sullivan, for their memories of Cub games going back over the decades.

Chris DeMain for help on Waveland Avenue and with tickets.

Angelo Louisa, who first encouraged my baseball writing and who provided support and advice that led directly to publication.

Jeff Musselman for his hospitality during visits to West Baden, Indiana, and for breaking the ice at the Lancaster, Pennsylvania, train station.

Mary Tiegreen for her advice and support.

Marlyce Tingstad for photographs of and information about the Pulliam family.

Dorothea Tobin for stories of her parents and the O'Connor family.

The staff at the Chicago History Museum, including Leslie A. Martin, research specialist, and Anne Marie F. Chase, circulation assistant, who helped so much with researching the museum's collections; and Erin Tikovitsch, rights and reproductions assistant, who expedited the reproduction of historic images.

The staff at the A. Bartlett Giamatti Research Center at the National Baseball Hall of Fame and Museum in Cooperstown, New York, including Freddie Berowksi, research assistant, who located and copied files on the Cubs, Harry Pulliam and others in the hall's collections; and Timothy J. Wiles, director of research, who provided invaluable advice and helped me discover that Harry Pulliam's stenographer was probably named Lenore.

Tom Boyle at Yesterday on Addison Street in Chicago, just west of Wrigley Field, for taking the time to search their wonderful collections for Cub artifacts, and for sharing his Cub memories with me.

Dave Ryan, University of Illinois at Chicago engineer, and the group in the shop whose names I am sorry I did not get, who directed us to West Side Park's home plate.

Debbie Turner, concierge, West Baden Springs Hotel, West Baden Springs, Indiana, who directed us to the site of spring training 1908; and Sandi Woodward, program manager, Historic Landmarks Foundation of Indiana, for advice concerning research into the Cubs 1908 spring training.

And finally, and most importantly, to the Sullivans and Meissners, and you know who you are and how you helped! Their work is duly noted within the pages of the book. However, Lucy's editorial work, ideas, critiques, contributions and participation in the Epilogue stories were especially crucial to the final product.

Table of Contents

Preface

"I was at that game."

Baseball fans love to tell the stories of memorable games they've seen in person, but too often for Cub fans those games have been more infamous than famous. One notorious example of this, Game Six of the 2003 National League Championship Series, has become baseball legend. We lived in Pennsylvania and so watched the horror of perhaps the worst disaster in Cubs history on television. Months later, while visiting Chicago, we sat with friends rehashing the monumental eighth inning meltdown.

"I was at that game," said our friend Dorothea.

"You're kidding."

"My sisters and I took my dad so he could be there with his seven daughters when the Cubs clinched. He went to the 1945 World Series."

The end of the story hung in the air like a dark fog, but was left unspoken: He would never see the Cubs win a World Series. But then no one alive has or perhaps ever will, either. Nonetheless, over the past half century of my baseball memories, there are dozens of Cub games, good and bad, that we love to relive, or can't avoid remembering, warts and all.

Which begs the question, of all the Cub games missed, which one would you choose to see in person if you could go back through the seasons and select a single game? It can be any game, any year, during your lifetime or before.

Kerry Wood's twenty strikeouts? I was on a business trip to New York for that one, sitting in a bar at LaGuardia waiting for my plane back to O'Hare to board. I overheard a couple of guys behind me talking about "that kid Wood in Chicago. Struck out twenty Astros this afternoon."

What? I found a pay phone and called home.

1

"It was unbelievable," said my wife, Lucy. "We had the game on, but I was in and out of the room, but then you just had to stop everything and watch."

Maybe Ernie Banks' 500th career home run?

Or Ryne Sandberg hitting two homers off Cardinal closer, and ex–Cub, Hall-of-Famer Bruce Sutter—the game that seemed to confirm the Cubs as true contenders in June of 1984?

Going back even further, and before my time, how about Gabby Hartnett's "Homer in the Gloamin'" that put the Cubs in first place to stay in late September 1938?

The question was first answered for me while watching Ken Burns' *Baseball* documentary on PBS in 1994. I had been following the Cubs my entire life (over four decades) but had never heard of "Merkle's Boner." How could such a crazy story all but disappear from the collective memory of Cub fans, especially since it led directly to the Cubs' last World Series championship?

So my choice is clear. I would want a seat in the front row of the upper level of the Polo Grounds in New York, September 23, 1908. I would want to have a bird's eye view and note the place of each actor in baseball's strangest tragicomedy, as New York Giant Al Bridwell steps up to the plate with two out in the bottom of the ninth inning of a Cubs–Giants 1–1 tie ballgame. As Cub pitcher Jack "the Giant Killer" Pfiester stands at the slab about to deliver his next pitch, I'd check Cub second baseman Johnny "the Crab" Evers, Cub center fielder Artie "Circus Solly" Hofman, and Giants base runners Harry "Moose" McCormick on third and poor Fred Merkle on first—too young at nineteen and too new to the big leagues to have established a nickname. The next play of the game, however, would saddle him with one of the most unfortunate and cruel monikers of all time.

And then I'd watch the ball because no one really knows what happened to the ball that day. There are as many versions of the story as there were players, fans, reporters and umpires who witnessed it, and authors, bloggers and historians who have interpreted the play ever since. There is no mechanical record of any kind. Although comparatively crude motion picture cameras and sound recording devices had been invented by 1908, it would be decades before such machines would be routinely put to use to document sporting events with film and sound.

Since watching "Inning Two" of Burns' film (although I've never been able to watch the entire series because its obvious East Coast–Boston bias made me ill), I've been somewhat obsessed by the events of 1908, and, from my point of view, their ultimately tragic conclusion in July 1909. Fred Merkle would perhaps have told you that for him, the consequences of that one play on that early autumn afternoon never ended.

My interest in that year has taken me to the Chicago Public Library's microfilm archives, the Chicago History Museum's Research Center, the A. Bartlett Giamatti Research Center at the National Baseball Hall of Fame in Cooperstown, New York, the sites of Chicago's West Side Park, Pittsburgh's Exposition Park, New York's Polo Grounds, the 1908 Cubs spring training grounds at West Baden Springs, Indiana, and the 1908 offices of the National League on the fourteenth floor of the St. James Building in Manhattan. Our daughter Anne Lise did research for me at the Louisville, Kentucky, Free Public Library.

And I've only just started.

As 2008 and the Cubs' dubious centennial approached, I thought it would be fun to document my experience of the season as it unfolded, and compare it to what I've learned about that last championship year. But as I wrote through the spring and summer months, memories of other Cub seasons, both memorable and to most fans better forgotten, came to mind and I found myself working those stories into the manuscript. And I realized that there was some symmetry at work.

The Cubs last won a World Series in Detroit on October 14, 1908. The infamous "Bartman" game occurred on October 14, 2003. My birthday is October 14. Plus my first game at Wrigley Field was in 1958, exactly fifty years after the 1908 championship season and halfway to the 100 years of frustration. True qualifications? Not really, but there's something in all of those coincidental dates that intensifies my personal connection to the Cubs.

Am I the only one? Certainly not. Are the Cubs the only team with a history of failure? No, but their story has become the most celebrated and they themselves, no matter who's on the roster, have become *the* symbol for hopelessness among all American professional sports franchises, and a metaphor for futility. I'm sick of it, and a lot of fans across the country are sick of it and would probably just as soon have the Cubs win it all so as not to be subjected to the now almost annual "Will this be the Year for the Cubs?" headlines in newspapers and sports magazines each spring. But it goes on, and 2008 was the most intense recent example of the speculation and media attention paid to the phenomenon.

This is the story of a family of Cub fans—Cub fans in exile, as we say it, for as I wrote the accounts of the games of 2008 we lived in York, Pennsylvania, and over the years had put 200,000 miles on our 2003 Accord driving to Cub games in most National League cities east of the Mississippi, plus Baltimore for interleague games. In May of 2009 we moved back home to Chicago and now walk to games from our home 1.6 miles west of Wrigley Field. We couldn't be happier.

And the 2009 Cubs that we've seen so often? As I write this it's all over but the weeping and gnashing of teeth. The promise of 2008 has typically crashed into another year of diminished expectations.

But today we sit at Montrose Harbor, looking along the lakeshore at the elegance of the Chicago skyline, a misty shadow on the horizon across the water, planning to walk to the ballpark again Thursday afternoon for a wonderfully meaningless afternoon of Cub baseball. We'll be at that game.

CHAPTER ONE

Spring Training

"We're going to win the World Series."

No, no, no, no, no, no, NO! How could he say it?

As pitchers and catchers report for spring training on Wednesday, February 13, 2008, Ryan Dempster, who is vying for a spot in the Cubs' starting rotation after four years in the bullpen, including three as closer, predicts: "I think we're going to win the World Series. I really do. I wouldn't have worked as hard as I did and everybody worked as hard as they did to not believe that."

The kiss of death! What is he thinking? And don't all ballplayers work as hard as they can every winter to prepare to earn their multi-million dollar salaries?

The hot stove league reports that Dempster has dedicated himself to getting into the best shape of his career in order to get back into the rotation. He had been a starting pitcher his first six years in the big leagues with Florida and Cincinnati, his best seasons being 2000 and 2001 when he went 14–10 and 15–12 respectively. After that he was strictly mediocre and so the Cubs acquired him in 2004 to pitch in relief.

"It's funny," Dempster continued, "when people make predictions and say things, and people say, 'How can you say that?'"

Not funny on the North Side.

"Enough of the curse this, the curse that, the goat this, the black cat, the 100 years, whatever it is. We're a better team than we were last year, I truly believe, and last year we made it to the playoffs and it was a battle to make it. I just feel our chances are better."

With him as a starter? I hope he worked *really* hard.

But in all fairness to Dempster, he's not the only one. *The Sporting*

5

News, *ESPN the Magazine*, *Sports Illustrated*, and Criswell of mlb.com all predict that the Cubs will return to the World Series for the first time since 1945. They all, however, pick the Cubs to lose against a variety of American League teams. But it's almost unanimous that they'll get there, which means it's all but impossible.

Frustration. Not an uncommon emotion for a Cub fan, and probably a bit mild considering the well-documented baseball horrors that have rained down on the Cubs over the decades. A full century of decades. But still not a good feeling to start the season as I await the first pitch of spring training 2008. It's five minutes away, a scheduled 12:05 P.M. start in Scottsdale where the Cubs will face the Giants, and 3:05 P.M. in Lebanon, Pennsylvania, where I sit facing my laptop. I am frantically searching for a site that features play-by-play, pitch-by-pitch coverage, like *Gameday* on the Cubs' website.

Gameday features an illustration of a baseball field with a cartoon pitcher and batter (both correctly shown as right-handed or left-handed), runners on base, the arc of each pitch, including speed at release and speed as it reaches home plate, along with a wealth of other statistical minutiae; it's more information than I will ever take in, especially since I'm supposed to be working. Under the illustration of the field a scrolling window gives word descriptions of every play. Pictures of the actual pitcher and batter, smiling their best baseball card smiles, are at top center. A running box score and a basic scoreboard keep the viewer up to date with the current balls-and-strikes count, number of outs, score by inning and individual player statistics.

A century ago, when the Cubs last won a World Series, fans who couldn't attend big games were treated to similar coverage, but via bulky, public contraptions that could be ten feet tall or more, featuring much more simply rendered diamonds and any combination of electric lights, pulleys, levers, lettered or numbered cards and actual baseballs to count outs and balls and strikes, keep score and indicate men on base. Think of the big green, mechanical center field scoreboard at Wrigley Field, but with a diamond rendered on it and actual electricity! Sometimes men stood by telegraph terminals and read the play-by-play through conical megaphones.

These score boards were often placed outside of the offices of the newspapers that sponsored them. Others were set on the stages of local theaters, like Orchestra Hall in Chicago or the Gotham Theater on East 125th Street in Harlem, New York City. As late as 1929 the *Chicago Herald and Examiner* mounted a Play-o-graph board on the superstructure of the elevated "el" tracks that still circle Chicago's Loop downtown business district. For the October 8, 1908, pennant-deciding game between the Cubs and the

Giants at the Polo Grounds in New York, the Giants put an electronic score-board on the façade of the St. James Building at Twenty-sixth and Broad-way, the location of both their team headquarters and the National League offices.

At 3:04 I can't find *Gameday* anywhere. It's not available on the Cubs' site, ESPN or the Giants' site. I am profoundly bugged. It's a conspiracy. Major League Baseball trying to force you to pay for something that used to be free, like the NFL Network fiasco of Thursday nights, or the Big Ten Network making a Penn State game unavailable on network TV, causing a fan uprising in Pennsylvania.

I e-mail a colleague in York, who is a Phillies fan.

"So there's no *Gameday* coverage of games anymore? Cubs are starting now and I can't find it anywhere, except audio that you have to pay for."

His reply is somewhat reassuring. "I think *Gameday* is regular season only, but don't quote me on that."

Okay, now I'm only disappointed, unless *Gameday* is dropped come Opening Day, at which point I'll be really ticked off.

I return to the Cubs' site and activate the live box score that, with a click of the refresh button, updates inning-by-inning progress and the stats. By deciphering the individual players' at bats, hits, rbi, and bases-on-balls, I can get a good idea of the details of the game.

And what a first game for the Cubs! They collect fifteen hits and beat the Giants 12–6. The starting lineup, which is almost the same as manager Lou Piniella's announced regular season Opening Day batting order, is out of the game by the third inning. Twenty-seven Cubs see action on February 28, 2008. But who cares? It's spring training! The most fun a fan can possibly have, short of winning the World Series.

On October 15, 2003, when the last out of the Cubs' season was recorded and one of the most infamous playoff chokes in baseball history was in the books, one day after a fan reached over Moises Alou's outstretched mitt to prevent the Cub left fielder from catching a foul fly down the third base line, we stared at the now darkened television screen, speechless. No calls to or from kids living in Indiana, Chicago or Brooklyn. No philosoph-ical life lessons learned. No getting up from chairs or couches to go to bed or fetch a beer. Just baseball shock. Cubs shock. Like 1984, but worse.

In Brooklyn, our daughter Jeanne had dressed her newborn twins, Lucy and Willa, in Cub onesies and invited friends to her apartment to watch baseball history being made. Jeanne and her husband, Brian, a newly con-verted Cub fan from Buffalo, wore Cub hats and shirts and cheered wildly when Kerry Wood homered. But by the sixth, their friends had to leave because they couldn't bear to see Jeanne become so profoundly depressed.

Because like the rest of us she knew it was over even with three innings left to play.

Lucy, my wife and the mother of four Cub fans, broke the funereal silence of our York home. "That's it," she said. "We're going to spring training."

"Damn right," I might have said, but don't remember. What I do remember is started making plans right then and there.

Later, we made calls to the kids living elsewhere, but we didn't talk about Bartman, Alex Gonzalez or Mark Prior. We said: "Okay. Here's the deal. We supply the hotel rooms, tickets to the games, food and booze. All you gotta do is get to Phoenix."

"I'm there," said Steve from Chicago.

"I'm there," said Anne Lise from Bloomington, Indiana.

"We're there," said Jeanne from Brooklyn.

That's how I know that spring training is the most fun you can possibly have—because we went for one week in March of 2004, and we had the most fun we've ever had. I chased ballplayers around like I was eight years old, autograph book and Sharpie in hand, sometimes, when necessary, nudging eight-year-olds out of my way. The Cubs won only one of the games we saw (fortunately, they beat the White Sox), but nobody cared! It was spring training!

This was our daily schedule for spring training in Arizona:

1. Wake up.
2. Breakfast by the hotel pool.
3. Get to the ballpark as early as allowed. Watch the workouts and chase players for autographs.
4. Watch the game and chase players not in the game, who often stroll around the ballpark, going to and from various practice facilities.
5. Hang around the park, chasing players for autographs. Chat with players, too.
6. Drinks by the hotel pool.
7. Dinner.
8. Sleep, because tomorrow's another big, meaningless day.

I realize there are a lot of spring training fans who know all the right hotels and bars for finding players after hours, but we didn't need that. We met Dusty Baker, Moises Alou, Corey Patterson and a slew of others right at the ballpark.

They're mostly gone now, on other teams, or out of baseball.

But we wish we were there this year, meeting the new players and the big names acquired during the Cubs' famous off-season spending sprees of the past couple of years, especially right fielder Kosuke Fukudome, late of the Dragons of Nagoya, Japan. In his first appearance as a Cub, Fukudome goes one-for-one with a walk, a run scored and a run batted in. He's batting 1.000!

When you arrive at the Cubs home page a video screen pops up, usually showing brief highlights from the most recent game played. But at the beginning of spring training we see a preview of the 2008 Cubs narrated by mlb.com reporter Brian McRae.

"It's been a hundred years since the Chicago Cubs last won a World Series Championship," says McRae. "This is a year the Cubs think they have all the right tools. But can the Cubs overcome an unsettled rotation, a questionable bullpen and a gap in center field? A hundred years of bad luck has to change sometime."

Yeah, but when? And why should it happen in my lifetime? Or my kids' lifetimes? Or in Willa and Lucy's lifetimes?

We know that there are Cub fans who are actually optimistic as each new season begins. We are not among them, and don't understand them. After one hundred years, why should we be optimistic? On the North Side of Chicago, optimism buys nothing but pain.

The mother of a dear Chicago friend recently lay dying, struggling to breathe, wearing an oxygen mask. She had been a Cub fan all her life. Two of her granddaughters have planned 2008 weddings, one of them scheduled for October. As the family gathered around the hospital bed, they talked about how sad it was that "Mommo" would miss the weddings. One granddaughter commented that the October wedding would fall on the same day as Game Five of the World Series. What if the Cubs get that far this year? Everybody's picking them. Mommo would probably want to watch the Cubs in the World Series rather than attend the wedding! The October bride volunteered that she and her fiancé had already changed the date to November, just in case.

Their grandmother opened her eyes and, glaring at her grandchildren, ripped the oxygen mask from her face. "Oh God," she said, struggling to breathe. "That's the stupidest thing I've ever heard. They'll never make it!"

This is a true story. And this is the kind of Cub fan we understand. Mommo passed away later that day.

A century ago, in March, 1908 the mood was quite the opposite of our perpetual gloom. As spring training got under way, the Cubs had established themselves as probably the best team in the Major Leagues. They had won the National League pennant two years running, and beat the Ty Cobb

Detroit Tigers in the 1907 World Series. In 1906 they set a major league record of 116 games won during the regular season. The Seattle Mariners, managed by Lou Piniella, tied the record in 2001, but it took them 162 games. The 1906 Cubs did it playing only 152 official games. They were a dynasty. They were expected to win, although they knew they would have to outdistance the Pittsburgh Pirates of Honus Wagner and John McGraw's New York Giants. They boasted the league's most famous double play combination in Tinker to Evers to Chance. They had arguably the best pitching staff in either league, including "Three Finger" Mordecai Brown, Ed Reulbach, Jack "The Giant Killer" Pfiester and Orval Overall.

As spring training 2008 gets underway, the final pitching rotation has not been determined beyond Carlos Zambrano, Ted Lilly and Rich Hill. And already there's controversy as Jason Marquis, brought in last year with a much-publicized three-year, twenty-one million dollar contract, complains that he has to win his spot in the rotation, instead of being inked in by Piniella in February. "If they don't want me in the rotation here in Chicago, we'll go from there. We'll see what happens," said Marquis. "I could take my services elsewhere if that's the case, and I could help another team in that capacity as a starter. My value doesn't lie in the bullpen in my mind." Great attitude. He should chat with Kerry Wood who, after years of struggling with injuries, seems not only content but pleased to have the opportunity to compete with Bob Howry and Carlos Marmol for the role of closer. This after being hailed as the best Cub starter since, well, Three Finger Brown. Manager "Sweet" Lou Piniella's response to Marquis? "If that's the case, he can go somewhere else." The Cubs get onboard the Love Train. And it's barely March.

Over the first few days of spring training we also learn that Aramis Ramirez, star third baseman and the first player to hold that position with any kind of continuity since Ron Santo, who left the Cubs in 1973, can't throw the baseball because of a tight right shoulder. Left fielder Alphonso Soriano fractured a finger. Second baseman Mark DeRosa has an irregular heartbeat. Center fielder Felix Pie, only twenty-three, needs surgery to correct testicular torsion and will be out three to five days, which generally means ten days, or perhaps the season.

"I thought this was going to be an easy spring training, I really did," Piniella said about the injuries. "I don't know, is there such a thing as an easy Cubs spring training?"

Not even a hundred years ago, Lou. In 1908 the Cubs trained in West Baden, Indiana, a resort known for its natural springs whose waters, like its namesake Baden Baden in Germany, were supposed to have health-restoring properties. The players didn't exactly have to rough it. The West Baden

Cubs' spring training in West Baden Springs, Indiana, more than a century ago. The hotel towers and world's largest dome at the time can be seen in the distance (Chicago History Museum, SDN-005537).

Springs Hotel, built in 1902, featured a six-story domed atrium, the largest in the world at the time. The luxury hotel was known as the "Eighth Wonder of the World" and was a favorite of celebrities, including Al Capone during the 1920s. It fell into disrepair for decades but has recently been restored to its original splendor.

The Cubs left for Indiana on March 4, 1908, having just hired a new trainer, A.B. Semmens. Good physical health was a concern even then. Semmens was hired, according to the *Chicago Tribune*, as "an expert on sprains and 'charley horses,' the only horses a dutiful player is supposed to know anything about." This was a not-so-veiled reference to gambling, the vice of greatest concern in 1908. Must not have been too much on the minds of Cub management, however, because the West Baden Springs Hotel was, and is, located within a mile of the French Lick Casino. Gambling, although technically illegal in 1908 Indiana, was somehow okay in French Lick. Political connections, then as now, meant everything when you wanted to make a buck.

Similar to the recent steroid scandals, the two major leagues turned a

The interior of the West Baden Springs Hotel atrium, 2009 (photograph by the author).

blind eye to the rampant betting and tampering with players and umpires by gamblers until a major scandal (the 1919 Chicago "Black Sox"), hearings and the resulting negative publicity forced them to deal with the issue. One 1908 American League player, Hal Chase of the New York Highlanders (whose nickname "Yankees" would soon become the official team name), was known to be the most talented first baseman of his era, if not of all time. He was also known to be amoral and easily convinced to throw games, or "lay down" in the language of the era, for a cut of a bookie's take. The attempted bribery of umpires at the very end of the 1908 regular season would figure prominently in the post-season disputes between National League president Harry Clay Pulliam and the owner magnates of the teams, and the tragic conclusion of those controversies.

In 2008 the issue is the Mitchell Report's revelations of steroid and human growth hormone (HGH) use among players, a mounting storm of a scandal that has finally grown too big to fight with mere public relations damage control strategies. The wordy official title of the report acts as a prelude, giving the reader a good idea of what's inside: *Report to the Commissioner of Baseball of an Independent Investigation into the Illegal Use of Steroids and Other Performance Enhancing Substances by Players in Major League Baseball.*

Named for former senator George Mitchell, who led the investigation for Commissioner Bud Selig, the report names names—89 names. The most celebrated case is that of legendary pitcher Roger Clemens, seven-time Cy Young Award winner. Going into spring training, the FBI is looking into his testimony before a House of Representatives committee investigating steroid and HGH use by players. He could be indicted for perjury and potentially go to jail.

Clemens' new-found notoriety seems to have dampened Barry Bonds' media predominance. During the 2007 season, reports of his alleged steroid use tainted his pursuit of Henry Aaron's career home run record, which he broke on August 7, hitting number 756 against the lowly Washington Nationals. His record now stands at 762. He was indicted in November of 2007 for perjury and obstruction of justice related to his steroids testimony before a grand jury. This means he could go to jail, too.

Neither Bonds nor Clemens appears on any Major League Baseball team's roster for 2008, although it was reported that Clemens would pitch batting practice to Houston Astro minor leaguers. Although they're both old by baseball standards, Bonds at 43 and Clemens at 45, chances are better than good that they would both be playing were it not for the performance-enhancing drug scandals. Then again, would they still be playing at a high level of skill if they hadn't used the drugs?

The *Mitchell Report* named dozens of other players. None concerned Cub fans too much, except perhaps Sammy Sosa who was only mentioned peripherally. Cub fans have mostly long since dismissed Sosa because of his refusal to join the team in the dugout for the last game of the 2004 season. An unforgivable sin. Corked bat? Okay, he gets the benefit of the doubt. Steroids? Perhaps, we shrug. Not suiting up? Damned forever in the hearts of Cub fans, who laugh and cheer at the story that Kerry Wood allegedly destroyed Sosa's boom box with a bat. But we'd be dishonest if we didn't admit that there's a hole in our baseball souls caused by the now stained memory of the 1998 home run race between Sosa and Mark McGwire, another superstar whose accomplishments have been tarnished by accusations of steroid use. Sosa could have had the sports god status of Michael Jordan (well, maybe almost) or Ernie Banks in Chicago. Now, we'd just as soon not think about him at all.

"CUBS BUNGED UP IN THE PHYSIQUE" screamed a headline in the March 8, 1908, edition of the *Tribune*. "MALARIA IN THE CAMP," detailed a subhead. Malaria? In Indiana? Pitcher Carl Lungren apparently had it and was taking oxygen cream and quinine to fight it. But he was improved and "resting easily in his pajamas," according to *Tribune* Cubs reporter Charles Dryden. Pitcher Jack "The Giant Killer" Pfiester was injured when a bowling ball stuck to his thumb and "dragged him half the length of the polished alley." And still the ball remained fastened to his hand until finally "released ... by soaking the entire outfit in a tub of alum water." Shortstop Joe Tinker had re-inflamed a "charley horse" suffered during an exhibition game the previous summer, giving the new trainer a chance to practice the expertise for which he was hired. Other than these health issues, and the diagnosis that most of the Cubs were "more or less bunged up," top on the list of worries was pitcher Ed Reulbach's lack of control.

We have the same concern about Rich Hill's curve, his money pitch, after watching him on television (our first chance to see the 2008 Cubs!) against the White Sox on March 13, 2008. But worst of all, there's Ryan Dempster's prediction. It looms large in the backs of our minds.

Backing up Dempster's forecast, somewhat, *The Sporting News* predicts that the Cubs will play in the World Series, their first since 1945, but lose, as they did in 1945. And in 1910, 1918, 1932, 1935 and 1938. Several of those World Series have since gone into baseball lore. The 1918 Series was famous as the last Boston Red Sox championship, until they won it twice this decade making most Cub fans, and Chicago fans in general, sick to death of Boston and its sports teams. They sold Babe Ruth to the Yankees two years later and supposedly suffered the "Curse of the Bambino," until

2004, as penance for this mortal sin. And speaking of Babe Ruth, his famous "called shot" home run happened (or didn't happen, depending on whom you believe) at Wrigley Field during the third game of the 1932 Series. The Cubs bench had been riding Ruth the entire game, and he was giving back as good as he got. In the fifth inning he gestured at ... what? The Cubs? Pitcher Charlie Root? Or the center field fence? What happened next is a matter of record. Ruth hit the ball perhaps 490 feet over the right center field fence and rounded the bases waving his arms and otherwise gloating at a silenced Cub dugout. Ruth himself didn't start verifying the story that he had pointed to the spot where he hit the ball until it became popularized. Charlie Root would hear none of it, claiming that if any batter ever tried to show him up like that, Babe Ruth or no Babe Ruth, he would have put him "on his ass."

The 1945 World Series became infamous for the origin of the Cubs' most notorious hex, the Curse of the Billy Goat. William Sianis, owner of the Billy Goat Tavern under Michigan Avenue (the inspiration for *Saturday Night Live*'s "cheeseborger! cheeseborger! cheeseborger!" skits), had two tickets to Game Four. He brought a pet goat as a publicity stunt for his restaurant. William Wrigley ordered Sianis and his goat to leave Wrigley Field because of the goat's objectionable odor. According to legend, Sianis placed a curse on the Cubs saying that they would never play another World Series at Wrigley Field. They lost that game and the next, thus losing the Series. Sianis reportedly sent a telegram to Wrigley asking the rhetorical question "Who stinks now?"

The Cubs haven't played in a World Series since. In fact, even though Wrigley Field is one of the most famous and best-loved ballparks in the world, the Cubs have never won a World Series there. In 1908, they played at West Side Park, also known as the West Side Grounds, bordered by Taylor, Polk, Wood and Lincoln (now Wolcott) on a block now occupied by the University of Illinois at Chicago Medical Center.* They played their first games at Wrigley Field, then called Weeghman Park, in 1916. The name was changed to Cubs Park in 1920 and then Wrigley Field in 1926.

The name of the ballpark, thought to be sacrosanct since then, has become the number one controversy of 2008 thus far. In April 2007, the Tri-

---

*While compiling images for this book we learned that in September of 2008 a historical marker was placed to commemorate the site of West Side Park. It is located north of Taylor Street on the west side of Wood Street, essentially left center field near the location of the ballpark's clubhouse. We returned to the site and photographed the plaque and other views of where the home of the last World Champion Cubs once stood. Upon entering a courtyard off Polk Street (third base line), a gentleman in a University of Illinois at Chicago work shirt glanced at us and asked, "Looking for home plate?" We laughed and confirmed his suspicion. He directed us to a hallway beyond a workshop on the ground floor. "Somewhere near there," he said, laughing. "Maybe in the men's room!"

West Side Park looking from right field toward home plate, 1908 (Chicago History Museum, SDN-006685).

bune Company announced that Chicago real estate mogul Sam Zell had purchased their eleven newspapers, twenty-three television stations, and the Cubs. Zell immediately announced that he would sell the Cubs, hopefully before Opening Day 2008, to help pay off debt. But that wasn't the controversial part of the deal. New owner? Okay, maybe whoever ends up with the Cubs will finally bring a World Series championship to Wrigley Field.

Wait a minute, though. Wrigley Field? Maybe not. In December of 2007, when the Tribune Company deal was completed, Zell announced that he might sell the naming rights to Wrigley Field. Baseball fans everywhere, not just Cub fans, were horrified. Change the name of Wrigley Field? Might as well sell the naming rights to Plymouth Rock, the Alamo or the battlefield at Gettysburg! How about our national landmarks? "COMCAST's Liberty Bell" has a nice rhythmic ring, so to speak.

In fact, the first Cub-related conversations I had during the hot stove league months were not about Zambrano's fragile mental health or whether Soriano would remain the leadoff man.

"They're going to rename Wrigley Field," a Yankee fan colleague said one day at work, perhaps a hint of taunting glee in his voice.

Looking from what used to be West Side Park's right field toward home plate, somewhere beyond the wall visible in the distance. Taken in a courtyard of the University of Illinois at Chicago, 835 S. Wolcott (photograph by the author).

"Yeah, well, at least it will still be standing," I retorted, dying inside. "And anyway, what's in a name? 'A rose by any other name would smell as sweet.'" But of course I do not for one minute believe that Shakespeare's words (*Romeo and Juliet*, II, ii, 1–2) apply to Wrigley Field. I, and many older Cub fans like me, don't even like it when our ballpark is referred to as "Wrigley" without the word "Field" attached, as in, "I've been to Wrigley and Fenway, and I think ..." which I hear often from, dare I say it, younger fans trying to impress with their nonchalance, baseball knowledge and profound experience. How can Red Sox fans, true Red Sox fans, stand it when they hear "Park" dropped from the name of their hallowed grounds? Fenway, by itself, is a highway and a neighborhood in Boston named for a swamp that was turned into a park by Frederick Law Olmstead, the same man who designed Riverside, Illinois, and Central Park in New York City. Okay, it's a fen, not a swamp. But a bog by any other name....

When did all this start? I don't remember anyone talking about the Cubs' ballpark as simply "Wrigley" until, say, the 1980s, when the Cubs first became hip to follow.

That's right. It wasn't always like this. The Cubs didn't use to raise their ticket prices every year and still draw over three million. Wrigley Field wasn't always one of three or four ballparks in the country that every true baseball fan just had to visit before death (Fenway Park, Yankee Stadium and Dodger Stadium being the only others I can think of as I write—and Yankee Stadium's days are numbered. There are those who say that the house that Ruth built actually died back when they remodeled it during the 1970s). Back in the Dark Ages of the 1950s and 1960s, the Cubs were lucky to get one million into the park. Three to five thousand a game was not unusual, especially in September when kids were back in school, the weather was cold and the Cubs were solidly under .500. The idea of selling the naming rights to Wrigley Field was as far from anyone's mind as, say, paying sixty-eight dollars for a seat in the bleachers.

Sixty-eight bucks? Yep. On March 14, 2008, the Cubs opened sales of tickets for dugout box seats, bullpen seats and something called Bud Light bleacher seats. (So the naming rights to at least part of the ballpark had already been sold!) Dugout Box Seats—$300 for prime games. Bullpen Seats—$220 for prime games. Bud Light bleacher seats—$68 for prime games.

What's a prime game? For several years now, the Cubs and other major league teams have maximized gate receipts by charging more for weekend, holiday and other games for which they anticipate heavy demand. Regular games are cheaper and value games can be less than half the price of prime games. For 2008, out of eighty-one home games, fifty are expensive prime dates, twenty-five are regular games and a whopping six are lower-priced value games. There will be no regular or value games during the months of June, July or August when school's out and kids could theoretically take the el to the ballpark. The generous six value games all take place weekday afternoons in April and May when kids are in school and can't take advantage of the lower prices. There will be no value games in September, a sign of management optimism that the Cubs will be in the pennant race come the end of the season and demand for tickets will be high. Even if they're not in the hunt, those tickets will all be sold long before school starts, snatched up by corporations, scalpers and other speculators buying Cub futures like so many pork bellies.

Value game tickets range from ten dollars for the second level of the upper deck above the bullpens to fifty dollars for box seats (except for the previously mentioned dugout, bullpen and Bud Light seats); regular game tickets go for sixteen to seventy dollars, and prime game tickets are twenty to eighty dollars.

It cost a dollar to get into the bleachers at the beginning of the 1970s. We usually sat in center field, under the scoreboard. Beer was fifty cents, but the beer man did not walk the bleacher aisles. Vendors stood at the bottom of the steps on either side of the center field bleachers, cases of bottles of Old Style and Schlitz stacked behind them. By the seventh inning, the Old Style was generally gone and you were stuck with Schlitz for the rest of the game, not that you could taste the difference by then. And beer sales did not end in the eighth inning. In fact, when you left the ballpark, you had to run a gauntlet of beer vendors standing at the exits trying to unload the last few beers in their racks. A common sight in the neighborhood back then was already over-served fans stumbling to their next destination (often one of the local bars) carrying full ballpark beer cups.

I don't doubt that the situation was the same in 1908. Drunkenness among baseball rooters was an issue, especially during an era when fans were encouraged to storm the field after home team wins. Ushers and police opened the gates onto the field to give them easier access to the diamond, their home team heroes, and, most dangerously, players on the visiting team.

During the 1970s we could watch the game and drink our beer in relative peace, with only five to twenty-five other fans in the center field bleachers. We'd have not just a whole row but hundreds of square feet to ourselves as one of the unwritten laws of sitting in the center field bleachers was, "Thou shalt not crowd the other fan sitting in the section." The left field bleachers were generally pretty full and the right field bleachers less so. Below us the gamblers sitting in the right center bleachers (made famous by the play *Bleacher Bums*, conceived by actor Joe Mantegna and written by members of Chicago's Organic Theater Company), were busy putting money on every play, every inning, and sometimes every pitch. "Even money nobody reaches," might be shouted out before the start of an inning. "I'll take a buck of that," comes a reply.

I recall discussing these guys with my sister Jeanne. She found it hard to believe that they were real people. I assured her that they were very real and that the play was in no way a study in caricature, and invited her to a game to experience that section of the bleachers for herself. So we went to a meaningless weekday game and sat among the gamblers. At one point a runner on first tried to steal on the Cubs. The throw to second went into center field (not unusual). One of the gamblers, the guy played by Joe Mantegna I was sure, said it was an E6 (error on the shortstop for missing the throw). I said, no, it had to be E2 (error on the catcher for a bad throw), at which point he said, "Four gets you five it's E6." And thus I was almost drawn into the action. However, before I could respond, the official scorer ruled it a stolen base. There could be no error because the runner did not advance to third, and so there could be no bet.

We rarely ventured down to the lower bleacher seats, visiting the gamblers' section only to observe the action. Mostly we stayed up under the scoreboard. On lazy summer days Lucy and I would sit in the sun until we got too hot. Then we would move up to the top bench, directly under the scoreboard and open to the winds off Lake Michigan. There was no electronic message board back then. The rest of the center field bleachers were blocked from lake breezes. It could be twenty degrees cooler up there, and protected from the sun by the shadow of the scoreboard. Soon we would be chilly, and so would move back down into the sun for a few innings. Back and forth, up and down, back and forth. Easy to do when there were only a handful of other fans in the section.

From our bleacher seats we could see the small crowd bunched around home plate, the seats beyond the dugouts and behind the bullpens mostly empty, and the upper deck completely closed. They used to post an Andy Frain usher up there to retrieve the foul balls that landed among the vacant upper box seats and grandstands.

We would continue to sit mostly in the center field bleachers after getting married and starting a family. Once I made the mistake of taking Anne Lise, who couldn't have been much older than five, to the left field bleachers. The language was so foul that within minutes she plaintively asked, "Daddy, can we sit somewhere else?" I felt like the total dope that I was and immediately gathered our treats and headed for center field. It was pretty crowded that afternoon (the upper deck was open), but I found a spot for us about halfway up to the scoreboard. We sat directly behind a group of four guys in their early twenties. One of them turned and looked at Anne Lise and said, somewhat in jest, "Oh man, you just ruined our fun," meaning that, out of respect for Anne Lise's tender ears, they would refrain from cursing for the duration of the game. I was grateful and told them so. But did I buy them a round of beers? I don't remember but I hope so.

Not that the left field bleachers was the only section of the ballpark where you heard unbridled profanity. During the 1976 season, Lucy hadn't moved back to Chicago from Arlington, Virginia, yet and I was living with roommate Charles Lyon in a dump we called the Hobo Jungle on Sunnyside near Kimball. Lucy's sister-in-law Bunny was in the area visiting her mother, who lived in Park Ridge. She called and said she had four tickets in the lower boxes, a few rows up from the visitors' dugout and directly behind first base. She would bring her two older kids, Stephanie and Jeff, who were ten and nine years old respectively.

When they picked me up, Bunny asked that I drive because she wasn't too familiar with the neighborhood around the ballpark, which I don't believe was called Wrigleyville yet. Driving east on Addison I worried about finding parking because it was a beautiful weekend afternoon and even the Cubs might draw over twenty thousand on a day like that. A few blocks west I got off Addison and looked for street parking. At one of the alleys an elderly man stood with a crude sign that read "Parking $2." Seemed reasonable, and much better than driving around the neighborhood for another fifteen minutes or more, so we pulled into the alley and followed him to a two-car garage behind a bungalow in the middle of the block. An elderly woman whom we took to be his wife stood next to the garage smiling. Bunny and the kids got out and I pulled the car in. We paid (probably Bunny paid, that is) the two bucks and chatted with the man for a minute. He handed me a business card and explained that he had two spaces in his garage available for all home games and I should tell all my friends. So he had a side business where he stood to make four dollars a day for 81 home games, minus any doubleheaders. In 1976 dollars were worth more than in 2008, but still, it seemed like a lot of effort for very little return. Plus he had invested in business cards and a sign during the era before computers and desktop publishing. He had to buy them from a printer which must have cost him at least a couple of days' business. In 2008 one could probably earn $40 or more per game for those two protected parking spots.

Two teenage girls sat in seats right behind us and from the start of the game blistered the air with profanity that was every bit as gross as anything I'd heard in the bleachers. Pete LaCock played first base for the Cubs that year and the girls had a field day with his name, including "Pete LaCock, you SUCK!" which was still a genuine profanity back then. Today it's in such wide, open use—I've seen it on billboards and heard it used by sportscasters on TV—that it's about as offensive as "you stink." But in 1976 it meant what it meant and was not used in polite company. Or in front of kids. I was at a loss as to what to do about it and let it go on too long until, having had enough by the third or fourth inning, I turned and said, "You girls don't seem to know any words with more than four letters, do you?" I probably should have threatened to complain to an Andy Frain usher, but my weak attempt at a scathing putdown seemed to work and they toned it down. This situation was very unusual for the box seats but would have gone unnoticed in the left field bleachers.

One difference between the left and center field bleachers, in our opinion, was that most fans under the scoreboard were there to watch the game. You would see scorecards and pencils everywhere. For example, on October 2, 1985, Rick Sutcliffe was scheduled to pitch against the Pirates at Wrigley Field after being on the DL for most of the season. He had won the Cy Young Award the year before as the Cubs' ace during the ill-fated Division Championship season of 1984 but had had hamstring and shoulder problems since

May. This would be his second start since returning to the roster and he was on a pitch count.

It was a Wednesday and I was at work. I wanted to be at the game, so when my boss pissed me off, and it was a genuine tiff we had over sending the company gofer out to go for something, I stormed out of the office at about 11:00 A.M. I called Lucy from the Grand and State subway station and told her what had happened and said I would be at the ballpark where my boss couldn't find me. When he called, which I knew he would, she was supposed to say I wasn't there and couldn't be reached. She was in total agreement, so I hopped on the CTA and got off at Addison.

This was also the second-to-last Cub home game of the year. We used to have a tradition of going to this game every year as one last visit to the bleachers. My brother Steve (a Sox fan), friends Charles Lyon, Bob Cooney and Mike "Frenchy" Cahill (if he was in town), or any combination thereof, would head out to the all but empty center field bleachers for a final afternoon of baseball, hotdogs and beer.

But then sometime in the late 1970s or early 1980s the Cubs seemed to play the Cardinals every year for their last home stand, usually over a weekend. And management started celebrating fan appreciation days to close out the year. Big crowds and thousands of Cardinal fans. Not our style at all. Plus, we started working real jobs and raising families. Outside life began to keep us away from the park more than we liked. But the tug of Sutcliffe's return, a meaningless Wednesday afternoon game against Pittsburgh (the Pirates would lose 104 games that year) and a second-to-last game were too much for me to resist.

Maybe twelve guys sat in the center field bleachers that afternoon, including Bill Veeck with four or five friends in his favorite spot in the bottom row next to the stairs on the right field side of the section. Veeck didn't look too good, thin and ravaged by age, cigarettes and disease. But he was obviously happy to be at the ballpark, regaling his friends with story after story. A lot of laughs rang up from that row.

The rest of us sat scattered around the benches. Two guys were stretched out asleep under newspapers. The ballpark looked almost empty. Paid attendance would be announced at 4,637.

During the fifth inning a fan above me and to my right, sitting alone like me and most of the others in the section, shouted, "Okay, how many pitches were they going to let Sutcliffe throw today?" By then Sutcliffe had all but lost it. After four shutout innings, and with a 3–0 lead, he was giving up single after single.

A guy about ten yards to my left answered, "Eighty."

"How many has he thrown so far?"

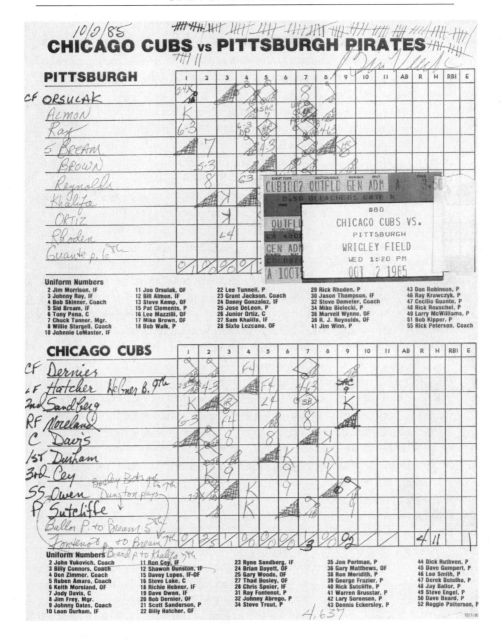

Author's scorecard and ticket stub, Cubs vs. Pirates, October 2, 1985. Bill Veeck's autograph and Rick Sutcliffe's pitch count are visible at top.

No one spoke.

"Oh, come on!" the first guy said. "This is Wrigley Field. This is the center field bleachers. You can't tell me that nobody here is counting pitches."

I looked down at my scorecard, counted my chicken scratches and said, "He's thrown eighty-three."

The first guy laughed. "I knew someone would be counting. They should have taken him out at eighty like they said they were going to."

A few pitches later, Sutcliffe gave up a home run to Johnny Ray with two on for the second, third and fourth runs of the inning, and was pulled. The Cubs went on to lose the game, and Sutcliffe got charged with the loss. I still have the scorecard with eighty-seven chicken scratches and Bill Veeck's autograph. He died exactly three months later, January 2, 1986.

Back then many big league teams played in huge multi-purpose sports facilities like Three Rivers Stadium in Pittsburgh, Riverfront Stadium in Cincinnati and Veterans Stadium in Philadelphia. We've been to many of them and are grateful they've almost all been imploded.

Not that we haven't seen some memorable games at these ... ballparks? Not the right word at all. That's why each was called a stadium instead of a park or field. Concrete monstrosity fits best.

On July 17, 2002, during our first summer living in York, Pennsylvania, we sat up at the top of Veterans Stadium in Philadelphia in seats just below the third base line sky boxes. We've sat in one of those boxes, too, thanks to the generosity of our friend Carl Scichili and his brother. One thing I did not understand about the design of "The Vet" was the location of those boxes—farther away from the field than the worst seats in the stadium. I guess you paid for the plush seats with cup holders, food, personal TV and other amenities, but it was still pretty tough to see the action. The ball looked like a kernel of Kix cereal from way up there. A comparable seat at Wrigley Field would have to be located high above the McDonald's across Clark Street.

The Cubs and Phillies were tied in the bottom of the tenth. Kerry Wood had pitched a great game into the ninth inning, spreading out four hits and striking out six, but gave up a lead-off double to Pat Burrell. With a 3–1 lead, Cub manager Bruce Kimm pulled Wood and brought in closer Antonio Alfonseca who, after Travis Lee popped out, promptly walked Scott Rolen and gave up a game-tying double to Mike Lieberthal. Typical, and profoundly depressing. The four of us—myself, Lucy, Patricia and Anne Lise (who won the attendance pool guessing 24,624 for an actual crowd numbered at 23,541)—sank into our seats and waited for the inevitable, which came in the tenth against Jeff Fassero. The Phillies loaded the bases, with the help of a free pass to Burrell, with one out. A ground ball could end the inning and Fassero obliged getting Lee to bounce a tailor-made, strictly routine, big fat no-doubt-about-it double play grounder to Cub second baseman Mark Bellhorn. All he had to do was turn to second, flip the ball to shortstop Alex Gonzalez and get out of the way of Gonzalez's relay to first baseman Fred McGriff. They're out of the inning, we thought, standing and cheering. "All right!"

Ha, ha, ha. Joke's on us! For some reason, the Cub second baseman looked at Burrell running from first to second, as if to tag him! Maybe he thought he could pull off a 4–3 double play without the 6. Whatever. Burrell pulled up short and Bellhorn kind of lunged at him, delaying the play long enough to make a double play impossible. Jason Michaels, who had pinch hit for Jeremy Giambi, was already across the plate with the winning run. The Cubs once again rescued painful tragedy from the cruel grasp of joyous victory—and an excellent Kerry Wood outing to boot.

We did not want to walk all the way down to our car through hordes of always friendly Phillies fans, so we just sat there for a while, staring at the celebrating Phillies and the dejected Cubs, and then the grounds crew cleaning up. The drive back to York was long and quiet.

Compared to these grotesque concrete bowls, Wrigley Field during the 1970s seemed more of an anachronism than a landmark. Rumors circulated that the Cubs would move to Schaumburg or some other suburb, or another city, and build a big new stadium. But the Wrigley family, still owners of the team and the ballpark, seemed overcome with the same inertia that prevented them from putting together a good team. So the Cubs continued playing in their "ivy covered burial ground" (Steve Goodman, *A Dying Cub Fan's Last Request*) to sparse crowds of crabby diehards, furiously scratching in their scorecards and drinking a six pack or more per game (a conservative estimate).

I must point out here that those beers came from twelve-ounce bottles, not sixteen-ounce cans as they do now. Six beers then would equal only four-and-a-half beers today. But there were beer vendors everywhere, except the bleachers. If you missed one going up or coming down your aisle, you only had to look behind him to see another. They scooted through the seating sections behind the foul lines like ants in an ant farm. Some days you would swear there were more beer vendors than fans. But beer was an important element of the Wrigley Field experience. Some used to call the ballpark the world's biggest beer garden, or worse.

Once, when Lucy and I had three little kids at home and no money, our friend Nia gave us two tickets for box seats behind home plate. It was a glorious, if brief, vacation for us, but we only had a couple of bucks to our name and so resolved to split one beer and a bag of peanuts. This would leave us just enough to catch the el back home to Albany Park. We bought the beer and set the cup on the concrete floor between us, each taking little sips in turn, trying to make it last. At the seventh inning stretch when the entire crowd stood, worried that one of us might accidentally kick the cup over and spill the remains of our precious golden nectar of the gods, we both reached for the cup at exactly the same time, bumping heads hard and giving each other ringing headaches. It made for a good laugh.

But then it all started to change. To me it felt like the shift in fan attitude began in the late 1970s. The Cubs became a treasure, in some warped kind of way, instead of an embarrassment. Wrigley Field was no longer the humble, ancient, outdated park that wasn't even near an interstate highway, but the jewel of all sports fields — not just quirky and somewhat quaint, like Fenway Park, but actually beautiful. The fact that there is no real parking nearby only added to its charm. So much so that the city has dutifully multiplied that charm by making it close to impossible to park on a street near the ballpark through a draconian permit system that dictates that you will be towed. This even though on the street is just about the only place to park, unless you can afford the small parking lots, if they're not full, that can be more expensive than your ticket to the game.

What brought about this change?

As with many cultural tectonic shifts of this kind over recent decades, it probably has something to do with baby boomers. In the late 1970s, the Vietnam War had ended, and rock and roll, in my opinion, was in the doldrums. Without anti-war protests to attend and fewer new music acts worth following, boomers returned to a favorite pastime of their childhood: baseball. And for many of us in Chicago, Wrigley Field was the most vivid and treasured memory that could be relived, virtually unchanged, for a few bucks in tickets, beers, hot dogs and el fares.

Others in town returned to Comiskey Park, then the oldest ballpark in the major leagues after the 1970 closing of Pittsburgh's Forbes Field. Its demolition was very sad for our family. Contrary to the reigning orthodoxy concerning the animosity between South Side and North Side ball fans, we loved going to Old Comiskey Park and still root for the Sox second only to the Cubs. We followed their championship 2005 season with great interest, and openly cheered for them during the playoffs and World Series. And we happened to be in Chicago on October 28, 2005, when the city honored them with a huge victory parade up LaSalle Street. It was Patricia's sixteenth birthday and we had a whole slate of fun things planned, but she wanted, and we all wanted, to be there to welcome the champion Sox. So there we stood at Randolph and LaSalle, next to City Hall, watching Mayor Daley (the Second) in his glory—more into it than even Ozzie Guillen—on the top of a double-decker bus leading the parade north through a blizzard of confetti.

Nineteen seventy-seven is the year that showed a demonstrable uptick in attendance for both teams. Cubs numbers went up over 400,000 to 1,439,834; the Sox added 700,000. Were the teams that good? The Sox played well, winning ninety games, but ended up in third place, twelve games out of first. And the Cubs? A perfect .500, 81 and 81 and twenty games out of first. Hardly worthy of an increase in attendance of 40 percent.

No, something else was in the air, and I propose it was boomers, now in their mid-twenties to mid-thirties and earning more money than ever before, returning to the game, and bringing their own kids to Wrigley Field to experience the bricks and the vines and the lush green of the field under the deep blue sky, and the lake breezes that can knock down a deep fly to right, or the southwesterly gales that send routine popups out over the left field bleachers and onto Waveland Avenue.

The Tribune Company saw this. When the Wrigleys, who apparently didn't understand what was happening in their own ballpark, decided to sell, the media giant was ready to expand into sports. A cozy setup to say the least: the newspaper, the team it covered and the TV and radio company, WGN, that broadcasts the games, all owned by one corporation.

But now, in 2008, the Tribune Company has sold itself to Zell, who will sell the Cubs and probably the rights to the name of the ballpark. How could this happen? What corporation would spend the money only to alienate the millions of baseball fans, Cub fans and others, who would view any other name on the iconic red marquee at the corner of Clark and Addison as an abomination? Those hideous Under Armour logos on the green outfield utility doors are bad enough. (And, anyway, what kind of company would give themselves a name whose first eight letters spell underarm?) How can Cub fans let this happen to their ballpark?

It's national news. On Friday morning, March 14, 2008, *Marketplace*, the National Public Radio business program, broadcast a short feature about Zell and the impending change darkening the skies over Wrigley Field. The program's business of sports commentator, Diana Nyad, said: "The Cubs fans are ... proud. They haven't won the World Series in ninety-four years, so they've got to hang on to something. And they just don't want the name of Wrigley Field changed." I hear this while driving to work. My cell phone rings immediately. It's Lucy. She and our eighteen-year-old daughter, Patricia, heard it on the way to Patricia's school. We are stunned. Shocked. Amazed. Not about the proposed selling of the naming rights, of which we are well aware, but about Ms. Nyad getting the World Series drought wrong by six years because the biggest story in baseball going into the 2008 season is the *centennial* of the Cubs' last world championship. How could someone billed as a business of sports analyst for a popular, nationally broadcast radio program get something like that wrong? I e-mail *Marketplace* to point out the error. I am probably one of thousands who call and e-mail about it. Two days later I go to the *Marketplace* Web site and print out a transcript of the segment. They have corrected the mistake with a footnote.

But she was right about one thing: Cub fans want Wrigley Field to stay Wrigley Field. As Ms. Nyad reported, "A recent survey said that 72 percent of the season ticket holders—72 percent—said 'We will just leave those seats empty this year, we won't go to one game, if they change that Wrigley Field name.'"

But what about fans who don't have season tickets? What kind of pressure can we exert on Zell not to mess with the name? Those of us who won't be able to get into many, if any, games at Wrigley Field because we can't afford it or don't live in Chicago? There are, as has been well noted, millions of Cub fans all over the country who show up at ballparks coast to coast wherever the Cubs play. We know this personally because we live in York, Pennsylvania, and go to games wherever we can. Pittsburgh often (including the game during which Sammy Sosa's helmet was shattered by a pitch); Philadelphia; Washington, DC; Baltimore (in June 2003, we saw a fan run onto the field at Camden Yards and throw corks at Sammy Sosa, and then kneel and bow in front of him); New York; Cincinnati; and once, Miami. Cub fans can account for as much as a third of the crowd. More sometimes, like a couple of games in Cincinnati. We've been to games when, in the late innings when the Cubs were winning (not too often), Cub fans took over the ballpark after many of the home team faithful gave up and left.

This is where our son comes in. Steve went to his first Cub game as an infant. As per usual, we sat in the bleachers. We bought scorecards for the whole family, except Steve, who could not as yet walk. His sisters, Jeanne, four years old at the time, and Anne Lise, two, sat in the last row in right center field, wearing their Cub hats, making marks on their scorecards. They watched the whole game and never complained as Lucy and I took turns walking Steve from center field to left, and then back all the way around as close to the right field foul pole as we could get. I don't want anyone to think that Steve is any more a Cub fan than Jeanne, Anne Lise or Patricia. Or me or his mother, Lucy. But, we got a call the first weekend of spring training 2008....

Steve and his roommate Dylan decided that they would keep Wrigley Field Wrigley Field by mounting a campaign called "Save the Name." They would sell T-shirts and solicit matching corporate and personal donations to compete with anticipated deep pocket corporations to be able to bid on the naming rights. Steve's strategy is to raise enough to make it not worth anyone's effort to change the name of Wrigley Field. Then his group will give the proceeds of their efforts to a charity. As I write this, Steve has everything in place, including the permits and licenses he needs to sell T-shirts in the city of Chicago. His girlfriend, Tara, is dubious but ready to hit the streets around the ballpark to help make it happen by passing out literature or selling T-shirts. They have joined forces with two other organizations with the same mission and have targeted Opening Day as D-Day.

The politics and business dealings of this could take years to resolve, but as spring training rolls into its last two weeks, we are personally committed to saving the name of Wrigley Field. More later.

Midway through the Cactus League season, the Cubs look promising, but not as ready to destroy the century-old demon as we would like. On March 16, 2008, Zambrano is magnificent and unstoppable in a six-inning performance that would have been without a hit, except for a deep fly to right center that Pie misjudged in three or four different ways. He is obviously not 100 percent, which leaves the Cubs doubtful up the middle.

In terms of team studs, Soriano went three for four with a home run deep to left. So the flow of spring training feels good, which usually means it will be a bad year for the Cubs. Pundits and more recently-arrived fans can be optimistic, but we can't. However, we will still drive to Pittsburgh, Philadelphia, Washington, New York, Cincinnati and Chicago to see the Cubs play.

The pitching as a whole looks okay. Any pitcher who wants to make the team has to pitch lights out because the competition is fierce.

Of major interest to Cub fans is Kerry Wood being named closer. He's had a good spring with excellent control. He hasn't walked a batter heading into the Cubs' last 2008 spring training game, to be played in Las Vegas. In the ninth inning he gives up his first base on balls, followed by a base hit. Man on first. Next guy up bounces one to the mound. Wood doesn't hesitate but reaches up with his bare hand (his pitching hand—OH NO!), snares it and turns to second base to start the double play, seemingly in one fluid movement. Next guy he fans with three sliders. Wonderful stuff. We pray it will continue all season long.

We all love Kerry Wood and want very badly for him to succeed. He plays ball. He wants to contribute however he can. I think he may feel bad about taking all that money while spending so much time on the disabled list. He loves every part of the game. He loves to hit, even though he probably never will again, as a closer (unless they use him as a pinch-hitter—I could see it, in a blowout).

How about the Dennis Eckersley path to baseball immortality? Eckersley was known as a quality starter for years. He played a key role in the Cubs' 1984 rotation, helping send the Cubs to the playoffs for the first time since 1945 (only to be dashed on the rocks of Cub inevitability as they blew the National League Championship Series by losing three in a row to San Diego, after winning the first two of the five game set). He wasn't the greatest starter around, though, overshadowed that year by Rick Sutcliffe's Cy Young season. But he became a closer with the Oakland A's, one of the most feared short relievers in baseball. And that's how he got into the Hall of Fame. The A's retired his number.

Why not Kerry Wood? He's still got heat, and mixing fast balls with his often very nasty slider could be, and has been, effective.

One hundred years ago Charles Dryden reported in the *Tribune* that "seldom have the Cubs been so fit at this state of the training season." They must have healed themselves of their earlier maladies. They were cocky, but they had every reason to be confident. They were arguably the best team in baseball, had been National League champions two years running and world champions in 1907. It would be up to the Pittsburgh Pirates and the New York Giants to come after them. Manager, first baseman and "Peerless Leader" Frank Chance was ready to play ball. So was second baseman Johnny Evers, known as the "Crab" as much for his temperament as his ability to swing his arms around his position to make plays. The Cubs were infamous for dugout brawls. If a player didn't follow orders, Manager Chance, an experienced pugilist, was as ready to fight as negotiate.

The Cubs players didn't like owner Charles "Chubby" Murphy. Most didn't like Frank Chance. Johnny Evers didn't like anybody, especially Tinker. Their best pitcher had only three fingers. They were a dream team.

CHAPTER TWO

Opening Day

At 8:36 A.M. Chicago time, March 31, 2008, it's thirty-seven degrees and raining. I just talked to our son, Steve, who is already at Murphy's, corner of Waveland and Sheffield. A couple of sports radio personalities are covering Opening Day from the landmark saloon. Steve's there because he has planned a big marketing push to launch Save the Name. He and his cohorts have T-shirts and fliers and hope to get on TV.

The Cubs announced their last roster moves before the beginning of the regular season. Left fielder Matt Murton and pitcher Sean Marshall were sent down to the minors. So here's the 2008 Chicago Cubs, as they stretch and get ready for Game One, directly from www.cubs.com.

Pitchers

46 Ryan Dempster
22 Kevin Hart
53 Rich Hill
62 Bob Howry
32 Jon Lieber
30 Ted Lilly
49 Carlos Marmol
21 Jason Marquis
63 Carmen Pignatiello
34 Kerry Wood
43 Michael Wuertz
38 Carlos Zambrano

Catchers

24 Henry Blanco
18 Geovany Soto

Infielders

5 Ronny Cedeno
7 Mark DeRosa
17 Mike Fontenot
25 Derrek Lee
16 Aramis Ramirez
2 Ryan Theriot
33 Daryle Ward

Outfielders

1 Kosuke Fukudome
9 Reed Johnson
20 Felix Pie
12 Alfonso Soriano

They have twelve pitchers and seem pretty strong both in terms of starters and the bullpen.

Our chief worry going into the first month of the season remains that

31

the Cubs are inexperienced up the middle. Catcher Geovany Soto is twenty-five. Shortstop Ryan Theriot is twenty-eight. Center fielder Felix Pie is twenty-three. All three began their major league careers just last year and only Theriot played what could be considered a full season. Pie played in eighty-seven games and Soto eighteen. Theriot and Pie had good springs at the plate. Soto, not so hot. But Derrek Lee had a mediocre spring, too (.179), so anything can happen. Right?

Most of the hitting talk centers around Kosuke Fukudome. Will he adjust to American pitching, which is apparently different from Japanese pitching? More movement, we hear. He hit okay in Mesa, .270 with a home run and eight RBI.

At game time, the temperature at Wrigley Field is fifty degrees Fahrenheit. The wind is out of the south at eleven miles per hour. There's a light rain falling and it's enough to delay the game.

In 1908, the Cubs' home opener at West Side Park was over three weeks later, on April 22. The Cubs the year on the road. The season was only 154 games and would extend into the first week of October without worry of playoff games being played in the cold because there was only the World's Series after the regular season. Also, doubleheaders were common, further shrinking the number of game dates. They are rare now and scheduled only to make up rainouts. A century ago, and up until relatively recently, they were promotional, two-for-the-price-of-one events with both games played either during the day, or during the evening, one right after the other with a short pause between.

For instance, on May 15, 1960, the Cubs played a traditional Sunday doubleheader against the St. Louis Cardinals. I was nine years old and my brother Steve was seven. We had moved into our new house, one of a long block of virtually identical red brick bungalows in suburban Oak Park, less than a year before. I say suburban but we lived only four blocks south of the city limits at North Avenue, and six blocks west of Austin Boulevard, Chicago's western boundary with Oak Park. Our neighbors two doors to the north invited us to the games. Their son, two years older than I, and daughter, a year or two younger than Steve, would be with us. My first doubleheader. I was in heaven.

The Cubs lost the first game 6–1 in typical fashion. Anemic hitting and mediocre pitching. It was expected. They had finished in fifth place (out of eight teams) the year before, six games under .500. They were already five games below .500 for the young 1960 season. The second game of the twin bill started very slowly for four young kids. Not much action at all. Our neighbor's daughter, only five years old, had had enough baseball for one day and was getting very restless. She wanted to go home. I didn't. There was no score, so anything could still happen. And the Cubs had Ernie Banks at shortstop, National League MVP two years running in spite of being on the Cubs. By the way, future Cubs manager Don Zimmer was also on this team and came in to play part of game two.

Our neighbor decided that it would be more painful for him to ignore his daughter's complaints than to listen to our pleas to stay. My brother and I would never protest too vehemently anyway. He was an adult and we had been taught to obey adults without question. And we had seen almost a game and a half of big league baseball, so we had no grounds for protest.

We left the ballpark, found the car and drove west, probably on Fullerton, to Austin Avenue and then south to Oak Park, the radio tuned to WGN. We listened as the Cubs scored a run in the fifth, two in the sixth and one more in the seventh. The Cardinals hadn't scored at all. But something more was happening. The buzz of the crowd grew more intense with every inning and with every block we passed driving through the Northwest Side. Palpable electricity filled the airwaves. You could hear it in the voices of the announcers whose pitch seemed to rise an octave over the course of the last innings.

We pulled into our neighbor's garage during the ninth. I ran down the alley, neglecting my little brother, through our postage stamp backyard, and finally burst through the back door of the house. My father sat chatting with a guest in the kitchen. Distracted and rude, I didn't pause to say hello.

I turned on the television just in time to see Joe Cunningham of the Cardinals come to the plate with two out in the top of the ninth. Jack Brickhouse's voice seemed to break with every pitch, each word lilting up and into the air, hanging out there dripping with the tension of the moment. "Everybody in the ballpark is standing up," he cried. The crowd screamed in anticipation, screeching whistles and shrill women's voices penetrating the chaos. Cunningham, a lefty, worked the count to three and two, getting in the home plate umpire's face to protest the call on strike two. The Cub pitcher, a new guy from the Phillies with whom I was completely unfamiliar, looked uncomfortable on the mound, picking up the rosin bag, circling the rubber, taking off his mitt and rubbing the ball. I found out later that he had given up two deep fly balls already that inning, one all the way to the right field wall, George Altman leaping high and stealing an extra base hit.

As the crowd roared, Brickhouse said his signature simple yet frantic, "Watch it!" as if all of us watching at home needed to be very, very careful about something. Cunningham connected on the three-two pitch going the opposite way, lining what looked like a base hit to left. Mixed feelings here.

If the ball fell safely it would mean that our early departure was not so tragic after all.

Out of the upper left corner of the little black and white screen Walt "Moose" Moran loped toward the ball. A somewhat chunky guy, not very fleet of foot, and not athletic enough to be enthusiastic about diving for balls, he reached down to his left side, at about ankle height, and grabbed the sinking line drive in the webbing of his mitt to preserve Don Cardwell's no-hitter.

Pandemonium reigned. The crowd rushed the field. Brickhouse's voice cracked noticeably. I know these details not because I have a great memory but because you can see the last inning of that game on YouTube, just as it was broadcast by WGN TV. I went there to refresh long forgotten details of my misery. It's still painful to watch.

We had walked out of a no-hitter, the greatest kind of baseball game one could ever see in person, and the kind of game only the luckiest of fans get a chance to witness. And it was a Cub no-hitter. What were the odds of ever being at Wrigley Field for one of those again? As of Opening Day 2008, forty-eight years after Cardwell's masterpiece, 255 no-hitters have been pitched in all of major league history, which goes back to 1876, the year the National League was formed. Do the math. Not even two no-hitters a year total, divided among all the major league teams divided by the few games we get to see each year....

Totally despondent and almost in tears, I turned the TV off. My father and his guest came into the room. He asked if I was okay. I blurted out, "We walked out of a NO-HITTER!" Not able to face anyone, I ran out of the room.

Behind me I could hear my father say, "I don't blame him."

His guest replied, "No. That's a tough one to handle." Or words to that effect.

Years later, sometime during the 1970s, I sat with some friends in the center field bleachers during the late innings of a Cub loss, the temperature dipping into the thirties. They wanted to retire to Ray's (now Murphy's) for something strong and warming. I had to explain to them why I couldn't leave, and in fact never left any sporting event, ever, before it ended. My friend Bob Cooney, whose law firm now gives away tickets through a promotion run during games on WGN Radio, listened politely all the way to the part where I said "to see Moose Moran make a shoestring catch to preserve Don Cardwell's no-hitter."

"Guess what," said Cooney, laughing. "I was at that game. We stormed the field. I still have dirt from the mound in a glass jar." I almost threw up my beer.

The tradition, or family law, of never leaving a game before it's over has been passed down to our kids. In December of 1989 a business associate gave me four tickets to see the Bears play the Green Bay Packers. Patricia was six weeks old so I took Jeanne, age twelve, Anne Lise, ten, and Steve, eight. We had seats about halfway up in the south end zone at Soldier Field. It was bitterly cold and windy on Chicago's lakefront that Sunday afternoon, but we were bundled up and so we stayed warm enough for three quarters.

It had been a depressing year for the Bears. They were 6–8 and head coach Mike Ditka had predicted weeks before that they wouldn't win another game that season. The fans believed him which is why the tickets were available. At the start of the fourth quarter the Bears were only two behind with the score 30–28, but when the Packers scored ten unanswered points the stadium emptied quickly. A Bear fan sitting above us began a mantra of "There's still time!" as the clock ticked down. The temperature fell as the Bears tumbled, and by the two minute warning with all but a handful of fans gone the protection of 55,000 bodies gave way to the equivalent of an open wind tunnel.

I turned to the three freezing kids and asked if they wanted to leave and seek warmth under the stands, or just head for the shuttle bus that would take us to the parking lot. They looked at me as if I had just put a Packer cheesehead hat on my head. I was suggesting mortal sin to them and they would have none of it. By the end of the game we were among about 200 people left in the end zone seats, including the guy still chanting, "There's still time," much to everyone's amusement.

Only serious illness, and it has to be debilitating, can remove us from a ballpark before the last out, and often, when the score is badly lopsided against the Cubs, it will be one of us claiming loudly that "there's still time." At a Cub doubleheader many years ago, I stood with business associates (it was my job!) under the Wrigley Field stands waiting out a rain delay. I told them I would stay until play resumed and stay for the second game even if it took all night, but they should feel free to leave any time if they had other obligations. I was at the ballpark for over eight hours and loved every minute of it.

Today, you usually have to pay for both games of a doubleheader and they are often day-night affairs. The owners will tell you that it's not their fault. It was the Players' Association that forced limitations on the number of consecutive games players would have to play. However, did the players force the owners to charge fans for both games individually? But I guess tickets have gotten so expensive that the owners can't afford to give a game away free. It would mean a loss of half a million dollars or more per game.

But it's gotten so pricey that fans can't afford to pay twice in the same day. The owners don't care, though. At Wrigley Field, they can easily get a whole new set of 40,000 fans in for a night game after an afternoon game.

We can breathe a collective sigh of relief on Opening Day because Gameday is indeed available. The format has changed a little, but so what? I can have the game minimized on my computer screen and reference it, in as much detail as I could ever want, as I work.

The 2008 Cub home opener on Monday, March 31, begins with the dedication of the new statue of Ernie Banks near the Clark and Addison box office and entrance. Henry Aaron, Ron Santo, Billy Williams, Jesse Jackson and a busload of Chicago politicos are on hand, mostly under umbrellas.

Later, Ernie takes the mound and tosses the ceremonial first pitch of 2008. He is still Mr. Cub and the fans love him, and why not?

In July 1998, WGN held an event called Sponsorfest at Wrigley Field while the Cubs were on the road. As a radio advertiser I was given two tickets. Anne Lise, who was eighteen at the time, and I drove to the ballpark and joined the other sponsors on the field where we could play catch, pitch from the mound, check out the ivy and then, best of all, meet Ernie and Jack Brickhouse, who sat in the Cubs' dugout signing autographs and chatting with fans. Ernie did not want to talk about himself but happily asked us about our jobs, Anne Lise's school and our family. When we answered his questions he found something in our answers to extend the conversation, seemingly endlessly fascinated by my job (marketing dinnerware and glassware!) and especially by Anne Lise's education and career goals. He wouldn't let us go. He was engaging and fun and generous with his time. He kept us so long that the people behind us became impatient so I had to take the initiative and thank Ernie and edge down the bench toward Jack who sat at the other end. But even as we moved on, Ernie kept asking questions and commenting on how great Anne Lise's plans were. We never got the chance to bring up baseball or his career with the Cubs at all.

In contrast, Jack had recently undergone brain surgery and did not look healthy. He struggled speaking which was sad for a man who made his living with his voice. Our visit with him was very brief. When he passed away a few weeks later, on August 6, 1998, one of the Chicago papers ran a large photograph of him standing on the concourse under the Wrigley Field grandstands. I noticed that he wore the same clothes he had on when we met him in the dugout. The photograph had no doubt been taken that same afternoon.

One hundred years ago legendary Cub first baseman and manager Cap Anson walked out to the West Side Park mound to throw the ceremonial first pitch before the Cubs' home opener, although Anson never played on any team named the Cubs. The Chicago National League team was known as the White Stockings for most of its history to that point in time. The name changed to the Colts (1894 to 1897), then the Orphans (because their symbolic father, Anson, had retired in 1896) and finally the Cubs, a name bestowed on them by the *Chicago Daily News* in 1902 because the Cubs had so many young players (the new American League, founded in 1900 and recognized as a major league in 1901, had raided the National League of many of its veterans), and because the brief, four-letter word could fit more easily and in larger type fonts in headlines.

Whatever the name of his team, Anson never would have given Ernie a place on his roster. Anson was known to be one of the most dedicated racists in baseball during an era when bigotry, racial and otherwise, was accepted behavior. Today it's normal but not always accepted.

The first game of 2008 couldn't be more Cub-like. After a ninety-minute rain delay Zambrano and Sheets look brilliant. Neither team scores going into the seventh inning when Zambrano leaves because of forearm cramps, after a fabulous pick-off of Brewers' third baseman Bill Hall at second base. Word is he needs to stay better hydrated, and eat more bananas to satisfy his daily potassium requirement.

I arrive home from work and ask Patricia what time she got home from school (her senior year of high school). "Fifth inning," she replies, staring intently at the screen.

Marmol comes in and looks lights-out brilliant, striking out three of the four batters he faces. He's unhittable, getting one guy with a tailing fastball that is just evil. The weather continues to live up to Opening Day standards—gray, wet and windy. The fans in the stands, amazingly, still fill the seats in the eighth, covered in parkas and hooded sheets of plastic.

Wood pitches the ninth. He immediately drills the first batter. What happened to the control he showed all spring? Maybe he was keeping the Brewers honest because they had hit DeRosa? But what's the point? Sure enough, by the end of the top of the inning the Brewers have scored three off Wood on two hits and an intentional walk and all is doom and gloom. This feels eerily familiar. Milwaukee is up 3–0 going into the bottom of the ninth.

Opening Day weather for April 8, 1969, was forecasted to be in the mid-sixties and cloudy, a fine day for baseball, especially considering that it was early April in Chicago. We expect at least one more blizzard every April. More often than not proper attire for the first Cub home game includes a winter coat, stocking hat, scarf, gloves and long underwear. Opening Days 1974 *and* 1975 were snowed out. I went to Opening Day 1988 with colleague Mark Fusello, who had just started his own business, and the temperature was 44° at game time. By the fourth inning it felt positively arctic. I dressed for spring weather and throughout the game Mark had to lend me gloves or his hat to keep one of his first clients from freezing to death. Strains of "Bear down, Chicago Bears" could be heard in the crowd.

But not 1969, so it was a no-brainer for a fellow student and me to cut classes at the University of Illinois at Chicago Circle, Circle for short and now called just the University of Illinois at Chicago, and head for the ballpark. I figured we'd sit in the bleachers where it would be a bit warmer in the sun. No problem getting in because there was almost *never* a problem getting into Wrigley Field and sitting just about anywhere you wanted. Opening Day 1968 had been crowded at 33,875, but not sold out. Only 16,462 attended Opening Day 1967, and 15,369 in 1966. So it was with confidence that we hopped in my 1968 Mustang (white with a blue houndstooth roof and a 289 V8 gas-guzzling engine—the fastest car I've ever driven) and took Lake Shore Drive north. The first sign that perhaps it would not be so easy to get in was the backup at the Belmont exit. I decided to continue north to Irving Park Road and double back into the Wrigley Field neighborhood. To this day it's easier to get to the ballpark exiting LSD at Irving.

The next clue that the crowd would be substantial was the parking problem. I could find no street parking within three blocks of Wrigley Field, unheard of for a weekday afternoon in those days, so I paid for parking at the Shell Station at the corner of Addison and Halsted, across the street from the Twenty-third Police District Station and a lot I was familiar with because it was my Dad's favorite place to park for Bear games during the years they played at Wrigley Field.

Fans jammed the sidewalks around the park. The bleachers were sold out. In 1969 bleacher seats (one dollar each) were put on sale day-of-game only, first come first served. This remained Wrigley Field policy until the Tribune Company bought the Cubs in the 1980s and made bleacher tickets available in advance.

I shouldn't have been surprised by the crowd, but the idea of a *good* Cub team took some getting used to. Hopes ran high in 1969. The young players brought on in the mid-sixties had matured. Don Kessinger at shortstop, Glenn Beckert at second, Randy Hundley behind the plate, Adolpho Phillips in center and pitchers Fergie Jenkins, Joe Niekro and Bill Hands, combined with veterans Billy Williams in left, Ernie Banks at first and Ron Santo at third for a solid lineup both at the plate and in the field. Leo Durocher had taken them from a 55–103 public embarrassment in 1966, a record-tying low and depressing even for Cub fans who are used to horrid won-lost records, to a third place 87–74 finish in 1967, one of the most stunning turnarounds in club history and an event that made Durocher the toast of Chicago and the baseball world. In 1968 they finished third again with a winning record for an unheard of two years in a row.

When Dusty Baker arrived in town in 2003, and then "Sweet Lou" Piniella became manager in 2007 and took the Cubs from last to first, those of us who remember Phil Wrigley hiring "Leo the Lip" over forty years earlier immediately saw history repeating itself. Our hope is that Sweet Lou won't follow the pattern established by Durocher, Jim Frey, Don Zimmer, Jim Riggleman and Baker and fall short of the ultimate goal.

My friend and I made our way around the park to the Clark Street ticket windows only to find that the game was a complete sellout, so we settled for standing room, the first time ever for me, and found a couple of spots on a crowded upper deck ramp above the grandstands between the plate and first base. Seeing Wrigley Field this crowded (paid attendance: 40,796; capacity: 36,644) was so odd that we as much reveled in the experience as enjoyed the game at first, especially since the Phillies scored a run in the top of the first inning to take an early lead. But then Ernie Banks hit a three-run homer in the bottom half of the inning and we were into the game, as was the huge crowd. And then in his second trip to the plate he hit another one, this time for two runs. By mid-game the Cubs seemed in total control, leading 5–1. Starting pitcher Fergie Jenkins was cruising along, striking out six through six innings. He gave up a solo shot to Don Money in the seventh, but then settled back in, struck out three more Phillies and took the mound in the top of the ninth with a comfortable 5–2 lead.

No beginning to any sports season ever, in my memory, felt as exhilarating. Was this a sign of things to come for the season? Were the Cubs to be this good all year? No one under the age of forty could remember anything like it.

But then, in the top of the ninth, grim Cub reality brought the crowd back down to earth. Fergie couldn't get anyone out. The first two batters reached on singles, bringing up Don Money. Surely Fergie would get him this time, we thought. But Money connected for his second homer of the day and all of a sudden the game was tied and our dreams of grandeur were squelched. Longtime Cub fans smelled an Opening Day tragedy in the works, a potential loss that could signal a franchise relapse to mediocrity as usual.

Many left when the Cubs failed to score in the bottom of the ninth, even though the game had breezed right along and was barely two hours old. We took advantage of this by grabbing vacated lower grandstand seats in the section immediately below us, and settled in for extra innings. We could now see the sky and the center field scoreboard! And anything could happen, right? After all, the Cubs had just had two consecutive winning seasons.

Phil Regan had relieved Jenkins after Money's homer and kept the Phillies hitless through the rest of the ninth inning and the tenth. But in the top of the eleventh, Money (again!) doubled home John Callison from second giving the Phillies a one-run lead. A lot more fans left, although it still looked crowded. We ventured down into the upper boxes, just above the Phillies on-deck circle, for whatever was left of the impending fiasco. The crowd's mood was gloomy at best and surly at worst.

Banks led off the Cubs half of the eleventh. They needed one to tie and two to win. Ernie was thirty-eight years old and nowhere near his peak strength of the late 1950s and early 1960s. But he already had two home runs and a single in the game and had batted in all five Cub runs, so he was exactly the guy we wanted to see step into the batter's box.

And he did connect, and from our vantage point low in the stands when the ball left his bat it looked to have a shot at leaving the yard as it sailed toward Sheffield Avenue. But the cheers turned to groans as the ball died and was pulled in by Phillies right fielder Callison. The Cubs had gone down one-two-three in both the ninth and the tenth and it felt like the eleventh would be more of the same with the lower half of the lineup due to bat after Banks. Catcher Randy Hundley stepped up to the plate with no hits in three official at-bats, although he had been on base twice, once on an error and once when he was hit by a pitch. The crowd grew silent. But Hundley came through with a base hit and represented the tying run at first with one out. Right fielder Jim Hickman was due up. It felt like a game-ending double play waiting to happen. Hickman was 0 for 4.

Durocher opted to send Willie Smith in to pinch hit. Smith was a substitute, journeyman outfielder who had batted a respectable .275 in only 142 at-bats after coming to the Cubs in 1968. But he got all of Phillies relief pitcher Barry Lersch's first pitch and sent it toward the right-center field bleachers. The crowd jumped to its feet and when it landed beyond the wall pandemonium ruled. The Cubs jumped out of the third base dugout and mobbed Smith as he crossed the plate with the winning run. Final score: Cubs 7, Phillies 6. And, as the lyrics to "Hey Hey, Holy Mackerel" suggested, the Cubs were on their way. They went on to win their first four games and eleven of their first twelve, going 16–7 for the month of April 1969.

During an interview a few years later, after he had retired, Ernie Banks was asked what his favorite game was and he said Opening Day 1969. But he didn't mention his two home runs or three-for-four day. He talked about Willie Smith's home run. That's Ernie. In a 2004 interview with *The Heck-*

ler (online at http://www.sportznutz.com/columns/fan_speaks_out/archives/
mr_cub_interview.htm) he is asked the same question and replied:

> A game July 2nd, 1967 and the Cubs were playing the Cincinnati Reds here.
> We won the game 4–2. Fergie Jenkins pitched against Sammy Ellis. I was up
> in the booth with Jack Brickhouse and we went into a tie for first place. It was
> the first time that late in the season that the Cubs were in a tie for first place
> and everybody at the park was so excited that they didn't want to leave. I was
> up there watching all of this and it was just a marvelous memory in my life to
> see the joy of the people because the Cubs were in a tie for first place that late
> in the season. They were cheering and shouting, and the fans and the players
> were really, really happy.

He described a game in which he didn't play. A different game from the one
he mentioned in the interview that I remembered from years before, but
Ernie is allowed to change his mind, isn't he? I recall watching that July 2,
1967, game on TV. WGN continued coverage longer than usual after the
game and focused a camera on the team pennants that fly above the center
field scoreboard indicating league standings. As the Cub flag was raised atop
all the other national league teams, and as the delirious crowd cheered madly,
refusing to leave the ballpark, Brickhouse said words to the effect of, "Let's
enjoy this moment. These fans have waited a long time to see it." Indeed,
the Cubs had not been in first place in July since 1945.

   Much like "Go, Cubs, Go" in 2008, "Hey Hey, Holy Mackerel" was
the Cub theme song in 1969. Fellow Cub fan and business colleague Bob
Ficks was a student at Stout State University (now the University of Wisconsin—Stout) in Menomonie, Wisconsin, during the summer of '69. Whenever the Cubs won, and just as Ron Santo would click his heels on the way
to the Cubs' clubhouse, Bob would put "Hey Hey, Holy Mackerel" on his
phonograph to celebrate. The recording of the song reminds one of nothing
so much as an extended cigarette jingle recorded by a sterile, 1950s style
chorus, the kind that might sing with Perry Como or Lawrence Welk. Bob
would crank the volume up as loud as it would go, specifically to annoy the
many Twins fans, especially his roommates, who attended Stout, which is
located about sixty miles east of Minneapolis–St. Paul. Then one day the
record disappeared! No one would own up to the heist, but later in the season when the Cubs began to falter, after every game they lost, plunging
them further and further behind the surging "Miracle" Mets, the song would
"magically" echo through the halls of the dorm whenever Bob approached
his room. "Hey Hey, Holy Mackerel" in mocking revenge. The Cubs theme
song morphed from jubilant celebration into merciless ridicule.

   In September 1969, I traveled to Norwalk, Connecticut, to visit a friend
who had moved from the Chicago area during high school. On the night of

September 8 my friend Pete and I drove to nearby Westchester County, New York, to find a bar with a television to watch the Cubs–Mets game. The Cubs were in the midst of their historic collapse, having lost four in a row. But they were still in first place, two and a half games ahead of the Mets. If they could win both scheduled games at Shea Stadium they could get their lead back to four and a half games and stop the downward momentum of the disastrous three game sweep, including an extra-inning loss, at the hands of the Pirates at Wrigley Field.

We sat at the bar of a small, cozy joint somewhere across the state line. We went to New York because I was eighteen and my friend nineteen, and the drinking age in New York back then was eighteen. The place was packed with Mets fans, so we tried to keep a relatively low profile, which wasn't hard because the Mets struck first scoring two in the third. But then the Cubs came back with two of their own in the sixth. I went to the men's room between the top half and bottom half of the inning with the score tied. There was a wait because the facility was small and the bar crowded. While there, down a short, dark hall, a huge roar went up in the bar. Something not good, obviously. When I got back to my stool the Mets were in the lead by one, a lead they would not relinquish. When Ken Rudolph and Randy Bobb struck out with the tying run on in the top of the ninth, the game ended amidst deafening cheers from the local fans. It felt like the season had ended, too, with everything going the Mets' way. We silently returned to Connecticut. The Cubs would go on to lose seven in a row and drop out of first place while the Miracle Mets went on to make baseball history.

Twenty years later, Opening Day 1989, set the tone for the entire season. I sat in the right field box seats (section 131; price—$11.50) with a "business colleague." It was crowded (33,361—1989 capacity 38,040), but not a sellout, reflecting the mixed expectations of fans as the season got under way. The Cubs had finished 1988 in fourth place with a disappointing 77–85 record, and had traded away legitimate budding superstar Raphael Palmeiro (.307 batting average in 1988) and fan favorite Jamie Moyer (still pitching!). We were worried that Sutcliffe's best years were behind him, and no one could know how well Jerome Walton and Dwight Smith would play.

Sutcliffe started against the Phillies and looked pretty strong until he got in trouble in the sixth and was pulled after giving up two runs. The highlight of the day came in the fourth inning when Sandberg led off with a double followed by a Dunston home run. Sutcliffe himself was two-for-two.

It wouldn't have been a true Cubs–Phillies game from that era without Philadelphia third baseman Mike Schmidt hurting the Cubs some way, and so he did with a home run in the eighth, whittling the Cub lead down to one run at 5–4. Schmidt should have played on the Cubs. Wrigley Field loved him. The ballpark, not the fans. For him they were truly the friendly confines as he seemed to murder the Cubs every time he came to town.

This game provided our first look at new short reliever Mitch Williams since the Cubs acquired him from Texas in the Palmeiro deal. It was scary. His first batter flew out, which was okay, but then he walked Dickie Thon and balked him over to second. He walked pinch hitter Rickie Jordan. Two on and two out. He got out of trouble when Steve Lake flew out to left field. Not satisfied with only one inning of excitement, Williams started the top of the ninth, ahead by only one run, by giving up singles to ex–1984 Cub Bobby Dernier, Tom Herr and Von Hayes in rapid succession, loading the bases with nobody out and Schmidt due up. I felt sick to my stomach. Loading the bases for Schmidt? Who was this guy Williams? He looked crazy projecting his whole body toward the plate and ending up facing the outfield after his follow-through. I didn't know much about him, but it didn't look good for the Cubs this Opening Day, or this season if he was to stay on as closer. So far he had faced seven batters giving up three hits and two walks.

Schmidt worked the count to 2–2 and then Williams reared back and ... got him swinging! A major sigh of relief rose from the crowd along with the wild cheering.

There was still only one out. Williams went full on the next hitter, outfielder Chris James. One more ball and he would force in the tying run. Strike three swinging again! This was nuts. He finished the inning and the game by striking out Curt Ford swinging. The ballpark erupted with joy, but we had all aged several years over those two last innings.

Over the course of the year Williams, nicknamed "Wild Thing," helped the Cubs clinch the division and supported the pitching staff by recording 36 saves. He was named to the National League All-Star team. His ERA was a sharp 2.76. He struck out 67 in 76 games, but also walked 52 and gave up 71 hits.

The Cubs finished in first place in the NL East behind the combined leadership of some of the most popular Cubs of the last thirty years including Ryne Sandberg, Andre Dawson, Mark Grace, Greg Maddux, Rick Sutcliffe, Scott Sanderson and Shawon Dunston, plus Rookie of the Year Jerome Walton and another budding superstar, Dwight Smith. With a roster like that, maybe nobody should have been surprised when manager Don Zimmer's "Boys of Zimmer" won their division.

Eric Gagne, legendary closer and new to the Brewers, comes on in the ninth inning, Opening Day 2008. Word is he's past his prime, and sure enough he can't find the plate. He puts two on with nobody out. Up comes Kosuke Fukudome, the one who's supposed to be puzzled by American pitching, but the only Cub with any hits all day. He's two for two with a walk. He works the count to three and one. There's a huge gap between right and center as the Brewers expect him to hit to left. From the center field camera we see the next pitch leave his bat headed directly for that gap. You know it's gonna be at least two. But then WGN cuts to a different camera and we watch the ball land in the right center field bleachers, not too far from where Willie Smith's 1969 homer came to rest. Wrigley Field erupts in utter pandemonium. Fans jump and scream and wave their arms as if the Cubs had won Game Seven of the World Series (they don't know any better). And a new Cub hero is born. I hope he has more staying power than Willie Smith, who played only two more seasons, hitting .216 in 1970 and .164 in 1971 when he appeared in only thirty-one games after being traded to the Cincinnati Reds.

The score is tied with nobody out.

The Cubs can't score the winning run. Howry comes in to pitch the tenth and gives up a run. The top of the Cubs batting order can't do squat in the bottom of the inning and that's it. Another ugly Cub roller coaster ride. You can see it in the faces of the fans as they stare at the field, unable to believe it's happened yet again. You can see it in the faces of the players. And you can hear it in the voices of the Cub announcers, Len Kasper and Bob Brenly. The players and Piniella will say that it was a tough loss but they have to put it behind them and get up in the morning, or the next morning, put their pants on one leg at a time and get out to the ballpark and be ready to play because there's nothing anybody can do about Opening Day and it's already yesterday and they just have to be prepared for tomorrow and learn from their mistakes and there's still one hundred sixty-one games to play—blah, blah, blah. But if the Cubs had to lose, why not a no-doubt-about-it seven to three, with the Brewers scoring first and never giving up the lead? And what does this portend for Kerry Wood? Our worst fears fulfilled and only one game has been played.

In 1908, the Cubs had opened on the road, and as they prepared for their home opener on April 22 they shared first place with the New York Giants, both teams at 5–1. Pre-game ceremonies included raising the world championship pennant on the center field flag pole at West Side Park. The pennant, according to Charles Dryden of the *Tribune*, featured "a white baseball on blue ground and a restful white bear armed with a bat." As the flag made its way up the pole, it got stuck about halfway and had to be brought back down. The second try was successful, but Dryden wondered, as did many Cub fans, whether the incident was "an evil omen that boded ill to our Cubs."

The flagpole was a long way out there. Center field was a roomy 560 ft. and the flagpole stood behind the center field bleachers. The left and right field lines were 340 ft. each. When examining photographs of the old ball park, what strikes one first is the presence of grandstands built on rooftops overlooking the field. The right field wall bordered an alley running behind buildings that fronted onto Taylor Street. The seating built on those roofs looked remarkably like the grandstands atop the buildings on Sheffield Avenue beyond Wrigley Field's right field bleachers. Across Wood Street, beyond left field, fans could stand or sit on apartment rooftops, or look out over the park from upper story windows. The similarity to the present ambience of Wrigley Field and the buildings along Waveland and Sheffield is almost spooky.

The Cubs' owner in 1908, Charles "Chubby" Murphy, did not like fans watching his team without paying and so finally built mammoth billboards above the right field seats to block the view from across the alley. Ads crowded the billboard, including a huge one for *The Daily News* that ran along the bottom, just above the small sections of bleachers, from right center to the foul line. The Fair, a discount department store located on Adams between State and Dearborn, across the street from The Berghoff, bought the position at the top of the billboard. But that was pretty much it for purchasing advertising to be viewed, or listened to, during ballgames. Broadcast coverage by radio, TV and the Internet was still a long way off. And not to be an old fuddy-duddy, but at least back then ball fans didn't have to be subjected to erectile dysfunction ads and now, new this year I believe, herpes commercials. Our youngest daughter is eighteen and it's uncomfortable enough watching these ads with her. I can't imagine what it must be like for parents watching Cub games with young children, trying to explain the infield fly rule and E.D. during the same inning. Some of the ads are actually comical, with "subtle" images of enormous, thick tree trunks dominating half the screen, or a happy couple approaching a very Freudian art gallery entryway. Or another during which, at the very beginning, a kitchen faucet malfunctions and ejaculates much to the happy amusement of the involuntarily celibate couple, who now have to fix the problem. Why are they so devil-may-care about the prospect of crawling under the sink with a pipe wrench?

And how about those twin bathtubs on the patio, or maybe it's a cliff, overlooking dramatic landscapes? Are we to believe that the happy couple responds when the time is right, or after the time was right, by exclaiming, "Hey! I got an idea! Let's disconnect the plumbing, push a couple of bathtubs outside and enjoy the view"?

The Cubs warm up before a game in 1908 at West Side Park. Note the stands built on the rooftops across the alley (Chicago History Museum, SDN-006868).

Attendance for Opening Day 1908, was only 15,000. West Side Park capacity was 16,000 meaning that even after winning the World Series the year before, the Cubs did not sell out. When they did fill the park, overflow fans, or bugs as they were called during those years, were allowed onto the spacious outfield grass, a practice common at most ballparks of the era. Wooden, double-deck grandstands ran around West Side Park's foul territory, from beyond first base to beyond third base. The outfield bleachers were open to the sun, as they are today, making the rooftop views possible.

Cubs Opening Day Lineup, April 22, 1908 (in batting order)

Jimmy Slagle, center field
Jimmy Sheckard, left field
Frank "Wildfire" Schulte, right field
Frank "Peerless Leader" Chance, first base (and manager)
Harry Steinfeldt, third base

Wrigley Field looking out toward Sheffield Avenue today. The seating on the rooftops is remarkably similar to the scene a century ago (photograph by the author).

Johnny Evers, second base
Joe Tinker, shortstop
Johnny Kling, catcher
Chick Fraser, pitcher

You will note the names Tinker, Evers and Chance, the famous double play combination, inducted into the Hall of Fame as such in 1946, largely, some argue, on the strength of the poem written about them by Franklin Pierce Adams, published in the *New York Evening Mail*, July 10, 1910.

> These are the saddest of possible words:
> "Tinker to Evers to Chance."
> Trio of bear cubs, and fleeter than birds,
> Tinker and Evers and Chance.
> Ruthlessly pricking our gonfalon bubble,
> Making a Giant hit into a double—
> Words that are heavy with nothing but trouble:
> "Tinker to Evers to Chance."

The Cubs took an early lead in the 1908 home opener. Cub pitcher, Chicago-born Chick Fraser, a resident of Park Ridge, went the distance and, although the Reds scored two in the eighth to get within two runs, the Cubs matched them with two in the bottom of the inning, cruising to a 7–3 win.

And speaking of Park Ridge residents, as we roll into the 2008 season, the second most important race of the year is the presidential election, pitting Hillary Rodham Clinton, who grew up in the northwest Chicago suburb, against the U.S. senator from Chicago's South Side, Barack Obama, for the Democratic nomination. The Republicans have long since settled on John McCain of Arizona. The next Democratic primary is in Pennsylvania on April 22 (centennial of Opening Day 1908!), so the candidates, plus Bill Clinton, Chelsea Clinton and Michelle Obama, have been bouncing around the state where we live in Cub exile. Chelsea actually made a stop in York. No one really expected Pennsylvania to be an important primary state, but since the contest is so close, we're getting a lot of attention.

I won't comment on whom we will vote for, nor about the policies of the individual candidates except for one small problem with Hillary Clinton, which applies to this memoir. When she was running for senator of New York, I recall her appearing on the Letterman show wearing a Yankee hat. I remember her saying something like, "I think I've always been a Yankee fan." This upset me very much. Always been a Yankee fan? You think? You don't know? Park Ridge may be a suburb, but it's closer to downtown Chicago than O'Hare, which is technically within the city limits. She grew up a Cub fan, and when you grow up a Cub fan you *know* it. And you don't then become a Yankee fan, unless, I guess, you're running for the U.S. Senate in New York. I'm curious as to what she's going to claim now that she's running for national office. That old Cub hat will no doubt come down from the top shelf of the closet and be dusted off as the Cubs are getting all kinds of publicity and are one of the most popular teams coast to coast. The Yankees are also very popular in terms of total fan base, but the Yankees are also hated by just about everyone who isn't a Yankee fan. Really hated. Which brings me to my last couple of points about how Hillary Clinton could not have been a Yankee fan. She's a political animal and always has been. It would not have been too politically astute, even if she was only running for president of a local teen club, to be a Yankee fan in Chicago. Also, she would have known she was a Yankee fan, as opposed to thinking that she was always a Yankee fan, which implies some memory lapse, because nobody would have let her forget it. Sounds a little like dodging bullets in Bosnia to me.

Nobody hates the Cubs, except some Sox fans. Please note that when I refer to the Sox, I mean the Chicago White Sox, the only team known as the Sox to me. One sees the national media reference the Boston Red Sox as just the Sox, but that only confuses me, and most other Chicago baseball fans. North Side it's the Cubs. South Side it's the Sox, although you will see Cub fans on the South Side and Sox fans on the North Side. West Side? I grew up in Oak Park, which is the first suburb due west. Madison Street, the dividing line between the North Side and the South Side, runs through Oak Park. So in my neighborhood one's favorite team was not predetermined by your home address. One of my oldest friends, with whom I went to grammar school and who now lives on Ridge way up on the North Side almost to Evanston, is a Sox fan. Most of my six sisters were Sox fans, and one, who lives in Inverness which is even further north and west than Park Ridge, remains one. My brother likes both, but the Sox more. Four of my sisters have moved away from Chicago and seem to like the Cubs, but have found themselves rooting for other teams like the Braves, the Mariners and, in the case of my sister in South Jersey, the Phillies. This last change of heart is the most puzzling because she was a Cub fan for years, raised her kids to be Cub fans in spite of my brother-in-law being a lifelong Phillies fan, and she only admitted being a Phillie fan to me for the first time this past year. And she's sixty years old!

If, in her youth, Hillary was looking for an American League team to balance her Cub fan-ness, as I read somewhere, she would have looked to the South Side because when Hillary was a kid, the Cubs stunk but the Sox were good, especially in the late 1950s when she would have been coming of age, baseball-wise. Those were the years of the "Go-Go White Sox" of Luis Aparicio, Nellie Fox and Jim Landis, over whom my sisters would swoon. They were contenders, ending up in second place behind the Yankees, it seemed, every year. Except 1959. The Sox clinched the pennant after beating the Indians in Cleveland one night in a game broadcast on WGNTV—unusual in that WGN at that time broadcast only the home games of whichever team was in town, the Cubs or the Sox, and unusual in that WGN rarely broadcast night games. The Sox turned a double play in the bottom of the ninth and Mayor Daley (the First), a lifelong Bridgeport resident, his modest home a few blocks from Comiskey Park, ordered the air raid sirens sounded all around the city to herald the joyous news—the first Sox pennant in forty years. At that time, forty years seemed a long baseball drought. This was no small matter as 1959 was the height of the Cold War and we schoolchildren were being drilled on how to crawl under our desks and hold our heads between our knees and, as the old joke went, kiss our little butts goodbye when those sirens went off. Scared the poop out of a lot of Chicagoans.

1908 was an election year, and as in 2008 the incumbent president was a Republican, Teddy Roosevelt. Unlike 2008, however, the Republican president of a century ago was very popular and therefore could name his successor. Roosevelt anointed William Howard Taft of Cincinnati to be his heir apparent. There was a Cub connection here. Taft's half-brother Charles, owner of the *Cincinnati Times-Star*, provided financial backing for Charles Murphy to buy the Cubs in 1905. Charles Taft would then buy the Cubs from Murphy in 1914 and own the team for two years.

We rely on historical distractions such as these to ease the pain of Opening Day 2008, which was one stinking, memorable loss. Why did it have to be memorable? Why did fan hopes, or rather delusions, have to be brought yet another time to the peak of the mountain of expectations only to be blown off by a SSW gale? Why do I ask these questions?

There's always another game tomorrow.

> Tomorrow, and tomorrow, and tomorrow,
> Creeps in this petty pace from day to day,
> To the last syllable of recorded time;
> And all our yesterdays have lighted fools
> The way to dusty death.
> *Macbeth, Act 5, scene 5, 19–23*

One week into the season, we see that when they say there are a lot of games left to play, they (whoever "they" may be) are right. We have calmed down, but remain skeptical at best and fatalistic. Five or six games don't tell us much of anything. As of Monday morning, April 7, 2008, the much maligned Baltimore Orioles sit atop the AL East, with the Yankees and Red Sox fighting it out for last place. (Oh, that this would continue through the rest of the year!) The Detroit Tigers, picked by several to win the World Series, haven't won a game. The Mets and Phillies are struggling, too. In the NL Central, the Brewers and Cardinals are tied for first, with the best records in baseball. And the Cubs? They've looked good the last couple of days, beating Houston two out of three to close out their first home stand. Zambrano has been great in his two starts and Kerry Wood, after blowing up in the opener, settled down to save all three games the Cubs have won. They are three and three heading into Pittsburgh. Derrek Lee, after a slow spring, is hitting like a madman, batting .400 with three home runs. Fukudome has three doubles and a homer, hitting .421. The slowest start at the plate belongs to Soriano, who has yet to break .100, although he hit the long ball yesterday (Sunday, April 6), and threw a guy out at the plate from left field.

CHAPTER THREE

Into the Season

During the second week of April, the Cubs travel to Pennsylvania to begin their first road trip of 2008. Checking the schedule we see that they play three in Pittsburgh, including the Pirates' home opener, followed by a weekend series in Philadelphia. We can drive to Pittsburgh from York, Pennsylvania, in three and half hours, door to ballpark, and to Citizen's Bank Park in Philadelphia in two hours, with luck and reasonable traffic. Because of various obligations, our only opportunity to see one of the Pittsburgh games will be Wednesday night. Since moving to York in 2002 we have made this drive often, including two weekend series when we stayed in a hotel. Most often I leave work early so we can get to PNC Park by seven o'clock and see the first pitch, watch the game and drive back, getting home around one-thirty or two in the morning. That's when the weather cooperates. The weather almost never cooperates.

To get to Pittsburgh we drive north on Interstate 83 and get on the Pennsylvania Turnpike near Harrisburg. Once, we drove in a torrential downpour, the kind where drops as big as quarters pound your car and flood your windshield like flowing sheets of bubble wrap so the windshield wipers' fastest setting can't clear the glass. We made it to the first service plaza before concluding that they would never get one in, and so turned back. We were wrong. We arrived back home in time to watch about half the game on television.

Another time we drove under a steady rain, but not the blinding kind, and kept going right past all of the service plazas between Harrisburg and Pittsburgh, certain that if they played the night of the biblical flood, they'd play that night, too. We arrived in Pittsburgh in time for the first pitch (which is important because the Cubs are the visitors and so bat first). We

51

paid ten bucks for protected parking in a multi-level lot about half a block down the street from the left field corner entrance. We walked to the ticket office only to hear that the game had been postponed because of rain. Why, we wondered, when a killer typhoon hadn't stopped the game we gave up on? I'd like to say we were merely disappointed, but we were way beyond that, thoroughly bummed that we had just driven three and a half hours in the rain on the always treacherous PA Turnpike (no center shoulder, constant construction so often no right shoulder either, winding mountain passes, tunnels, lots of semis that don't seem to care that the conditions are lethal and so barrel on past us flooding our windshield and making us blind) and would now have to drive back in the rain and descending darkness without seeing the Cubs. Seven plus hours of white knuckles for nothing. And the parking lot wouldn't give us our money back.

At work we have MSN as our home page. I keep several cities' weather permanently posted in the lower right corner. Chicago; York, Pennsylvania; New York (for Brooklyn, where our daughter and grandchildren live and so the place we drive to most often) and wherever the Cubs are playing (the location we drive to most often after Brooklyn). On Wednesday the forecast includes a small, yet frighteningly ominous icon—an illustration of a dark gray thunderhead ripped asunder by a thick, fire-red bolt of lightning. Hovering the mouse's cursor over the cloud I see that it symbolizes thunderstorms. Why I need to confirm this by doing anything like hovering a cursor is symptomatic of Cub fan-ness. We often can't believe what is as plain as day and right in front of our faces, even though we've been beaten over the head with brutal facts and irrefutable evidence of endless futility for a century.

Our choice then is simple. Drive through a monsoon only to arrive in Pittsburgh for a rainout, or stay home which will guarantee that they'll play the game, which we'll watch on TV. I will not claim that we are unique in this belief that our behavior has a direct influence on the fortunes, or more often the misfortunes, of our favorite team. This kind of sick logic is common. It is a popular sports superstition. If you wear a certain shirt your team will win etc. We believe that the decision to play or not play Cub games in Pittsburgh is determined by whether or not we drive through torrents of rain to get to PNC Park.

So we stay home, only to discover that the game isn't televised. We have Comcast cable and in previous years if the Cubs–Pirates games weren't on WGN, whether in Chicago or Pittsburgh, they were on a Pittsburgh station that is part of our cable package. Why aren't they on? The second Pirates home game of the year and the first home night game, after all? What kind of broadcast support is that?

Of course, the April ninth game turns out to be the game of the year so far, and will no doubt be remembered forever by all who played in it or saw it. The Cubs blow a one run lead in the bottom of the ninth, on a home run served up by Kerry Wood (Oh no! Not again!). The Cubs score two in the fourteenth inning only to give up two to the Pirates in the bottom of the inning. The Cubs score two more in the top of the fifteenth and hang on to win their second consecutive extra-inning game. And we missed it. Moped out and missed it. So what that we wouldn't have made it home much before four in the morning? Ah, we tell ourselves, but if we had gone, the Cubs would have lost.

The Cubs win again Thursday night (televised), sweeping the Pirates' first home series. Now we must decide which games to go to in Philadelphia. We can't go Sunday, but feel like we can make it to both other games. On Friday I take a half day of vacation. Patricia has a piano lesson until four, so we're on the road by 4:15. Plenty of time, right?

The Schuylkill Expressway is the main road into Philadelphia from the northwest, kind of like the Kennedy in Chicago. But for most of its distance from King of Prussia, where you exit the turnpike, into Center City it is only two lanes in each direction. Now, Philadelphia is one of America's largest cities. A major metropolis. So imagine, if you're from Chicago, the Kennedy Expressway with only two lanes from O'Hare to the Edens split. Frightening, isn't it?

We breeze through the EZ Pass lane in the toll booth and come to an almost immediate dead stop. Okay, it's rush hour, but still. The jam continues all the way into the city and doesn't open up until we're past downtown. So although it only took us a little over an hour to get from York to King of Prussia (Valley Forge exit), it takes us almost ninety minutes to get from the outskirts of the city to the Broad Street exit near Citizens Bank Park, and then another half hour to get down Broad Street to the entrance of the first parking lot, a short par three away. On our way from the lot to the ticket office we hear cheers, and then a few moments later more cheers. We get into the ballpark and discover that the Cubs scored two in the top of the first on consecutive solo home runs by Derrek Lee and Aramis Ramirez. So the roars we heard were from the thousands of Cub fans that show up, like us, at every road game they can. Those two homers would prove to be two-thirds of the Cubs' offense, the last run also a home run with nobody on base, this one by Alfonso Soriano. We watch it sail by us in our nosebleed, 400 level seats, and make it into the first couple of rows just to the right of the left field foul pole. And that is that. Zambrano doesn't have his good stuff. He labors the entire time he's on the mound, which isn't long by his standards. The big scoreboard monitor shows him sweating heavily. He

spends a lot of time adjusting his athletic supporter and seems to be aiming
the ball and pushing it at the plate like a shot putter. Piniella lifts him in
the fifth. Maybe he's eating too many bananas, which he's being force-fed,
we hear, because he still has a potassium deficiency which contributes to
cramping in his pitching arm, the ongoing problem that surfaced during
spring training.

The Cubs lose 5–3. They look sloppy again. Errors. Misjudged foul flies
and an ugly incident in left center field when Fukudome runs down a deep
fly to the gap and makes a running belt-high catch only to bump into Soriano sprinting over from left, causing the ball to plop out of his mitt. Whose
fault? Who cares? Their fundamentals are poor.

On our way to our car we feel drops, but we're optimistic that we'll make
it home before midnight because the game ended around 9:30. Ha, ha, ha,
ha, ha. Joke's on us! The God of Cub Fan Misery will punish us for being
wimps and not going to Pittsburgh on Wednesday. We sit in the parking lot
forever, moving one half car length in an hour. We don't know why, but
finally get out by backing up, swerving around other cars, ignoring legal
parking lot lanes and driving all the way across the lot in the wrong direction to exit near the ballpark. We all have to go to the bathroom and hope
that the park is perhaps still open. It is not. The game ended over an hour
ago, for heaven's sake. We double back toward Broad Street, but it takes
another twenty minutes to make our way the quarter mile to the entrance
of Interstate 76. But it's open and clear! Woo hoo! We may make it home
in good time after all.

Not so fast, sucker. We follow the curve around to the section of the
highway that passes Center City and can see that it's backed up forever!
Solid brake lights ahead. And our bladders are screaming for relief! Where
to get off? Thirtieth Street Station? I know there are some hotels near the
art museum. But it could take as long to figure all that out as getting on the
turnpike and driving to the first service plaza. We take a poll and decide
that, although hurting, none of us are going to have an accident and so are
determined to get the hell out of Philadelphia and deal with the pressure
somewhere along the turnpike. An hour later, approaching the I476 junction, traffic eases a little and we can pick up some speed.

But the God of Cub Fan Misery is not done with us. The heavens open
up and crush us with the storm we thought we were avoiding two nights
earlier. Although traffic is very light (only emergency vehicles and idiots
venture out on nights like this), it is moving at forty miles per hour, hazard
lights blinking everywhere. Distant lightning illuminates the sky, but we
can't hear the thunder because the rain pounding our Accord's roof is too
loud. The right lane is blocked twice by accidents, bad ones it looks like but

I can't be sure because I can't really see anything. We make it to the service plaza and pull right up to the door in a no parking area. Lucy and Patricia jump out and are drenched hopping over puddles that cover the ten feet between our car and the door.

We arrive home at about 12:45 A.M., over three hours after the game ended. We could have been coming home from Pittsburgh! We've made it home from Brooklyn in less time.

Saturday's forecast is for more of the same, so we, in respect to the God of Cub Fan Misery, decline to try it again. They play the game and the Cubs lose again. However, the game was a sellout, so we would have ended up standing if we got in at all, which isn't bad, necessarily. We like standing room at Wrigley Field. But it certainly would've taken hours to get out of Philadelphia again.

We wimped out again, no doubt about it.

I have a prior commitment on Sunday so we can't go to the game. The Cubs win in the tenth inning on an error as the Phillies play a very Cub-like defensive game. The big controversy comes when DeRosa hits a home run down the left field line. Replays show that it was definitely foul. And the Cubs win by only a run! We'll take it.

Four wins and two losses on their first road trip. Not bad. Ugly, but not bad at all considering they look like minor leaguers and don't seem to have a starter who can get anybody out just now.

But on April 23, 2008, the Cubs beat the Colorado Rockies in the tenth inning for their sixth win in a row. They are now tied with the Diamondbacks for the best record in Major League Baseball, playing .714 ball. Everything seems to be clicking. Pretty good starting pitching—even the two starters who looked a bit off the first few weeks of the season, Lilly and Hill, seem to be coming around—excellent relief work, and hot, timely hitting. But what should make the rest of the baseball world take notice is that the win in Colorado was number 10,000 for the franchise. Only the New York–San Francisco Giants have won more. For fans around the world who assume that the Cubs have always been horrible, this should be a bit of a wakeup call concerning the team's hallowed, if largely forgotten, history. From 1876 until 1945 the Cubs were usually good, often contenders and fairly regular pennant-winners. Not even the dark ages of the post–1945 teams could erase all of that past glory. American League fans might point out that the Cubs had a quarter of a century head start since the Junior Circuit has only been around since 1901. But then National League fans will point out that the American League hasn't even been playing real baseball since the designated hitter rule became part of their game in 1973. As far as we're concerned, if a player takes the field, he has to pick up a bat, too.

We plan to attend our second Cub game of the year at Nationals Park in Washington, D.C., the night of Saturday, April 26, 2008. The evening before the Cubs are on WGN TV and we watch. Dempster pitches well enough and the game is close, the Cubs tying it at two in the top of the fifth.

In the bottom of the inning, Felipe Lopez sends a high drive deep to left center. Reed Johnson (we call him "Poop" Johnson for a reason that makes sense only to our family. It is actually a term of endearment, I promise.) takes off to his right, running hard on an angle toward the warning track. As the ball comes into view on our screen, we see that there is no way in hell he can get to it. He's going to a) hurt himself, and b) miss the ball which will bounce around in the outfield allowing Lopez at least two bases. From the left we see DeRosa, who's playing left field tonight, angling to back Johnson up and play the ball off the carom. Then Johnson dives, stretching full out in the air parallel to the ground, and snares the nasty little white orb just before he lands flat and slides into the padded base of the bullpen fence as Kerry Wood, sitting on a stool right at the fence, enjoying the game, looks on. Johnson jumps to his feet, the bill of his cap flipped comically up by the impact, and raises his mitt as he runs toward the infield, showing the umpires that he does indeed have the ball. DeRosa and Wood just stare at each other in disbelief.

"Poop!" shouts Lucy.

"Poop!" I shout.

"Oh my God! Wo, Poop!" shouts Patricia.

Bling! A text message arrives from Steve—*Poop!*

That's one you'll be seeing on the highlight reels for a long time, we say to each other.

But it isn't enough to save the game. And Howry doesn't have what it takes to save the game, either, although when he takes the mound in the bottom of the ninth the score is tied 3–3, so it's not a save situation. In protest, Howry decides to just flat out lose the game, giving up a two-run, walk-off homer to substitute catcher Wil Nieves.

Nothing can dampen the thrill of Poop Johnson's catch, though. Not even a typically horrible Cub loss.

I check the MSN Home Page weather predictions and once again the dark cloud with the bolt of lightning splitting its middle warns of trouble, specifically Saturday evening thunderstorms. I don't even mention it to Patricia and Lucy. We will not be dissuaded. We will not wimp out.

Checking the Nationals' Web site, I see that they open the center field gate a couple of hours before game time so you can watch batting practice from the outfield, and then open the rest of the stands ninety minutes before the first pitch to let the fans move around the park to the lower boxes, the better to see the players. So we leave at about 2:45 for a 7:10 start.

Web research also tells me that you can park for fifteen dollars in Lot HH north of the ballpark near where I395 and I295 run together. It looks to be at least half a mile away, but all of the lots look about as far, except the fifty dollar lot just outside the ballpark behind left field.

Driving toward the park from the east we cross the Anacostia River and know we missed an exit. We double back and approach from the south. From the outside it looks huge, all gleaming metal, white stone and glass. It could be the exterior of an indoor shopping mall. We continue north on South Capital, pass the ballpark and follow the convoluted Web directions to the entrance for 395 and the exit for D Street, bearing right on Washington Avenue to the parking lot which sits directly under the Interstate. A small triangular space dominated by the concrete underside of the highway overhead, concrete pillars and high chain link fences, it resembles the setting for the rumble in *West Side Story*. We are the first car to arrive and so, remembering the hour it took to get out of the lot at Citizens Bank Park in Philadelphia, we park right next to the exit.

To call the walk from Lot HH to Nationals Park ugly would be to insult the parts of our nation's capital that are merely ugly. We proceed under the highway across the street, not quite sure where the sidewalk leads. We end up on a median strip where Washington Avenue feeds into South Capital. How did we get there? We don't know! We find a sidewalk and pass several closed gas stations, empty lots and an old gray stone Catholic Church, its skin darkened by centuries of smoke and exhaust fumes, the last vestige of a neighborhood that has disappeared. To the east, on our left, everything is under construction, block after block dominated by cranes, the naked beams of unfinished buildings, white construction trailers, port-a-potties and tall, temporary wooden fences that wall off the sites, festooned with illustrations of what the new neighborhood will look like, according to the imaginations, or marketing departments, of the developers: all bright lights, condos, shops, boutiques and trendy restaurants. To the west, across busy South Capitol, the neighborhood of aging townhouses and small brick apartment houses looks threatened by the encroaching, continuously redeveloping city that has been Washington, D.C., for over thirty years, since Lucy and I both lived here in the mid–1970s. Southwest D.C. can't survive as a lower income neighborhood. It's the city's smallest quadrant, and it's too close to the government buildings that run along Independence Avenue from the Capitol, past L'Enfant Plaza and on to Fourteenth Street, to the Smithsonian and the Mall, and to the waterfront along the Anacostia where it flows into the wide Potomac. So maybe one day soon, the neighborhood around the park will be a D.C. version of Wrigleyville, only with a lot more glass and steel.

We enter through the center field gate, presenting the sheets of paper that are our tickets, printed using the online printing option. Right away we see that there will be a lot of Cub fans at this game. Among the several hundred that arrive early for BP, most wear something that screams Cubness, including Cub hats of all vintages, solid blue or white pin-striped shirts with players' names and numbers on the back, Wrigley Field (est. 1914) jerseys, "shut up and drink your beer" shirts, etc. But we've seen this often before, especially in Cincinnati and Pittsburgh.

Nationals Park, from the outfield seats, looks nice enough, but we suspect that its attraction lies in its newness. It is pristine, but without much personality, resembling most of the new ballparks we have visited over the years, from the South Side to Detroit to Philadelphia to Cincinnati. Four decks wrap around the infield, all dark blue seats, radiating shiny steel railings and clean white concrete aisles and stairs. The low wall behind home plate is composed of large rectangular blocks of gray-green stone of various sizes, reminiscent of the outer walls of the Catholic Church we passed on South Capital, only cleaner. There is a notch (as first called, in our memory, to describe the big gap in the third base upper deck at the Great American Ballpark in Cincinnati) above first base so you can see a little of the outside of the park to the south. But you have no sense of where you are. Nothing to indicate that the new ballpark resides in Washington, D.C. High above the backstop, really high, the huge, red and white, multi-level press box sits bolted to the highest reaches of the ballpark, even higher than the cheap seats. It looks like a misplaced, two-story industrial park office building floating above a sports arena.

We look up and see that Len and Bob have the worst view in the place, and indeed, during the Friday night broadcast, the two Cubs broadcasters commented early and often on how far up and away from the action they sat. Most of their jabs were meant to be humorous, jokes about thin air and sky-high pop fouls getting nowhere close to their altitude, but they also complained that from their stratospheric vantage point they have a difficult time judging the trajectory of fly balls. Back before the era of luxury boxes, broadcasters had great seats. Jack Brickhouse and Vince Lloyd sat in a broadcast booth that hung below the Wrigley Field upper deck, just to the left of the backstop screen. But when the park was remodeled and the new suites were added, a new press box was built high at the top of Wrigley Field, although the top of Wrigley Field is still closer to the field than some luxury boxes at other ballparks.

When we get to our seats, Row Z in the lower deck along the right field line, we see the real problem with the park. The view toward the outfield is not pretty. Beyond left field, behind the foul pole, is a non-descript, multi-level concrete parking lot (the $50 valet lot that I read about online). Huge Nationals-themed banners do little to hide its blandness. A two-story, circular pavilion, a refugee from an amusement park or boardwalk, dominates center field above the seats—two levels of bars and restaurants. An enormous Jumbotron scoreboard towers above the two decks of right field seats. Maybe from the highest deck you can see the Capitol in the distance, but down at field level, you may as well be in Generic Big League Ballpark USA.

At 5:30 they open the sections in foul territory, from foul pole to foul pole. We go directly to the seats behind the Cubs' third base dugout. The players are already out on the field doing their stretching exercises as the Nationals finish BP. We comment on how big Derrek Lee looks, and how small Mike Fontenot. We watch the game's starter, Carlos Zambrano, take swings from both sides of the plate. He looks real big, too. Sweet Lou stands behind the batting cage for a while, but then strolls out to shallow left to watch the progress of the pre-game warm-up. Kerry Wood comes in from the field; Lucy and Patricia comment that he's aging into his thirties really well. We watch Japanese media set up video cameras and wield microphone booms. When Fukudome returns to the dugout after shagging fly balls in right field, alongside a Japanese colleague in street clothes who also wears a mitt and runs down hits, he is surrounded by admirers and signs many autographs. A couple of Caucasian fans shout greetings in Japanese. A young man wearing a Boston hat comments dismissively that, oh, Cub fans are into learning some Japanese, too, mere trend-followers of fans in Seattle and elsewhere where Japanese players are on the roster. One of the Cub fans turns to him and says, "Hey, we're just trying to be neighborly." The Red Sox fan doesn't reply.

The Cubs get the top three hitters in the batting order, Johnson, Theriot and Lee, on base in both of the first two innings, and score five runs. Zambrano doesn't look like he has his best control, going deep into a lot of counts and walking too many, building his pitch count early, but he gets out of every jam and pitches seven scoreless innings, striking out five including the last batter he faces in the seventh, Nationals third baseman Ryan Zimmerman. Unlike the game we saw in Philadelphia, he works quickly and spends little time off the mound regrouping himself, if that description makes sense. Cub hitters give him great support right from the start. Every Cub ground ball has eyes. Anything down the third base line ends up in the corner for a double, and the Cubs will hit five doubles in the game, including two each for Ramirez and Cedeno.

During one of Fukudome's at-bats Lucy glances up at his stats and personal info on the right field scoreboard and notices that it's his birthday. But he doesn't celebrate the day with any kind of hit, settling for only a walk in the first, finishing the game 0-for-4, striking out twice. Every other Cub gets a hit except Soto, who is struggling mightily at the plate. He strikes out five times, three times looking, for a dubious achievement of eight consecutive K's over two games. Lou will sit him on Sunday.

By the ninth inning a lot of fans have left, leaving Cub fans to virtually take over the stands. As John Lieber, in relief, faces the last Nationals batter in the bottom of the ninth with a 7–0 lead, the crowd rises and it is loud with Cub supporters screaming. Lieber accommodates us by fanning Lopez, and Nationals Park erupts with Cub fan exuberance. On the way out, Cub fans high five each other, shout "Cubs!" at the sky and sing Steve Goodman's "Go Cubs Go." Most are more calmly pleased, knowing that it's April and it's ... well, it's the Cubs. Once in a while you make eye contact with a fan who, like most Cub fans you know, has been here before and all you do is exchange quick, shallow nods and move on, ready for whatever comes next.

What comes next for us is another storm. We first feel drops as we approach the center field gate. The rain steadily increases in intensity as we approach South Capital and begins to pour somewhere around that Catholic church. By the time we reach Lot HH we are drenched, and the wisdom of parking next to the exit is moot because we are among the last five cars in the lot. But now the question is how the hell do we get out of D.C.? We don't know Southeast and Southwest as well as we know Northwest, and even the route out of the district via New York Avenue Northeast. But we know we don't want to head back toward the ballpark, or even get on the Interstate that runs directly over our heads, not with 35,188 fans (I won the attendance pool with a guess of 36,421 vs. Lucy's very high 41,652 and Patricia's very low 30,185 — not to brag, but I felt pretty good about it considering it was our first time in that ballpark) with the same idea. We decide to head north to either find New York Avenue or turn east toward RFK Stadium and find our way out of town from there, which we have done before after previous Cubs–Nationals games pre–Nationals Park.

By now I have the wipers on full-tilt. I somehow miss Independence and then for some reason do not turn right on East Capitol after passing in the shadow of the Library of Congress. We end up on Maryland Avenue. We drive through Capitol Hill neighborhoods, long since gentrified, young professionals and students spilling out of bars and visible through uncovered front windows partying in the warmly lighted living rooms of refurbished row houses and brownstones. We see signs for I95 and follow them, but then they disappear! So we continue through Northeast, hardly able to see, through the low income neighborhoods that haven't changed in thirty years, finally finding Rhode Island Avenue, which I remember from my days in D.C., and following it all the way past the University of Maryland to an entrance to the Beltway beyond. We had crossed a hypotenuse of the city, from Southwest through Northeast and, through sheer luck, did it in perhaps less time than it would have taken to wait in traffic on the interstates and the Baltimore–Washington Parkway. Perhaps the storm had kept traffic light.

But we still had I95 and I83 to deal with. The skies put on a fireworks display of thunder and lightning, once again, as during the drive home from Philadelphia, the lanes of the highway all but impossible to see. But we arrive home at about 12:30 A.M., two hours from Lot HH to our driveway, just as it should have been.

The next day I feel hungover from the exertion, having had nothing to drink at the ballpark! What a waste! We can't afford to return to D.C. on Sunday (the total tab for Saturday night's game, including tickets, courtesy fees and other charges for purchasing them online, gas, parking and refreshments, was around $300), so we watch Sunday's game on WGN, the Cubs losing two-zip. Where every hit fell safely Saturday night, every line drive and ground ball is right at a Nationals fielder on Sunday. Lilly looks good, but the Cubs can't buy a run, squandering a bases loaded fifth, and so end the series against maybe the worst team in baseball losing two out of three.

On April 30, 2008, they are 9 percentage points ahead of the Cardinals, just barely in first place with a 17–10 record.

Similarly, on April 30, 1908, the Cubs sat alone in first place, only a game ahead of the Pirates and a game and a half ahead of the New York Giants. But they had played only eleven games, while the 2008 Cubs are well into the season having played twenty-seven.

They continue to lose series after series, two games to one, including three-game sets against the Brewers at Wrigley Field, the Cardinals in St. Louis, and the Reds in Cincinnati, losing the last game 9–0 under a barrage of seven Cincinnati home runs, four off Lieber (brought into the rotation from the bullpen for the first time this year) in the second inning alone.

Good teams and bad teams. Home and away. The Cubs seem to be able to lose to anybody.

On an off day, Thursday, May 8, they await the arrival in Chicago of the best team in baseball, and the team that swept them three games to none in the 2007 National League first round playoffs, the Arizona Diamondbacks. The Cubs are in second place, two games behind the Cardinals, and four games over .500. I have been a Cub fan for over half a century, and I believe this should be a pretty good start, historically speaking. But the trends are bad. Soriano has been back from his leg injury for a week and continues his slow start, hitting far south of .200. Hill doesn't look too good, and Lilly and Howry need to hit mid-season form.

We check the schedule and decide to travel to Pittsburgh for games on Saturday, May 24, and Sunday, May 25. To insure that we (I) don't wimp out, I book a hotel on Priceline where you name your own price and then pay for the room. No refunds. So either we go or eat the cost of the hotel, which is located near the universities, not far from the location of Forbes Field. On a previous trip to Pittsburgh we visited the area and touched the portion of the center field wall that still remains as a monument to baseball seasons past.

Forbes Field opened on June 30, 1909, but was already a firm plan in the mind of Pirates owner Barney Dreyfuss the year before. It would be the first among the next generation of National League ballparks to replace wooden grandstands with concrete and steel, and second only to Shibe Park, home of the Philadelphia Athletics of the new American League, which opened earlier that same year.

Wrigley Field and Fenway Park are the last among those parks to survive and thrive as baseball's most historic distinations. Makes one wish they could have done something to save some of the others, especially, as far as I'm concerned, Old Comiskey Park on Chicago's South Side, built in 1910 as "The Baseball Palace of the World," and the oldest ballpark in the majors when it was demolished after the 1990 season. That year, I brought our three older kids—Jeanne, 12; Anne Lise, 10; and Steve, 8 (Patricia was not yet one and so remained home with her Mom)—to the second-to-last game. It was sparsely attended, which was fine with us because I was able to take the kids on a tour around the park, from our seats along the first base line, to the right field upper deck, around to the outfield seats and across the ramps that ran behind the original exploding scoreboard. Sure I'm a Cub fan, but I loved Old Comiskey Park second only to Wrigley Field. It was unique and somehow elegant with its broad, arched windows opening onto the streets beyond, and to the lush trees in the public park outside left field.

Dreyfuss built Forbes Field on higher ground because Exposition Park, where the Pirates played through 1908, sat right on the Allegheny River, between the current sites of PNC Park and Heinz Field, home of the Steelers. The problem was water. Sitting on low ground, drainage after the frequent (don't we know they're frequent!) Pittsburgh rains was poor. Dreyfuss had a tarpaulin designed in 1908, the first of the modern era, made of "1,800 yards of brown parafinned duck," as reported by *Sporting Life*. "The center ... will be attached to a truck 10 × 15 feet and 3 feet high. Before and after a game in threatening weather, the truck will be run out and the playing ground covered with the tarpaulin.... There should be no more deferred games on account of wet grounds." But he knew that better drainage in a new park high above the rivers was the answer.

In addition, all of the teams needed more seats. The largest of the ballparks held about 20,000, but demand for tickets to see contending teams, like the Cubs, Giants and Pirates, often exceeded that by several thousand, especially when they played each other. And the owners, with an almost universal reputation for avariciousness, were loath to deny anyone admission.

There were already complaints about fans sitting on the grass in the outfield or in foul territory. For example, the Giants' April 22, 1908, home opener began an extraordinarily controversial year at the Polo Grounds with a victory that was bitterly protested by visiting Brooklyn Superbas (later the Dodgers) owner Charlie Ebbetts. A routine fly ball to right, hit by the soon-to-be infamous Fred Merkle in the bottom of the ninth, was ruled a double when it landed among the fans sitting on the field. The ruling set up a two-out walk-off home run by Giant "Turkey" Mike Donlin (although they didn't use the term "walk-off" back then. It was first used in the *San Francisco Chronicle* in 1988). Ebbetts protested vehemently to National League president Harry Pulliam, who was very familiar with the problems of the old ballparks and the teams' policies regarding fans on the field, having worked for Barney Dreyfuss in the Pittsburgh organization before being named president of the league in 1902. Pulliam sympathized with Ebbetts but supported the umpire's ruling on the field.

A couple of years ago, after arriving in one of the PNC parking lots before a game, we asked the attendant if he knew where Exposition Park stood. He smiled and told us that the locations of home plate and the three bases are painted on the blacktop, a rather humble commemoration of the old ballpark, it seemed to us, especially considering the fact that four games of the first World Series, between the Pirates and the Boston Americans (soon to be known as the Red Sox), were played there in 1903. Boston, led by Hall of Fame pitcher Cy Young, won the scheduled nine game series in eight, five games to three.

The lot attendant pointed in the direction of PNC Park and said, "Right over there, near the highway overpass." We learned later that there is an official Pennsylvania Historical and Museum Commission marker (the same kind of marker you see all over the state) along the Riverwalk, but seeing the bases plotted out on the parking lot asphalt in the same paint as the parking space lines is somehow more moving. And they're not that easy to find because they blend in with the rest of the lot.

Each year we park in that lot for at least one game and stand at Exposition Park's home plate and look out toward the junction of the rivers and the steep hills beyond and pay homage to Tinker, Evers, Chance, Brown and the rest of the 1908 Cubs who played there, and even Honus Wagner.*

Who would have the energy and dedication to plot the old infield? There is an essay on the Society for American Baseball Research website called "Finding Exposition Park by Denis Repp" by David Finoli [*sic*]† (www.sabr.org/ sabr.cfm?a=cms,c,572,9,0) that tells the story of dedicated fans and baseball researchers heading out to the parking lot with old maps and surveys to locate the site of the diamond.

The painted marker at the site of Exposition Park's home plate in Pittsburgh. The Pirates moved to Forbes Field in 1909 (photograph by the author).

Forbes Field held 25,000 when it opened, and its capacity grew to 35,000 by 1938. Exposition Park, by comparison, had a capacity of 16,000. The Cubs would not move into a concrete and steel ballpark until 1916, but the Cubs organization did not construct it themselves as most other teams had. Weeghman Park was built in 1914 on the grounds of a Lutheran seminary, bordered by Addison Street, Clark Street, Waveland Avenue and Sheffield Avenue on Chicago's North Side. It was the home of the Chicago

---

*While compiling images for this book we visited the parking lot to photograph the painted home plate. As I crouched down to shoot, several fans sat tailgating in camping chairs behind a minivan.

"You from the newspaper?" one man asked. "Take a picture of this guy." He pointed at his friend. "He's wanted by the police in four states."

"No. I'm taking a picture of home plate here."

"Of what?"

I explained the significance of the painted marker. They marveled. They had been sitting within ten feet of it and hadn't even noticed it was there, had no idea there used to be a ballpark on the spot, other than Three Rivers Stadium, and surely didn't know the first World Series was played there. They told me I had made their day.

†The dual byline, "By Denis Repp" and "by David Finoli" is as it appears on the listed Web site as of the final edit of this book.

Exposition Park in Pittsburgh, 1903. Note the Allegheny River and what is now downtown Pittsburgh just beyond the ballpark. Photograph by F.M. Hull (Carnegie Library of Pittsburgh).

Whales of the Federal League until that league folded after the 1915 season. Whales owner Charles Weeghman then acquired a piece of the Cubs and moved them to his now vacant park for the 1916 season. So what was to become Wrigley Field was kind of "ready-made" for the Cubs.

So we're set to go to Pittsburgh. In the meantime, the Cubs get hot and win nine out of eleven games, returning to first place. Alphonso Soriano is a mad man, raising his batting average from under .200 to .300 in a week, even though it drops back into the .200s pretty quickly. They lose two out of three in Houston, but put their hitting clothes on and trounce the Pirates 12–3 at PNC Park Friday night, May 23, as we watch on the Pittsburgh channel. Zambrano looks strong and as the Cubs come to bat in the top of the eighth inning, he's three for four at the plate and due up. But he's thrown over a hundred pitches, so we anticipate a pinch hitter. As the camera pans the Cubs dugout, however, there he is rummaging around for a bat wearing a batting helmet. Sure enough, Piniella lets him hit and he delivers his fourth hit of the game, this time batting from the left side. We think to ourselves, what fun! But worry that maybe Piniella is showing up the Pirates—rubbing it in their faces a little. Whether or not he means any disrespect, it feels a bit off.

The Pirate announcers state that they will all be glad when the series ends on Sunday and the Pirates won't have to face the Cubs again until late in the season. The Cubs have had the Pirates' number all year so far, winning nine out of ten through the first game of this final Chicago–Pittsburgh series of the first half of the season. So it is with lightness in our hearts that Lucy, Patricia and I hit the road at about half past noon on Saturday the 24th, heading for Pittsburgh. We have plenty of time to drive the two hundred and twenty miles in about three and half hours, check into our hotel and make it to the ballpark for batting practice. Scattered, billowing white clouds gently roll across a deep blue sky as we motor west on the Pennsylvania Turnpike. Pennsylvania is a beautiful state, and once through the twin Blue Mountain and Kittatinny Mountain tunnels, which seem about as close to each other as home plate and the center field wall at Wrigley Field, maybe closer, we're in the rolling mountains, lush with new, late spring foliage; and we smile and ooh and ahh as we admire the often dramatic vistas, spinning rock 'n' roll CDs as we go.

We exit I376 and find Forbes Avenue, only to discover it's a one way street, and our hotel is in the wrong direction. We double back around, and after a couple more miscues arrive at the hotel. As we park the car we discuss the pros and cons of driving to the ballpark, and decide to leave the car and take a cab.

The cabbie looks like a refugee from a Jimmy Buffet festival, with dirty, long, disheveled blond hair and a wrinkled, very loud green Hawaiian shirt. He laughs when we suggest that he guess where we're going, Cub shirts, hats and even earrings proudly on display.

I have to note here that the proliferation of team logo wardrobe at ballgames seems to me a relatively recent phenomenon. Looking at historic photographs of 1908 games, for instance, one sees a sea of bowlers and straw boaters, with most men wearing dark suits and ties. The few women in the crowd look very formal with full-length bustled skirts and long-sleeved white blouses buttoned to the neck. They also sport huge, wide-brimmed Merry Widow hats festooned with ribbons, bows, feathers and more lace that look to rise a foot above their heads. As more and more women attended games, these hats became a problem, blocking the sight lines of fans for several rows behind them, and were often written about by the era's sportswriters. In fact, large women's hats were becoming a controversy at a variety of entertainment venues to the point where one of the earliest films by D.W. Griffith (director of *Birth of a Nation*, *Intolerance* and other silent era classics, and considered by many film historians to be one of the first truly great movie directors) is a brief farce that shows stubborn women in a Nickelodeon refusing to remove ridiculously decorated Merry Widow hats, causing a near riot. The message, "Ladies, please remove your hats," was the 1908 equivalent of our own era's "Please silence your cell phones" projected before movies.

Because team gear is almost dress code at ballparks these days, it is easy to spot the Cub fans at PNC Park. They are everywhere, as usual. Paid attendance will be announced as 29,929 and I swear 10,000 must be Cub fans. And they (we) are loud. "Let's go Cubs" rings out loudly and often throughout the game. Pirates fans try to counterattack with "Let's Go Bucs" but because "Cubs" and "Bucs" almost rhyme, the stands echo with a chaotic, "Let's Go _u_s!" Similarly, during the seventh inning stretch, they play "Take Me Out to the Ballgame" on the organ, the words displayed on the scoreboard with the fans exhorted to follow the bouncing cookie. When it comes time to shout your team's name in the "it's root, root, root for the (home team)" verse, it's a mash of "CUBbies" and "BUCKos" so you can't make out either.

As has been widely publicized this year, in addition to the centennial of the last Cubs World Series championship, 2008 is the centennial of the publication of "Take Me Out to the Ballgame." However, it was not sung during the seventh inning stretch back then. In fact, there was no seventh inning stretch in 1908, and probably wasn't needed as games rarely went longer than two hours. Jack Norworth wrote the lyrics, the story of a girl named Katie Casey. The music is by Albert Von Tilzer. Neither, as the story goes, had ever been to a baseball game, but because of the frenzy surrounding the 1908 race, even two non-fans from the world of popular songs had to notice. And Norworth was a star, having written the huge hit "Shine on Harvest Moon" with Tilzer, and engaged to marry Nora Bayes, star of Florenz Ziegfeld's "Follies," the most popular show on Broadway for the second year in a row. Norworth and Bayes were the Brad Pitt and Angelina Jolie of 1908. Norworth was inspired by a sign he saw, depending on what you read, in a train station or on a platform of the Ninth Avenue Elevated in Manhattan. I tend to think it might have been the Sixth Avenue el that ran from Central Park downtown. The "Follies" were in production at the Jardin de Paris, a rooftop theater at Forty-fourth and Broadway. It would have been a straight shot for him to walk a couple of blocks south and east to the Sixth Avenue el, which stopped at Twenty-eighth and Sixth, a half block from Von Tilzer's office, York Music Publishing in Tin Pan Alley. As of this writing, the building is still there at 40 W. 28th Street.

According to the song, Katie Casey is "baseball mad," to the apparent bewilderment of the author, who describes her "beau" as competing with the game for her affection.

> Katie Casey was baseball mad,
> Had the fever and had it bad.
> Just to root for the home town crew,
> Ev'ry sou Katie blew.
> On a Saturday her young beau
> Called to see if she'd like to go
> To see a show, but Miss Kate said
> "No, I'll tell you what you can do:
>
> Take me out to the ball game.
> Take me out with the crowd.
> Buy me some peanuts and Cracker Jack.
> I don't care if I never get back.
> Let me root, root, root for the home team.
> If they don't win it's a shame.
> For it's one, two, three strikes; you're OUT.
> At the old ball game."
>
> Katie Casey saw all the games,
> Knew the players by their first names.
> Told the umpire he was wrong,
> All along, good and strong.
> When the score was just two to two,
> Katie Casey knew what to do,
> Just to cheer up the boys she knew,
> She made the gang sing this song:
>
> Take me out to the ball game.
> Take me out with the crowd.
> Buy me some peanuts and Cracker Jack.
> I don't care if I never get back.
> Let me root, root, root for the home team.
> If they don't win it's a shame.
> For it's one, two, three strikes; you're OUT.
> At the old ball game.

The verses are almost never sung, as we know, which makes me wonder why the song is so strongly connected to Norworth instead of Von Tilzer, the composer of the melody. The melancholy swing of the chorus reflects the fatalistic, almost defeatist lyrics, as if written for the Cubs of fifty years later. "If they don't win it's a shame." No celebration of victory here! And "it's one, two, three strikes; you're OUT!"

The beauty of the strikeout! The best contact hitters in the game will swing and miss on strike three hundreds of times (Ty Cobb, 357), power hitters perhaps thousands of times (Sammy Sosa, 2306) and face that long, lonely walk back to the dugout amid the cheers and jeers of a hostile crowd or the sighs and groans and maybe boos of hometown fans. The strikeout is one of the elements of baseball that makes the game truly unique. In any other sport a great player, like Michael Jordan or Walter Payton for instance, can play game after game after game seemingly flawlessly as far as the typical fan in the stands can see. But in baseball, even the best major league players fail at the plate more often than they succeed, and with alarming frequency look ridiculous waving at a pitch that has completely fooled them. That is why the chorus of the most celebrated song about baseball ends with a strikeout, and the most celebrated baseball poem is all about a strikeout. No other short piece of baseball writing captures the game as well as "Take Me Out to the Ballgame" by Norworth and "Casey at the Bat" by Ernest Thayer, the latter an elegy to a star player who whiffs in the clutch. Baseball futility enshrined forever in music and verse. No walk-off home runs in these baseball literary gems.

My research tells me that "Take Me Out to the Ballgame" was first performed in October of 1908, after the season ended, even though copyrighted the previous spring. It became an instant hit, perhaps because the lyrics matched the mood of New Yorkers who had just lost the pennant to the Cubs in the most controversial sequence of events in baseball history.

But back in Pittsburgh, in May 2008, the Cubs would soon give new meaning to walk-off. Saturday's game begins well enough, as Marquis looks strong in the first three innings, and then the Cubs take a one-nothing lead in the top of the fourth. The game goes back and forth until the Cubs are up 4–3 as the Pirates come to bat in the bottom of the ninth. Kerry Wood trots to the mound to close it out, and we start feeling sick. As previously stated, we want Wood to succeed more than any Cub in recent memory, but he makes it excruciatingly hard to watch. And this game is no different. He throws a first pitch strike, but then hits Chavez, the Pirates' catcher, with a pitch. Nady pinch bats and raps a single. Sanchez bunts the runners to second and third and then Rivas hits a sacrifice fly to right to bring in the tying run. Blown save. Crap. It feels like we will now wait for the inevitable walk-off hit, whenever it comes. Defeatist like the song? You bet.

We wait until after 11:00. Patricia and I keep score in Dick's Sporting Goods scoring books in which we can squeeze innings ten through thirteen in by keeping score in the totals boxes at the far right. But, in spite of the

Cubs getting the leadoff man on in both the 12th and the 13th innings, it goes to 14. More than half the 29,929 fans in attendance (Lucy won the attendance pool, guessing 27,582!) have left, leaving mostly Cub fans screaming for a clutch hit or two. But there are none. Freddy Sanchez reaches first on a throwing error by shortstop Ryan Theriot to start the bottom of the 14th. But the good news is that Sanchez bats first in the order so we can just go on to the next page of our score books and start at the top with no messy arrows, circles or footnotes. In fact, Soriano led off the Cub half of the inning, so we could start their 14th on a brand new page, too! What are the chances of that happening—the two teams sending the tops of their batting orders up in the 14th inning just to make scoring easier for us?

A wild pitch by Michael Wuertz sends Sanchez to second. Rivas hits into a routine ground out to Theriot (the wild pitch took the double play away), sending Sanchez to third. Wuertz puts McClouth on first with an intentional walk. But they decide to pitch to Jason Bay. Why? we ask ourselves. Why not put him on, too, and have a play at every base? Bay is three for five with a homer, while the next guy, LaRoche, is only two for six including two strikeouts. Ah, but they pull in the outfield and pitch to Bay who promptly hits the dreaded walk-off line drive over the heads of the pulled in outfielders to the left-center field corner. So ugly.

And then we can't get a taxi back to the hotel. We wait at a cab stand on Federal Street, outside the back wall of the SpringHill Suites Hotel across General Robinson Street from the ballpark, with about a dozen other Cub fans. But no cabs come to the cab stand. A couple of Pirate fans wait with us and explain that Pittsburgh isn't Chicago or New York, where there are always plenty of cabs everywhere. They are waiting to be picked up by some friends. A cab pulls up and the driver offers to drive a Cub fan and his young son to their hotel, our hotel coincidentally, for twenty-five bucks. I can't help myself and loudly tell the guy not to take it. The cabbie is robbing him. We took a cab from that hotel to the ballpark for less than ten dollars about seven hours earlier. Seven hours! I am suddenly very tired. The Pittsburgh fans feel genuine pity for the guy with his son, and so offer them a ride as soon as they're picked up by their friends. Even though we're trying to get to the same hotel, we wouldn't fit in the car, so we say nothing and wait. And wait. And wait. Walking through downtown Pittsburgh after midnight, and then up Forbes Avenue to Oakland, is not an option.

We eventually find a cab and live to tell the tale, but the next day we plunge into the netherworld of Yogi Berra's "déjà vu all over again." Sunday we drive to the game and park between PNC Park and Heinz Field. We find the humble, painted home plate marking the location of Exposition Park, and then continue through the parking lots, sparsely populated by Pirates fans tailgating, to PNC Park. We sit in the last row of the lower deck, just below the concourse along the left field line. The Cubs take a 5–4 lead in the top of the eighth. But I turn to Lucy and Patricia and say, "Why do I feel that a one run lead for the Cubs is actually an insurmountable Pirates lead?" They nod and brace themselves.

Carlos Marmol comes in to close out the bottom of the ninth. There are many Cub fans who wonder whether it would have been wise to let him close Saturday night, too, which we hate to think because we *love* Kerry Wood. Marmol gets pinch hitter Chris Gomez to pop up to short, but then walks Sanchez. The Pirates put in Brian Bixler to pinch run. Marmol then fans Rivas. Two out, man on first. This should be it, right? Large pockets of Cub fans below us stand and cheer for the last out. This we don't particularly like to see because they are blocking the view of Pirates fans sitting behind them. Not good baseball etiquette, especially for visiting fans.

What happens next is the kind of play you want to witness in person only once in your life. But I've seen it twice!

Marmol gets McClouth to hit a routine fly to left. We stand (there is no one behind us) and cheer the win for the Cubs. Soriano drifts toward the line, the ball clearly in his sights. He is soon out of our line of vision, blocked by the upward slope of the third base line wall. But then we are completely confused because at the exact moment that Pirates fans should be disgustedly rising to leave, they instead jump to their feet and cheer even louder than the Cub fans had been cheering. What the heck? I look toward the diamond to see Bixler racing down the third base line to score. We have a view of television monitors mounted on the underside of the upper deck. The replay shows that the ball hit Soriano's mitt and bounced onto the ground. He appeared to have lost it in the sun.

The game is tied, but we mercifully only have to wait until the 11th inning this time. But it happens almost exactly the same way as the night before. With a man on second with two out, the Cubs walk McClouth to get to Bay. Just like the night before, instead of loading the bases by walking Bay, too, they choose to challenge him, and just like the night before he drills a single, this time off Jon Lieber, to win the game.

We can't get out of Pittsburgh fast enough. At the historic Midway service plaza on the turnpike we run into a couple of Cub fans and, instead of the normal "Go Cubs" exchange, we can only shrug.

Along the way Lucy reiterates a conclusion reached by Anne Lise several years ago: "We are the goat."

Almost ten years ago, in September of 1998, colleague Bob Ficks put together a baseball outing. He hired a stretch limo, stocked it with beer and snacks, and drove a bunch of us, including myself and co-employee Ellen Ladd, from Chicago up to Milwaukee to see the Cubs play the Brewers. That morning, the Cubs were tied for the lead in the National League Wild Card race. Sammy Sosa hadn't hit a homer for quite some time (this during the fabled McGwire–Sosa steroid-fueled home run contest of that year) but anxious anticipation ran high among us.

We had beautiful seats, first row of the upper deck along the right field line, directly above Sosa. And he produced for the thousands of Cub fans who had made the trip, hitting two home runs and fueling a 7–0 lead going into the late innings. The Brewers, however, fought back, getting within two by the bottom of the ninth. Cub closer Rod Beck loaded the bases with a single, a double and an intentional walk. With two out, Geoff Jenkins hit a routine fly to left. We Cub fans rose to our feet, cheering wildly. Game over, right? Cub left fielder Brant Brown planted himself under the lofting ball and then ... dropped it. With two out, all three runners were going with the pitch, and before I could even shift my eyes from Brown to the infield, the man who had been on first was halfway to home with the winning run. Within an instant the game went from a two-run win to an excruciating loss.

Ellen grew up a Cardinal fan in Edwardsville, Illinois, across the Mississippi from St. Louis. She sat bemusedly watching the celebratory Cub fans return to our normal, depressed state in the time it takes to ... drop a fly ball.

There are a lot of Cardinal fans in Southern Illinois. My grandmother, who lived in Macedonia, Illinois (population: 51), claimed to like the Cubs, the Sox and the Cardinals, but I suspected that she included the Chicago teams only to please her eight Chicago-raised grandchildren.

Earlier in that wild, home run–crazy 1998 season, Bob Ficks invited Ellen and me to a Cubs–Cardinals game at Wrigley Field. Much has been written about the magic of that contest between two popular power hitters and how it brought legions of strike-soured fans back to baseball and thousands more new fans to the game for the first time. Fans weren't just following the individual accomplishments of a single player, as with Roger Maris' 61 homers in 1961, the record Sosa and McGwire were chasing, or Rickey Henderson's base-stealing record of 130 set in 1982, as exciting as those feats were. This was a contest between two baseball giants, both larger than life, to see who would first break and then set the most celebrated record in baseball. From early in the season few doubted that Maris' mark of 61 home runs would fall. The questions were who would reach 62 first, when, and then who would end the year with the new home run record because whoever hit number 62 first did not necessarily have a lock on being on top at the end of the regular season.

The new back grill along Waveland Avenue at Murphy's Bleachers, corner of Waveland and Sheffield, Chicago (photograph by author).

The morning of August 19, 1998, Sosa and McGwire were in a dead heat at 47 homers each. It was a pleasant day for mid–August, even a little cool. There were clouds but no hint of rain. Bob picked me up at my suburban Arlington Heights office, about twenty miles from Wrigley Field. Ellen, who lived a couple blocks east of the ballpark, would meet us at Murphy's back grill for a pregame burger and beer. Cubs–Cardinals games are always crowded, but with the Sosa–McGwire story dominating baseball news from coast to coast, the atmosphere around the ballpark was that much more electric. The scalped ticket market along Waveland and Sheffield was more brisk and animated than was normal for a mid–August weekday afternoon on the North Side. The Cubs were in second place, 7½ games behind the Houston Astros, but still in the wild card race; St. Louis sat in third place, 16½ games out of first. But most of us were thinking about the long ball more than possible postseason baseball.

We found our seats in the lower grandstand above the Cubs' bullpen and below the I-beam posts that support the upper deck, so we had clear, unobstructed sightlines of almost the entire playing field. Only the far left field corner was out of our view. The stands were packed—SRO. The announced attendance would be 39,689; in 1998 Wrigley Field's capacity was

38,884. By checking the flags above the center field scoreboard, we saw the wind appeared to be blowing in pretty hard from the east, or right field, but not enough, we felt, to stop a well hit ball by either Sosa or McGwire.

The game began badly with Cub starter Mark Clark giving up two runs on four hits. The Cubs tied it in the bottom of the second on a two-run homer by José Hernandez, so Ellen and the thousands of other Cardinal fans on hand couldn't celebrate a Cardinals lead for long. And then it was our turn to lord it over our guests when Henry Rodriguez hit a two-run dinger in the fourth to put the Cubs up 4–2. But that's not what we came for, at least not entirely. Sosa had been called out on strikes in the first and thrown out at second in the third trying to stretch a single into a double. Maybe he was too anxious. Pressing. McGwire had flown out to deep left in the first, putting a charge into the crowd, and popped out weakly to Hernandez at third in the third.

In the top of the fifth Clark walked McGwire, drawing a loud chorus of boos from the Cardinal fans. Bob and I agree that no pitcher in their right mind would purposefully give McGwire anything to swing at during any season, but especially in 1998. Same with Sosa. Cardinal fans didn't agree and felt Clark should challenge McGwire. Pitch to him, for God's sake!

In the bottom of the fifth Sosa came to the plate with two out and Cub second baseman Mickey Morandini on first with a single. Would Cardinal pitcher Kent Bottenfield pitch to him? In addition to his 47 home runs Sosa was batting .311 with 119 runs batted in. He was dangerous in every way. But Mark Grace, hitting .320 and one of the best contact hitters in the game, followed Sosa giving him great protection in the lineup. A man on first with two out is not often considered a serious jam for a pitcher, especially against the Cubs, but in 1998 the Sosa–Grace one-two punch was a problem even with nobody on base.

From our seats we couldn't really tell what Bottenfield threw to Sosa for his first pitch, but we knew when it left the bat with that special, sweet, satisfying crack that it was tagged. We jumped to our feet as it sailed right past us, deep to left field and out for Sosa's 48th, giving him the season home run lead, and the Cubs a four-run cushion at 6–2. Ellen didn't stand. She sat quietly, grinning slightly, sardonically as if to say, okay okay, you guys take round one but there's a lot of baseball still to be played. Bob and I hooted with joy and slapped high fives with every Cub fan within reach.

McGwire came up again in the top of the sixth with the bases loaded and two out. Cub manager Jim Riggleman brought in relief pitcher Terry Adams to face him. Cardinal fans started making a lot of noise knowing that the Cubs would have to pitch to McGwire or walk in a run. Even with a four run lead, and McGwire representing the tying run at the plate, walking him would look like a complete capitulation even to Cub fans. Then, with the count at one ball and two strikes and the whole ballpark screaming—Cub fans for strike three and Cardinal fans for the long ball—a passed ball scored the runner from third and sent the other two runners to second and third leaving first base open. McGwire looked at ball three and ball four and took his base. Cardinal fans howled in protest as Riggleman slowly returned to the mound and called on Felix Heredia to come in for Adams. Heredia got Cardinal center fielder Ray Lankford to ground out to second base to end the Cardinal threat with minimum damage done.

The game held nothing but promise. If the Cub bullpen could hold on, McGwire would only bat one more time and could at best tie Sosa at 48. Or the Cubs could walk him again! No one would vocalize such a sentiment, but to say it didn't cross our minds wouldn't be honest. In the meantime, Sosa would hit one more time, too. And the Cubs still held a three run lead.

But the Cardinals scored twice in the seventh on a Delino DeShields pinch-hit home run off Matt Karchner, the Cubs' fourth pitcher of the afternoon, to cut the Cubs' lead to one. Ellen's smile changed from sardonic to expectant. Cub fans began to fidget uneasily in their seats. A one run lead felt like a tie or worse. The cheerful buzz of a couple of innings ago had turned into a murmur of dread.

Sosa came to the plate in the bottom of the seventh with a man on first and two out, and walked on five pitches. It was our turn to scream bloody murder. Gutless Cardinal cowards! Pitch to him! Ellen laughed openly as Grace flied to center for the third out.

In the top of the eighth McGwire hit second and quickly drew a count of three balls and one strike. Cardinal fans, sensing a third walk, groaned loudly, many standing and blistering the air with colorful curses directed at pitcher Matt Karchner and Cub manager Jim Riggleman, as well as their mothers, ancestors and descendants, before the Cubs even had the chance to pitch ball four.

They never got the chance to really let the Cubs have it because on the next pitch McGwire crushed it, sending it screaming down the left field line, from our point of view almost a carbon copy of Sosa's homer as if he was thumbing his nose at Cub fans saying, "Sammy can do it? So can I." The Cubs and Cardinals were tied at six, and Sosa and McGwire were tied at 48.

Neither team scored in the final two innings of regulation, the Cubs going out meekly, three up and three down in both the eighth and the ninth. Looking on the bright side, Sosa was due up in the tenth!

But so was McGwire.

Terry Mulholland, the Cubs' fifth pitcher of the afternoon, looked good having faced seven Cardinal hitters and giving up only one hit and a walk. And he looked sharp striking out Brian Jordan on three pitches to start the tenth. Up stepped "Big Mac." First pitch, ball one. Then ball two. Again, Cardinal fans grew restless sensing that Mulholland was pitching around McGwire and would unintentionally intentionally walk him. But McGwire made an honest man out of Mulholland by taking his next pitch deep for his second home run of the day, giving the Cardinals a one-run lead, and himself a one home run lead. Bob and I sat glumly in our seats, unable to see the field for all of the standing, jumping and delirious Cardinal fans, including Ellen. When Lankford followed McGwire with another homer, she again laughed and without saying it aloud seemed to join in with the general Cardinal fan message to Cub fans: "You see, Cub fan chumps! No matter how good you think things are, no matter how good you think the Cubs are, no matter how much hope you summon up from your worthless souls, the Cardinals will play in and probably win another World Series long before the Cubs."

Perhaps we project. Ellen would never say such a thing, and probably thinks about baseball in terms of the Cardinals and rarely wastes her time considering Cub futility at all. But sometimes it feels like everyone in baseball believes this about the Cubs, maybe especially Cub fans themselves, and especially after games like these.

Sosa came up second in the bottom of the tenth and Cub fans managed a loud standing ovation, urging him to match McGwire homer for homer. But he hit it to the pitcher for an easy put-out at first. The Cubs threatened with two out but failed to score and it was over. They lost 8–6 and Sosa fell behind McGwire 49–48.

Bob and I were very happy that Ellen lived in Wrigleyville and wouldn't be with us for the long, slow rush hour drive back to the far western suburbs.

For us, the home run contest seemed to end that day. Less than a month later, on September 8, 1998, McGwire would be the first to pass Roger Maris when he hit number 62 against the Cubs in St. Louis. The Cubs and Sosa showed class as they congratulated him, Sosa trotting in from right field to hug and be bear-hugged by McGwire. But the moment was bittersweet, as are our memories of that splendid season of home runs and Cub Wild Card hopes. Ten years later the sadness of the steroid scandal and the baffling behavior of Sosa as his love affair with Cub fans soured, make it almost impossible to relive that year with the same thrills we get when, for instance, reliving the Bulls' great seasons of the same decade. Perhaps we understand a little bit how Sox fans felt during the Black Sox scandal of almost ninety years ago.

CHAPTER FOUR

Midsummer Dreams

All media report it. My colleague, the Phillies fan, brings it up at work, as if it's news to us.

The Cubs, going into June, have the best record in Major League Baseball, National League and American League. This has not happened since 1908. After the debacle in Pittsburgh they beat the Dodgers three straight at Wrigley Field, followed by three straight against the Rockies to make them 35 and 21, playing .625 ball. But they are only two and a half games ahead of the Cardinals. They have one more to play against Colorado on Sunday, June 1.

On May 31, 1908, the Cubs were in first place with a record of 23 and 13 and a winning percentage of .639, ahead of the Phillies by three and a half games. The Giants were tied for third with Cincinnati at 19 and 16, mere percentage points behind the Phillies. The Pirates were next at 18 and 16.

Lucy and I can't watch the fourth game against the Rockies because we have other obligations, as does Patricia, but she arrives home well ahead of us. When we do pull into the driveway and stumble into our townhouse, after an enjoyable if exhausting tour of Hershey, Pennsylvania, we ask Patricia what happened.

"Cubs won," she says. "And Steve [our son who lives on Waveland Avenue across the street from Wrigley Field] called. I was talking to him as I was watching the game. Soriano connected and I started screaming and Steve said, 'Yeah, I'm looking out my window. The ball is rolling down my street.'"

The Cubs start June having gone 7 and 0 at Wrigley Field after the miserable finish to the three game series in Pittsburgh. All is sweetness and

77

light, and we are planning a trip to Chicago over the weekend of the Sox series. I know that it is already sold out, but Steve can get tickets to anything, so we're confident we'll see at least one game this year at Wrigley Field.

We, however, wonder about our luck. Of all the games they've won over the last several weeks, why did we see two of the very few losses, and probably the two most miserable, depressing losses at that? "We are the goat," indeed. But this is baseball and as any major league player will tell any interviewer after a horrible loss, as Soriano did after he lost the ball in the sun in the bottom of the ninth inning of the last game in Pittsburgh, there's always another game. So you put the bad ones behind you and look forward to the next one. Which is what we'll do. We will be Chicago bound.

The Cubs maintain their position as the best team in baseball through the first couple of weeks of June, winning like crazy at home and going 4 and 3 on a West Coast road trip. The usual horrors raise their ugly heads— Soriano drops another fly ball, but then throws the runner out at second base; Zambrano loses a lead, with the help of a defensive meltdown, and then loses his cool waging war on dugout Gatorade coolers and his hat—but all in all, the Miracle on Clark Street continues into mid-month.

The presidential election distracts most of the rest of the country. Barack Obama finally wins enough delegates to assure his nomination on Tuesday, June 3. Hillary Clinton doesn't concede that night, preferring to put off the inevitable for a few more days, but then throws her support behind Obama the following Saturday. If all goes as expected from now through the Democratic National Convention in Denver this August, Obama will be the first African American man in history to be nominated president of the United States.

Just as the Cubs seem to have their everyday lineup set, with periodic changes in center field (Johnson or Jim Edmonds, released by the Padres on May 9 and signed by the Cubs a few days later, much to the displeasure of many Cub fans who still think of him as the enemy from his years killing the Cubs as a Cardinal), and the infield (Cedeno subbing at second for DeRosa or at shortstop for Theriot), Atlanta Braves pitcher Jeff Bennett pitches Soriano high and tight in the second inning of a night game played at Wrigley Field on Wednesday, June 11. Soriano appears to start swinging, but then pulls his hands back toward his chest as the ball tails inside. It hits him on his left hand and ricochets up to the right side of his face, near where his jaw meets his ear. He drops to the dirt in obvious pain.

In spite of his adventures in left field, since returning from his first stint on the disabled list Soriano has been key to the Cubs' winning ways. He leads the team in home runs with fifteen, even though out for fifteen days in late April. He's hitting over .280 for the year after an abysmal start that saw him below .200 for weeks. Since his return on May 1, he's been hitting .323.

The Cubs announce that he has a fracture in his left hand and will be out for six weeks, which, as far as we're concerned, means eight. We could be wrong. Maybe we're too used to Prior and Wood never returning from injuries, until Wood came back this most recent time and went to the bullpen.

Tuesday night, June 10, Albert Pujols of the St. Louis Cardinals hit a routine ground ball and left the batters box to run it out, only to pull up lame a few yards up the first base line. It was nothing special. He didn't appear to trip or lose his balance. He took off for first as he had done hundreds, maybe thousands, of times before. He'll be out for three weeks.

As the players, managers and press say over and over again, injuries are part of the game, someone's got to step up, the Cubs have the depth to hang in there while Soriano mends (but do the Cardinals have the same depth to deal with Pujols' absence?) etc., etc. But it's depressing, watching both injuries happen, and makes Dempster's 7–2 complete game masterpiece a little less exhilarating.

Dempster continues to amaze, striking out eleven and making only one real mistake, giving up a two-run homer to pinch hitter Corky Miller in the seventh inning. He's now 8–2. He could win twenty games as a starter this year.

Before play on June 12, the Cubs remain the best team in the majors, and are still two and a half games ahead of the Cardinals. By June 17, they are twenty games above .500 and off to their best start since ... not 1908 this time, but 1906, the year of their record 116 wins. We would never presume to suggest that such a thing could happen again in 2008. A prediction like that? Kiss of death.

We leave York, Pennsylvania, the morning of June 19 at about 9:00. We plan to drive straight through to Chicago, with a brief stop in Maumee, Ohio, to pick up Steve's girlfriend, Tara. No problem because Maumee, a Toledo suburb, is right on the Ohio Turnpike. It will take no more time than a stop for gas—which is right at $4.00 a gallon (on June 13, my total at the gas pump was over $50.00 for the first time)—so we anticipate that the trip will take the normal ten and a half hours, which will get us into Chicago at about 7:30 P.M. Central Time. It's a beautiful day for driving, so we look forward to the Pennsylvania landscape. And it is lovely, alternately pastoral and dramatic as we drive through the lush green Allegheny Mountains. We pass Pittsburgh at about 12:30, right on schedule.

Steve's birthday was June 15, which was also Father's Day in 2008. This happens every now and then, and so ever since Steve was little we called such a conjunction of festive occasions "Men's Day." We plan this weekend to be a big blowout of celebrations which include, in addition to Men's Day, Mom's last day of work June 18, Patricia's graduation from high school (straight A's and top 10!), Steve's last day on one of his two jobs which he is finishing up even as we drive west, and the last weekend before Lucy is scheduled for major surgery, which will put her out of commission for at least six weeks. So we plan to do it up.

Steve is very happy because instead of working ninety or so hours a week, and every weekend, he will have a more human Monday-through-Friday schedule. Lucy isn't exactly looking forward to the surgery, but it will correct a nagging problem and prevent a potentially more threatening condition in the future.

We bought Steve a bunch of bulky presents for his birthday, and cleaned out the basement of his last remaining possessions still at home, so our trunk is full. It's difficult to fit Tara's small suitcase, but we shift things around and make room for it and head off again from Maumee for our Monster Men's Day Weekend Blowout, and a three-game series against the White Sox at Wrigley Field.

Somewhere along the Indiana Toll Road we pick up WGN Radio and listen as the Cubs get swept by the Tampa Bay Rays (formerly Devil Rays— I don't recall when or why the "Devil" was dropped, but can guess). The Cubs sound bad, which does not bode well going into the series with the Sox.

Yesterday Steve wasn't sure when he could get off work. His last day at the wine shop at Racine and Taylor includes an evening tasting that could last until 10:00. But we talk to him as we pass McCormick Place and he tells us he's done—the tasters were apparently in the right mood and ready to sample and thus went through the allotted bottles more quickly than usual. He'll meet us in the parking lot of our hotel, the Holiday Inn Mart Plaza, one of the few Downtown or River North hotels where you can actually pull into an adjacent parking lot.

Chicago looks beautiful. Radiant red and golden yellow flowers line the Lake Shore Drive median. Trees, lush with deep green leaves, gently billow over the roadway. Cyclists, joggers and walkers crowd the paths along the lake from Hays in Jackson Park, which we always take to Lake Shore Drive in order to pass the brilliantly glowing, gold leaf, twenty-four-foot replica of the *Republic* statue that stood in the reflecting pool of the White City that was the 1893 Chicago World's Fair.

As we approach Downtown, we notice two new, very tall buildings. One appears to be at the south end of Grant Park, on the east side of Michi-

gan Avenue. The other is the as yet uncompleted Trump Tower on the site
where the Sun-Times Building once stood on the north bank of the Chicago
River behind the Wrigley Building. We don't know what to think of it yet,
but our first impression is that it is something of an intrusion, breaking the
elegant sweep of the cityscape that used to be bookended by the John Han-
cock Building on the northeast and Sears Tower on the southwest.

We turn left onto Monroe and pass the new wing of the Art Institute.
Not too sure about that either. It looks a bit retro to me, harkening back to
the 1950s or 1960s, an era of some rather unfortunate architectural deci-
sions, like Lincoln Center in New York and the University of Illinois at
Chicago (still Circle to us—Lucy and I both alumni). The thin vertical elements of the wing's skin are eerily, to me, reminiscent of the World Trade
Towers. Continuing through the Loop, we marvel at how busy it is, crowded
with foot traffic. Ten or twenty years ago, on a Thursday evening such as
this it would have been dead.

We turn north on Franklin and cross the river onto Orleans, turning
into the hotel parking lot across the street from the mammoth, gray stone
hippo of a building that is the Merchandise Mart. I glance up toward the
top of the southwest corner of what was until very recently the largest private office building in the world, in spite of the fact that it is only eighteen
stories tall. Twenty years ago I worked in an office on the fifteenth floor, my
desk pushed up against a window I can now see from the street. At the end
of most workdays I watched orange-red sunsets over the sprawling West
Side of Chicago, Braun Bottles below me and University Hall at Circle visible in the distance to my left at Morgan and Harrison. Sometimes violent
weather fronts rolled in from the horizon, visible long before they broke over
the Loop, lightning illuminating thick black clouds thundering, literally,
right at us. On Wednesdays during late spring I would stand and look down
onto the junction of the north and south branches of the river at Wolf Point
as sailboats and luxury craft lined up waiting for the bridges to rise so they
could coast out to their berths at one of Lake Michigan's harbors. Then, on
Wednesdays during the fall, they would return to dry dock.

The hotel's parking lot is on Wolf Point. We pull in and find Steve
already there. We drive a few spaces down and marvel at the views, one looking south down the river, under the Lake Street el bridge and beyond, a
canyon formed by the skyscrapers that shadow the river on both sides; and
east toward the lake, a wall of mostly sparkling new glass and steel or glass
and stone high rise office buildings and hotels that run along Wacker Drive
to Lake Shore Drive.

We wonder at the fact that Wolf Point, what must be among the most
coveted locations in Chicago, is an open air parking lot. Our friend Bob

Cooney (who didn't walk out of Cardwell's no-hitter) used to tell the story of one of his ancestors who settled in Chicago during the middle of the nineteenth century. He ran a tavern on Wolf Point, but then, perceiving that the city was growing to the west, traded it for a roadside saloon at Lake and Kedzie. The comparative worth of those two properties now? Doesn't matter. Our friend has his name on the shingle of one of the most successful law firms in Chicago. My parents wanted me to go to law school with him, but ... that's another story.

We're all so happy to see Steve, and he's especially jubilant because he just closed the wine shop for the last time. We exchange gifts right then and there, popping trunks to store our loot. After checking in, we head to our rooms which face north, looking down on the East Bank Club. Steve has a wonderful bottle of champagne which we quaff as we toast the weekend, our myriad of celebrations and the Cubs, who we are certain are on a one-way trip to the middle of the division, having lost two out of three to Philadelphia at Wrigley Field, and, as we just heard on WGN, three out of three to Tampa Bay in Tampa.

Steve needs to turn in his store keys so we agree to meet in an hour at a nearby boite to figure out the rest of the weekend.

Do we have tickets? No! That would have required planning, at which we are not good. Are there any tickets available? Of course not! This is the Cubs vs. the Sox, for God's sake. All three games have been sold out for weeks, if not months, and seats are going for hundreds of dollars on the street. So here's the plan: Steve will get up early, cross Waveland Avenue and stand in line to buy us all standing room tickets. Great idea! We love standing room. It's always a party, populated by serious ball fans who are determined to get in no matter what, and who are quick to talk baseball with total strangers and who form a kind of standing room brotherhood, watching out for each others' spaces, keeping lines of vision clear and popping for rounds of beer. And at fifteen bucks a ticket, it's the best baseball value in town.

We sleep well and get up early. I go down to the little shop on the first floor to get coffee and a paper. The Cubs–Sox Crosstown Showdown dominates the front page of the *Sun-Times*. Stories and columnists follow through page 8 ... but wait! It's a fake front page. The real paper starts after this special sports opening section.

On fake page 5, Jay Mariotti writes about a war of words, or at least a preemptive strike of words from the South Side. Sox general manager Ken Williams is quoted as follows:

> It is so different. You might as well build a border, a Great Wall of China on Madison, because we are so different. We might as well be in two different cities.

The unfortunate thing for me is it's a shame that a certain segment of Chicago refused to enjoy a baseball championship being brought to their city. The only thing I can say is "Happy Anniversary [the 100th anniversary, that is]."

Sox manager Ozzie Guillen is also quoted complaining about rats at Wrigley Field, calling it "the worst field in baseball," and stating that Sox fans show up and watch the game while Wrigley Field is populated by tourists. Sox pitcher John Danks chimes in by saying (in a separate piece on page 15), "We'll all be bringing our nose plugs (to Wrigley Field), try not to smell all the urine over there." Wanting everyone to understand that it was only a joke, he continued, "Nah, we're looking to have fun over there, but that place is a [bleep] hole."

The Cubs are silent but Mariotti feels the need to defend them, calling Williams "bitter (that the Cubs are) the blueblooded phenomenon with the national identity and charming shrine, (while the Sox are) the other team that no hotel concierge ever recommends." As for Guillen, as far as Mariotti is concerned, he "is a jerk being a jerk. If you want to like the jerk, fine, but that's what he is." We had no idea that this kind of poison is festering in Sweet Home Chicago. A bit silly.

We cross the enclosed walking bridge over Orleans Street and head through the Merchandise Mart, past its windows of upscale home furnishings and radio stations, and past the elevator bank where I caught my lift up to the fifteenth floor every working day for over five years, to the second floor el station. It's all automated now, but there's a cheerful CTA employee posted at the entrance to help anyone who is challenged by the fare vending machines. She recommends all-day passes for five bucks each, but we doubt that we'll need them, so I put six bucks on a card and that pays for Patricia, Lucy and me one way to Wrigley Field. The fare card celebrates the Crosstown Showdown series with a 1950s retro illustration (very reminiscent of the covers of Cubs scorecards of that era) of a ballplayer about to throw with the heading "2008 Cubs vs Sox." A subhead that reads "TAKE CTA OUT TO THE BALLPARK" runs vertically along the magnetic strip.

We look for the Ravenswood, but remember that since we moved from Chicago the names of the various CTA train lines have been changed to colors. The Ravenswood is now the Brown Line.

There are no more conductors. The train driver has the additional responsibility of looking out his window to make sure there are no passengers dangerously close to the train, or stuck in a door, before continuing on down the line. And instead of the conductor's distorted, crackling, scratchy voice coming over the train PA system to announce stations and transfer points with all the audible pleasure of fingernails scraping across a blackboard, it's a pre-recorded, disembodied professional voice talent that booms in deep, woofer-like fidelity that we are indeed on the Brown Line and the next stop is Chicago Avenue and Franklin.

While on the train, we get a call from Steve. Apparently the line for standing room is around the block and the word is out that each fan will be allowed only one ticket. This does us no good because, even if he makes it to the ticket window, we need five. As we pull into Fullerton, where we will change for the Howard, errr ... Red Line ... to Addison, we arrange to meet Steve, go to breakfast and decide on our next step.

We run into him at Harry Caray's statue near Sheffield and Addison. We collectively shrug and decide to see our brick before eating.

Our brick? Yes. The Cubs had a promotion offering commemorative bricks to be set in the sidewalk around Wrigley Field for perpetuity, or at least until this recent surge of ridiculous popularity (okay, it's over twenty years running now, but it still seems recent to us) ebbs and the Cubs then decide, because of dwindling attendance and the evil machinations of a greedy and heartless owner, or owners, to move to a new city or suburb, or replace the holiest temple of baseball in the world with a sterile amusement park-like stadium with computerized everything and huge Jumbotrons that dwarf the playing field.

Upon these bricks you may inscribe any message you wish, as long as it's clean and mostly pro–Cubs. As a family Christmas gift, Steve purchased one for the Sullivans (of Chicago, York, PA, and Bloomington, IN) and Meissners (of Brooklyn). On

The Chicago Transit Authority celebrates the June 2008 crosstown series between the Sox and Cubs with this special farecard.

Christmas Eve we discussed what to put on the brick. I encouraged using our names so future generations could go to the ballpark and note the fierce Cub loyalty of their ancestors. I took notes. Here's what was suggested:

SULLIVANS
MEISSNERS

or

LIFE IS CUBS

or

WE WERE
AT THAT GAME

or

WE WERE AT THAT
GAME—SULLIVANS
AND MEISSNERS

The eggnog-fueled debate raged and finally I was overruled on every suggestion (as is normal) and the following was adapted with loud acclaim:

THANKS DAD.

Why? Because I am blamed

The Sullivan-Meissner families' "Thanks Dad" brick outside Wrigley Field's Clark Street entrance and near Ernie Banks' statue, dedicated Opening Day 2008 (photograph by author).

for the insane Cub-based behavior of every member of our family, including Lucy (raised in White Plains, NY), and Jeanne's husband, Brian (raised in Buffalo, NY), although Jeanne herself gets most, if not all, of the credit for that conversion.

"Thanks Dad" is a little obscure and can be interpreted many ways. Most might conclude that it was cast in the spirit of gratitude, as in, "Oh, wow, thanks, Dad. We are the luckiest humans on earth to be Cub fans and we owe it all to you. It's a privilege. No, an honor. No, a *blessing!*"

Others might read it with a more sarcastic lilt, as in, "Thanks, Dad. Yeah. Thanks a-friggin' lot. We compromised our educations, our personal relationships, our health, our mental stability, our incomes, our ability to accomplish anything in this life other than the ability to keep score, and we all risk basal cell skin cancer, or worse, from too many afternoons in the bleachers. Time squandered when we could have been pursuing art, music, world health or saving the environment. And what do we have to show for it? Not one ... NOT ONE ... World Series championship in our, or your, lifetime. Yeah, thanks, Dad, because up until now getting in the playoffs for the Cubs only means we gotta turn off the TV after the Cubs lose the last game they play for the year as some other team (like the Marlins, goddamnit) celebrates. Yeah. Thanks, Dad. Thanks a bunch."

We start toward Clark Street, walking on hundreds of other bricks, most of which have people's names on them, only to be met by a horde of fans just told by the ticket office that standing room is now also sold out. Presumably they're all heading for the ticket brokers located on Addison between Sheffield and the el station. Continuing on around the corner, we pass under the famous marquee and find our brick almost under Ernie Banks' new statue. We marvel at what a good likeness of Ernie it is, then Patricia takes a picture of our brick.

A scalper approaches and offers four box seats for a hundred bucks. Somebody comments that the price is way too cheap and the tickets must be counterfeit. We need five anyway, so I don't pursue it, telling the guy that I don't have the cash.

"ATM right over there," he replies.

"Okay," I say. "I'll think about it. I'll find you if I want them." He nods and turns away. I wonder to myself why he is on this side of the street. Used to be Wrigley Field security, and the police, kept scalpers across Clark, Addison, Waveland and Sheffield. There used to be a thriving open air ticket market in front of Murphy's, and Ray's before it was Murphy's.

Ray's was our favorite pre-game meeting spot until Murphy bought him out. Back in the 1970s you could actually stand on the southeast corner of Sheffield and Waveland and have elbow room. It was a humble, typical Chicago neighborhood corner bar with an illuminated Budweiser sign hanging off the front corner of the one-story building. Only the window to the outside, where you could order a beer and a hot dog until the city decided they couldn't sell beer through the window anymore, made it at all unique. Inside it was dark, the main room and a small back room taking up only a small fraction of the current Murphy's footprint. You can see where Murphy added on. Along its Waveland Avenue side the color of the brick changes from yellow to red where the back addition begins. There were no additional bars or grills at Ray's, let alone the beer garden in the back that today extends all the way to the alley under the el tracks. We'd sit at the bar and have a hot dog and an Old Style, right out of the can, as Ray helped tend bar, serving himself periodically from a gallon jug of wine. When we heard the first notes of the national anthem, it was time to wander across the street with plenty of time to buy a ticket ($1.25, raised to $1.50 by 1978, and $2 by 1980), a scorecard ($.20, raised to $.25 in 1977) and a beer ($.50) and find a seat under the scoreboard.

One evening in the late 1970s, the phone rang. I answered it. Lucy was sitting in the living room of our apartment, the second floor of an Albany Park two-flat at the end of the Ravenswood line. Here's what she heard (my end of the conversation):

"Hello? Yeah ... yeah ... yeah ... yeah ... yeah. I'm there."

I hung up. When I returned to the living room, Lucy said, "Don't tell me. Frenchy's in town and you're meeting him at Ray's tomorrow." Frenchy grew up on the next street over from us in Oak Park. He's a Cub fan in exile, too, living on Long Island.

"Yeah," I replied.

She laughed, and probably would have gone to the game, too, except that it was late September and we had babies, and it would be cold at Wrigley Field. But somebody had to represent the family....

Hungry, having skipped breakfast at the hotel, we walk down Clark to the Salt & Pepper Diner to discuss our next move. Over variations of eggs, potatoes, sausage, juice, coffee, etc. we determine to check the scalpers with storefronts and addresses first, before talking to anyone on the street. Steve has a business meeting a few blocks south at Sheffield and School Street, so the two of us leave the diner while Patricia, Lucy and Tara finish their breakfasts. Several doors down we pass a group of four guys standing in front of a bar. "Need tickets?" one of them asks.

"Yeah," I say.

"You okay, Pops?" asks Steve.

"Go ahead," I say. "I'll be fine." Steve continues on to his meeting and I follow one of the guys into the bar. Just inside the door is a closet-sized office with another guy at a laptop. The first guy asks how many and I say five and he says that's kinda tough. But he has three here, in the far reaches of the third base upper deck, and then two more in the boxes in the section right below. Total price? $850.

I don't know what to think about that price. Is it good, bad or fair?

Or how about this? He's got these four together, then we do one standing room and see if a seat opens up near the four. But standing room is sold out, I tell him.

"We have standing room," he says.

"Do you have five?"

"Sure." I wonder for a moment how he has so many, if each customer was allowed only one standing room ticket when they went on sale this morning. But then I realize I don't know what I'm doing, and so forget the question entirely. You see, back when we went all the time, you could walk up to the ticket office and get in. And even recently you could buy as many standing room tickets as you wanted and didn't have to wait in line at dawn. We indeed waited for and bought standing room tickets for a Cubs–Sox game during batting practice just a few years ago. We stood in line along the old red brick Waveland Avenue outer wall, watching the ballhawks chase down the many balls that were hit out of the park. One ball landed on the street, bounced high and off the yellow brick façade of the apartment building at the corner of Kenmore and Waveland. It caromed up and over the heads of the knot of guys running after it, back across Waveland, and came to rest along the ballpark wall, not five yards from where I stood. I jumped at it, thinking that I had it made, and that I would have my first ever souvenir baseball, even if was only a BP ball. But those guys are quick and fierce. An old guy like me didn't have a prayer. They ran over me like a herd of buffalo. I hit the sidewalk, scraping my hands and bruising my knee. Returning to the standing room line, I tried to shake it off.

"Are you okay?" asked Lucy, frowning, worried.

"Where's the ball?" asked Patricia.

We got our tickets and had a great afternoon standing with a couple of Sox fans, who—after I asked some fans who had stopped in the aisle and blocked our view to move along—offered to buy us a round of beers. After the game, we shook hands and wished each other well.

So we have never bought scalped tickets. I have sold tickets on the street when I had extras, but always at face value, and never to scalpers but to guys looking for good tickets to go to the game. We would often then meet the buyers in the park and have a good old time at the old ball game.

"How much for standing room?" I ask.

"One hundred apiece."

My first thought is of our president's economic stimulus package. We received our check a few weeks ago. The five hundred bucks would be less than half!

Maybe I should negotiate. Not maybe, buster. I know I should negotiate. But I am not a good negotiator. We've bought four houses in our lives and our motto might as well be "Buy high, sell low," because we have never gotten any sellers down below their asking prices. And cars? We pay for Steve to fly to York to get us the best prices on cars, whether bought or leased, because in the long run we save money. And right now I wish Steve was in that bar with me because he would know what to do.

Maybe I should tell the guy I'll come back after I shop the other prices in the neighborhood. I'll cruise Addison and check out the action at Murphy's and get back to him. No doubt he would think that if I leave his bar, I'm lost. But do I do any of this? No. Why? Because I just want the whole thing settled. I want to go back inside the Salt & Pepper Diner with tickets in hand without further ado.

"You take credit?" I asked. He did, which made me feel, at least, that the tickets would not be counterfeit. But I would be charged tax, totaling $550 or so for five standing room tickets, face value $15 each.

Back at the diner, all are a bit aghast, but in the spirit of economic stimulus, we are beyond the insanity of it all and look forward to entering the park. And this is Patricia's last Chicago fling before she goes off to college, and Steve's big weekend blowout after quitting one of his jobs and having his first three-day weekend in as long as anyone can remember, and Lucy's celebration after quitting the job for which she was way overqualified. We finish breakfast, leave the diner and turn north toward Wrigley Field.

Passing Ernie's statue, I overhear someone say to a friend, "We shoulda taken them for sixty." This means that even if he was paying for standing room, he was paying forty bucks less than me, but it was unlikely that he was looking for standing room. No, no, no, no, no, no, no. I won't think about it any more. We'll go to Steve's and wait for the gates to open for batting practice.

As we pass the parking lot adjacent to the Cubs clubhouse, we see a black Mercedes two-door pull in through the Waveland Avenue gate.

"Patricia, who's that?" I ask.

"Marmol," she says with no hesitation.

Carlos Marmol jumps out, wearing a white tee shirt and shades, and entrusts his vehicle to a valet. Hey, we think, this is pretty cool, so we pause at the chain link fence and watch, spacing ourselves so from any given angle one of us has a good view of the cars, the gate and the approach to the clubhouse entrance. Why not? We have hours to kill. Soon enough Matt Murton arrives, and then Alfonso Soriano, limping. A cab is allowed into the lot and Jim Edmonds gets out. Then a white Maserati. A Maserati? I haven't seen one of those for decades except maybe in the movies.

"Patricia?"

"Aramis."

"Nice car."

Then a big, creamy white sedan pulls up and Derrek Lee steps out, looking tall and cool. We are all nuts by now, just loving the parade of Cub stars, running up and down the length of the fence to get the best view. But what is that car? The ornament on the trunk seems to be a set of wings, but

Whose Bentley is this, parked in the Cubs' team parking lot at Wrigley Field? (photograph by author).

it just cannot be a Chrysler product. D-Lee? No way. Straining my failing eyes, I see a "B" in the middle of the wings, but it doesn't mean anything to me. I ask a couple of guys chatting nearby.

"Bentley," one of them says.

Bentley? Nice. Class. I haven't seen a Bentley since John Pazdan's family, who lived across Columbian Avenue from St. Giles in Oak Park, had one. The old models looked like Rolls-Royces.

Jon Lieber shows up and stops at the gate on Waveland to sign autographs. I run around and wait with the small group and he signs my little notebook. Feels almost like spring training. We see Kerry Wood, Ron Santo and Bob Howry. We notice Billy Williams walking through the lot, seemingly unrecognized.

I yell out, "Hey, Billy!"

He waves and replies, "How you doin'?"

"Great," I say. "How're you?"

"Just fine."

A Pontiac pulls up and Kosuke Fukudome gets out. Kosuke drives a Pontiac? What's up with THAT? Maybe he has some kind of endorsement deal with GM.

This reminds me for the second time today of my years working at the Merchandise Mart for Noritake, a Japanese dinnerware company headquartered in Nagoya where, coincidentally, Fukudome played for the Chunichi Dragons. In Japan teams are named after the company that owns them. Chunichi Shimbun Co., Ltd., owns the Dragons. If American baseball had the same policy, the Cubs would be called the Tribune Company Cubs. When the Cubs signed Fukudome I was sure he'd feel at home because the Dragons were the Cubs of Japan, winning the Japan Series in 2007 for the first time since 1957—the longest stretch of futility in Japanese baseball. My friends at Noritake were always as disgusted with the Dragons as I was with the Cubs. Anyway, concerning cars, while American employees of Noritake drove cars from all over the world—Japan, Germany, Sweden etc.—all Japanese employees drove American cars to the point where I assumed it must be company policy for visiting Japanese staff, although I never asked.

Climbing the steps into the Wrigley Field stands, be it box seats, grandstands, upper deck or bleachers, still gives me the same emotional rush that I experienced when I entered the park with my Dad for the first time in 1958. It's a physical, tactile sensation that you feel in your gut and along your arms and up to the top of your head—a shiver of pure love of place and delight with life. The lush green of the grass and the ivy on the outfield wall, the monumental green mechanical scoreboard rising broad and tall above the center field bleachers, the cityscape beyond and deep blue sky above; and the promise of baseball to come and the eternal hope that the Cubs just might win today. There is no other place on earth that gives me the same feeling. Today that feeling is enriched by the comfort of the park's familiarity and the sense of coming home because so far, no matter how much they've tinkered with Wrigley Field, it's still the same place to me.

I've done some research and have narrowed down my first game at Wrigley Field, and first Major League baseball game, to two possible dates. I remember the Cubs played San Francisco during the Giants' first season on the West Coast after moving from the Polo Grounds in New York, and I remember that school was out and it was a weekday. And I remember that the Cubs won. So it was either Tuesday, July 1 (Cubs 9, Giants 5) or Tuesday, August 5, 1958 (Cubs 10, Giants 9). I was seven years old and too young to remember momentous dates other than family birthdays, so the date didn't register. I don't recall it being a close game, so I'm going with July 1. Now there's all kinds of symmetry here. As we enter Wrigley Field on June 20, 2008, it will soon be the 50th anniversary of my first game, in this the 100th anniversary of the last Cubs World Series championship.

I remember two incidents very vividly. First, the stars of the TV western series *Broken Arrow*, Michael Ansara and John Lupton, in full costume as Apache chief Cochise and U.S. government Indian agent Tom Jeffords, arrived and sat in the next section. My dad got Ansara's autograph on my scorecard. He signed it "Cochise." I had that scorecard hanging in my bedroom for years. I don't know what happened to it.

Second, sometime in the early innings an Andy Frain usher came to our seats, second tier boxes back when box seats were actually boxes, delineated by metal pipe surrounding groups of seats. He checked our tickets, as a couple of late-arriving fans looked on. It seemed they had tickets for the same seats. Upon inspection it was discovered that the ticket office had sold my dad seats for the wrong day. So we had to get up and follow the usher to the customer service office on the concourse behind home plate. As we made our way along the aisle that runs between the box seats and grandstands, I scraped the side of my head, just above my right ear, on a hot dog vendor's metal box. The small wound started to bleed.

So Cubs customer service not only had in their office an angry fan who had been sold tickets to the wrong game, but a bleeding kid. They made nice. Real nice. My dad, a combat veteran of World War II, could see that my wound was very superficial, but he made the most of it, which probably wasn't too tough. After a few words, everyone joking and joshing as a nurse put a bandage on my cut, we were led out of customer service and straight to the best seats in the house. Some Cub executive must not have attended that day because we were definitely reseated in a very rarified location—first box, second row, just to the right of the Cubs dugout. For the rest of the afternoon I watched Ernie Banks, Bobby "Shot-Heard-Round-the-World" Thomson, Dale Long, Alvin Dark and my favorite Cub, Tony Taylor (I was crushed when the Cubs traded him to Philadelphia in the 1960 deal that included Don Cardwell coming to the Cubs), step out of the dugout and into the on-deck circle, not more than a few yards away.

As I write this, a couple of weeks later, a news article depresses me. Another seven-year-old boy sat watching his first major league game behind the Cubs dugout on Thursday, July 10, 2008, not too far from where I sat fifty years ago. Cub pitcher Ted Lilly lined a foul ball that hit him in the head. His father, afraid that he might be dead, took him in his arms and ran for first aid trying to give him mouth-to-mouth as he went. Today, the boy is in serious condition, but out of life-threatening danger. His parents worry about permanent brain damage. I don't want to dwell on how something like this, or war, or famine, or earthquakes, or terrorist attacks can make baseball seem frivolous. But it gives one pause, as the game goes on, along with work and meals and driving to the store. Perspective.

Our $500 "seats" for the June 20, 2008 Cubs–Sox game. The last ramp to the upper deck along the left field line at Wrigley Field (photograph by author).

We take our spots leaning against the metal pipe railing along the last ramp up to the upper deck along the left field line. We especially like this standing room area because the luxury boxes that hang below the upper deck and obscure the view from much of standing room, end several yards to our right so we can actually see the scoreboard very clearly.

The tarp is on the field. The weatherman forecasted scattered showers, but it isn't raining at game time, and it had been dry as we made our way to the park, ate breakfast, got hosed by scalpers and then watched Cubs arrive at the players' parking lot. But there is substantial water on the tarp.

Soon the grounds crew runs enthusiastically out of the door in the left field corner (formerly the players' field entrance to the clubhouse) to the first big ovation of the afternoon. They keep coming out and coming out and coming out. How many guys do they need to roll up the tarp? There are dozens of them! Well, we conclude, it must be pretty heavy with all the water on its shimmering Cub-blue surface, so they need all the muscle they can muster. We watch with rapt interest as they line up along the first base-line edge of the tarp. We love everything about being at the game! They each take a grip and quickly pull the tarp over itself so that soon it covers left field, exposing the infield, which still shows some wet areas. Then they turn around and cover the infield again. NO! They're supposed to take the tarp *off* the field!

Calm down everyone. The first pass, we remember, was simply to dump the water off the surface of the tarp so they can better roll it up with the huge corduroy metal tube lying in right center field. Which is what they proceed to do.

But what about all that water in left field! Not to worry. During the off-season the Cubs completely resurfaced the playing field, leveling its notorious slope, improving drainage and fixing all of the potholes and irregular areas about which visiting outfielders complained very bluntly. Even Alphonso Soriano was quoted as saying, "It's not comfortable. There are like a lot of little holes ... you have to be careful ... I'm just more worried when the ball is coming, I'm not worried about my legs because it's not that bad. I'm more worried about the holes. They can give you a tricky bounce."

But not anymore, supposedly.

The tarp is finally rolled to its storage area near the visitors' bullpen along the right field line. Players appear and begin stretching. The umpires lumber onto the field and gather around home plate, joined by the two managers, Lou Piniella and Ozzie Guillen. From our vantage point, admittedly pretty far away, they seem to be laughing and joshing each other, probably over a pre-series exchange in the press and in television interviews about who is better looking and more trim. Guillen said something about how difficult it was for film crews to find a body double for Piniella, for commercials, I guess. For himself, Guillen said, one would only have to quickly search the files of a modeling agency, implying that his trim, buff figure could be matched only by the best-looking, best-built talent in the advertising and entertainment industries. Piniella, in response, said that he would never trade either looks or physique with Ozzie.

Finally, the Cubs take the field and sign autographs on baseballs for the kids that trot out to meet the players before each game. Then, the national anthem. All is still as the organ rings out and the words are sung. The players' uniforms are crisp and unsoiled. The sun is now high and bright. The grass and vines seemingly glow their most pristine, lush green. Anything is possible, and we are at the threshold of heaven.

We soon learn that there is a beer stand just to our right that sells sixteen ounces of Heineken or Becks for six bucks. Sixteen ounces of bad American beer, Bud, Bud Light, Old Style (sorry—it's our traditional Chicago favorite, but it's still watery American beer) or Old Style Light cost six twenty-five. Where's the decision? We are happy.

Lilly is on the mound and looks good in the first, getting the Sox one-two-three. Fukudome leads off the Cubs first with a single and goes to third on a single by Theriot. First and third, nobody out. A great beginning. Lee comes up after a three-for-four day against the Rays in a losing cause. But he's only batting .289. For Lee, this is at least thirty points below where he should be, as far as we're concerned.

The crowd is keyed up. Many fans stand, stomping and screaming for a Lee hit.

He grounds into a six-four-three double play, scoring Fukudome, but ending what could have been a first inning rally. This makes us sad. We *love* Derrek Lee. Since coming to the Cubs, after killing them in the 2003 play-offs, he's become one of our favorite Cubs *of all time*. In the field, he's gotta be one of the best, if not *the* best first baseman in either league. And, as I've noted, he should be hitting north of .300. When he heats up, he's craaazy! You can't get him out. But lately, he's been struggling. Maybe in ... July. Second half. When they need him most?

The Sox score three runs in the second and third, including two home runs (Pierzynski and Dye, whose blast over the left field bleachers and over Waveland Avenue and down Kenmore Avenue may still be heading north), and the score remains three to one until the Cubs half of the seventh when Derrek Lee comes through for us with a dinger, followed back to back by a long ball off the bat of Aramis Ramirez. Tie game, 3–3. No one scores in the eighth. With Kerry Wood on the mound, the Sox start the top of the ninth with a double by center fielder Brian Anderson, putting the potential lead run on second with no one out. Oh, no. We feared just this as we watched Wood trot in from the bullpen directly below us. He makes everyone very nervous.

But this is classic Cubs–Sox stuff. Dare we think it? Dare we say it out loud? In fact, as I type this, I worry that I'm cursing the Cubs without speaking a word, just by allowing these words to pop up on my computer monitor. But many speculate that it could be a Cubs–Sox World Series in 2008. On June 20 they are both in first place in their divisions and look strong.

As noted before, the Cubs and Sox played in the first cross-town World Series in 1906. The fact that it was only the third World Series played matters not. Chicago owned baseball with more fans attending games at West Side Park or the South Side Park, home of the Sox at 39th and Princeton, than anywhere else in the country. The Cubs had the best record in baseball history, and the Sox couldn't hit but had a great pitching staff. In 1908, many expected the 1906 Worlds Series to be repeated. The Sox and the Cubs were in the pennant race down to the last game of the season for both leagues.

After the lead-off double, Wood settles down and gets the next three batters, striking out Pierzynski to end the top of the ninth.

As Aramis Ramirez steps to the plate to lead off the bottom of the ninth, the crowd stands, cheering wildly. Our view blocked, we climb up onto the sloping concrete wall that borders the ramp to the upper deck, trying to balance beer, pencils and scorecards in one hand as we hold onto the steel pipe railing with the other. And so keeping score is out of the question. It's precarious up there, but we don't have to wait long because on the second pitch from Sox reliever Scott Linebrink, Ramirez connects and sends it deep to center field. We lose the ball behind the overhanging luxury boxes, but watch as Anderson backs up to the warning track. We can see by the way he carries himself that he knows it's gone, and sure enough, it lands, or rather plops, in the bushes just beyond the wall.

The crowd goes berserk, jumping and slapping five with total strangers. Screaming like banshees, not leaving, waiting for Steve Goodman's song to come on and then shouting the inane lyrics, but who cares that the words are inane? For this moment, it's glorious. And let the moment last forever. Leaving the park, the hooting and hollering and slapping hands continue down the ramps and out onto Waveland. The Sox fans look a little shell-shocked, and we know how they feel. We've left PNC Park and Shea Stadium and Citizens Bank Park and RFK and old Milwaukee County Stadium feeling exactly the same. And that's baseball. I guess that's sports. You go through those horrible games and wait and pray for a game like this and hope you're lucky enough to be there. This could be our only game at Wrigley Field this year and it makes up for that weekend in the hell known as Pittsburgh.

Not having another $500 for Saturday's game, we join Steve on Waveland Avenue for a street party. He puts a flat panel screen in his first floor bedroom window and tunes in the game. His roommates set up a bean-bag toss called cornhole and Steve brings out two round-back metal chairs with soft green plastic cushions hooked on their frames for Lucy and me. We sit and face the TV with the noise of the bleachers crowd to our back and fans walking to and fro on the sidewalk and street. Steve brings out beer in red plastic cups.

"My roommates have a keg of Coors Light, or some other garbage," says Steve, "so I bought us a twelve of Stella."

The game starts out close, with the Sox scoring two in the first answered by one from the Cubs in the bottom of the inning. In the top of the fourth the Sox take a 4–1 lead, but the game pretty much ends in the Cubs' half. They bring twelve batters to the plate, score nine runs, including two homers by Jim Edmonds in the inning and one each by Fontenot and Ramirez, and put it out of reach, although the Sox score a lot of runs, too. Just not quite as many as the Cubs. Final score: 11–7.

The weather is ideal, about 70 degrees and sunny with a light breeze. We are about as comfortable as we can stand. During big moments in the game, passersby stop and stare at the TV, chatting and providing their own color commentary. Steve and Patricia grab mitts and play catch in the middle of Waveland as the tourist buses line up waiting to take their charges back to Naperville or Joliet or Racine, Wisconsin. As the beer flows, the volume on the street goes up. Cub fans are raucous, getting primed for Saturday night. Sox fans are glum and hurry by, as anxious to get away from the North Side as we were to get out of Pittsburgh.

Bean-bag toss on Waveland Avenue before a game (photograph by author).

Just as we watched the Cubs arrive in their parking lot the day before, we watch them speed by after the game. We wave and call them by name. We notice that Derrek Lee gives Jim Edmonds a lift. Edmonds must not have a car in town yet. We cheer. In just over a month he has won over the fans with his clutch hitting (I haven't calculated it yet or seen a newspaper but by the end of the game today he must be over .300) and excellent fielding.

Ozzie Guillen drives away, eyes set dead ahead, ignoring the Cub fans who say nothing worse than "Hey Ozzie!" They have no time to give him any grief. He is gone in an instant.

Our goal on Sunday is to leave town early enough to get home to York in time to watch the last game of the series on TV. It is ESPN's *Sunday Night*

Baseball game. We drive up to Waveland Avenue to pick up Tara. The sidewalk and street in front of Steve's place are spotless. He and his roommates cleaned up after their party. Around the corner on Sheffield, however, the first stoop on the left is a mess of crushed cups, empty bottles and a concrete planter toppled and spewing cigarette butts. "They were still going strong when we got back last night," Tara explains. We had celebrated Taste of Randolph in the old produce and meat packing district that is now a row of restaurants ranging from the great to the merely trendy. Had an Italian Beef, which is de rigueur whenever we travel home, and a couple of other tasty morsels before settling in at an outdoor table at a tapas café, whiling away the evening over small plates and Spanish wines.

Passing Wrigley Field for the last time we see a long line already formed early in the morning of a night game, waiting for standing room tickets to go on sale.

The Cubs sweep the Sox, winning Sunday's game seven to one. Dempster looks great, going eight complete innings. One curious note concerning the game: After an Eric Patterson home run into the right field basket, ESPN commentator and ex–Red Hall of Fame second baseman Joe Morgan, who we've always considered a major Cub-hater, suggests that Ernie Banks depended on the baskets attached to the Wrigley Field outfield walls for a large percentage of his 512 career home runs. He calls the baskets Banks Boulevard. It has since been pointed out that the baskets were installed in 1970. Ernie retired in 1971 so he would have had to hit several hundred home runs his final two years in the majors for a large percentage of them to be basket homers. In fact, he hit only a total of fifteen during 1970 and 1971.

One week later, the Sox return the favor at the Cell, sweeping the Cubs.

As we head into the second half of the season, the Cubs are solidly in first place; the Sox not so solidly. Zambrano returns from the DL and looks fabulous in two outings. Soriano is due back after the All-Star break. In the meantime, the Cubs pick up Rich Harden, the brilliant young pitcher from the A's, and send Gallagher, Murton and Patterson to Oakland. Harden looks great his first time out against the Giants on July 12, but Marmol gives up five in the ninth to send the game into extra innings, saddling Harden with a no decision. Welcome to the Cubs.

And speaking of the All-Star Game, the Cubs will send eight players, the most in either league, although Marmol is added at the last minute because Kerry Wood has a blister and won't pitch. The other Cubs are Soriano (who won't play either), Dempster, Zambrano, Fukudome, Soto and Ramirez. Lou Piniella is selected to be one of the National League coaches.

CHAPTER FIVE

At the Break

The All-Star Game is scheduled for July 15 at Yankee Stadium as a kind of farewell nod to the ballpark before its demolition after the 2008 season. This year's break is four days with regular games resuming Friday, July 17. The Cubs reside in first place in the National League Central Division, four and a half games in front of the Cardinals. In a season of tight races, only the Los Angeles Angels enjoy a larger lead—six games over the Oakland A's in the American League West.

Will this be a season just like 1908 when both races were decided on the last day of the season, or in the Cubs' case after the season? In the American League, the Sox are up by only a game and a half, while Boston just edged into first place before the break and leads a slumping Tampa Bay team by only a half game. In the National League East the Phillies are ahead of the sizzling hot Mets (they have won nine in a row and could continue the streak after the break) by only a half game. In the West the Arizona Diamondbacks are a game ahead of the Dodgers in a division where no team is above .500. And how about the All-Star break itself? Josh Hamilton of the Texas Rangers puts on quite a show in the Home Run Derby competition, hitting 28 homers in the first round, the most *ever*, including 13 straight at one stretch. It's a record. But then he lost in the final round five home runs to three. Wild stuff!

The game itself is a classic, going fifteen innings and lasting four hours and fifty minutes. The longest *ever*! The American League won 4–3 (yet again—we're pretty sick of the Junior Circuit winning every year) on a sacrifice fly at 1:37 A.M.

And it's not just baseball! The 2008 Super Bowl is ranked by many as the best *ever* with the New York Giants beating the New England Patriots

99

with an insane fourth quarter drive including the most impossible catch in football championship history. The NCAA championship was sent into overtime by Kansas after an amazing comeback and clutch three-pointer as the final seconds ticked away. And what about Tiger Woods' injury-plagued performance on the links, winning the U.S. Open in sudden death after some of the most amazing shots and putts *ever* just to stay even with journeyman golfer Rocco Mediate through 72 holes and then 18 holes of a playoff round. "I think this is probably the best (victory) ever," said Woods, who has won a lot of major golf tournaments! And at Wimbledon? Rafael Nadal and Roger Federer fought into the darkness of night through five grueling sets, Nadal winning what many have called the greatest tennis match *ever*! And the Olympics haven't begun yet! Indeed, writers for Fox Sports and NBC Sports have dubbed this the greatest sports year *ever* with five and a half months yet to go.

With only baseball as a major team sport, and only primitive coverage of that available to only a comparative few, how could 1908 compete with the stratospheric highs of 2008 sports?

Concerning baseball, at least three books have been written claiming it the greatest season *in history*, right in their titles: *Crazy '08: How a Cast of Cranks, Rogues, Boneheads and Magnates Created the Greatest Year in Baseball History* by Cait Murphy, published in 2007 in anticipation of the Cubs' dubious centennial; *More than Merkle: A History of the Best and Most Exciting Baseball Season in Human History* by David W. Anderson, published in 2000; and *The Unforgettable Season* by G.H. Fleming, published in 1981. And there's a book published last year that argues the case that 1908 was just a hell of year all the way around: *America 1908* by Jim Rasenberger.*

The year began with the first illuminated ball dropping down the flagpole atop the New York Times Building to signal the end of 1907 and the beginning of 1908. Times Square was packed with young revelers ringing bells and blowing horns and howling drunkenly at the sky as a blizzard of confetti filled the air, much like every New Year's Eve since. The *Times* management had been persuaded to try something less dangerous than the fireworks that had been traditionally set off every year since the newspaper moved there in 1904.

Traffic could not move, horse-drawn carriages, wagons and trolleys stalled by the crowd. There were few automobiles in 1908. Rasenberger details that the modern American auto industry was truly established that

---

**Since composing this memoir,* When the Cubs Won It All: The 1908 Championship Season *by George R. Matthews was published by McFarland. Unlike the other baseball histories covering that year, Matthews focuses almost exclusively on the Cubs with other teams' games referenced only when they influenced the progress of the Cubs' season.*

year when the first Model T came out of Henry Ford's factory in Detroit and General Motors was founded. But most of America knew nothing of these key events. Horses still provided the power behind almost all local transportation.

But 2008 often feels like the *end* of the American auto industry. In July Ford announces a second quarter loss of $8.7 billion! For years they've been living on their pickup truck and SUV sales, but with gasoline stabilizing at around $4.00/gallon, consumers are turning away from the gas-guzzlers. And General Motors is no longer the world's number one automaker. Toyota now claims that honor. Business analysts question whether either Ford or GM can survive the losses.

We bought our first car in the early 1980s—a Ford Escort wagon. We took the el to Bert Weiman Ford on Ashland Avenue and chose the Escort because it was about all we could afford, and it had a nifty kid's wagon as a gift-with-purchase for an additional penny. The free wagon was great. We used to pull our kids to the corner store on Lawrence, and later, after we moved to Hermitage near Ridge, roll it up to Devon Avenue to cart back Halloween pumpkins. The Escort didn't last nearly as long. It was a piece of junk. In fact, they had to take apart the engine before we had been driving it for a month. Finally, on a trip to Wisconsin, the radiator gave out and we coasted into a Ford dealership in Woodruff. But did we learn our lesson? Oh no, not at all. We thought maybe we had a lemon so we actually traded up to a brown Ford Taurus station wagon. We thought we were Rockefellers on the drive back to Chicago; it felt so smooth and powerful with a lush interior and a fabulous radio. But not for long. Just as the warranty and our payments ended, at, I believe, *exactly* 60,000 miles, the car broke down monthly, each time in a new way, so that our monthly shop payments were higher than our car payments had been.

In 1990, on one of our early baseball outings, as we drove our Taurus wagon out of the parking lot at Three Rivers Stadium in hilly Pittsburgh after seeing the Cubs play the Pirates, facing a long drive back to Chicago, the brake pedal went all the way to the floor. This with four little kids in the car. Horrified, we found a car repair shop in suburban Pittsburgh and lived in a Red Roof Inn for two days while the damn thing got fixed. Recurring transmission problems finally forced us to dump Fords for Hondas. Our current 2003 Accord has over 200,000 miles on it (driving to Cub games in Chicago, Cincinnati, Philadelphia, New York, Miami, Baltimore, Washington, D.C., and, of course, Pittsburgh, will do that in a hurry) and is cruising right along. It has had one $300 repair in that time.

The point is that if we figured this out, it's no surprise that millions of other American car buyers figured it out, too, and started buying cars based on dependability. So American automakers are in rapid decline while oil companies reap record profits.

Ironically, John D. Rockefeller, founder of Standard Oil in 1870 (parts of which later became Amoco and then BP/Amoco and then just BP, Exxon, Mobil, and then Exxon/Mobil and a bunch of other oil companies) and the richest man *ever* (corrected for inflation), made his money from lamp oil and kerosene, not gasoline. There was little demand for gasoline through the first decade of the twentieth century because there were so few automobiles. In fact, during the nineteenth century many oil companies dumped gasoline as waste generated by the refining process. By 1908 Rockefeller was already retired from running Standard Oil's day-to-day business and, much like Bill Gates, who officially retired from Microsoft in 2008, spent his time trying to figure out how to give his vast fortune away to worthy causes. The main threat to his business, besides the federal government's ongoing trust-busting efforts led by President Theodore Roosevelt, was Edison's electricity, which was slowly wiring America and replacing kerosene and oil-burning lamps with electric lights, although Rockefeller hedged his exposure by investing heavily in the growing electricity business. How lucky for Rockefeller, though, that Henry Ford and William Durant of General Motors had figured out a way to make the nation, and soon the entire world, entirely dependent on fuels refined from oil.

Including the airlines. The oil crisis of 2008 is making life difficult for everyone, but the major carriers seem most affected. We hear regularly that passengers will now be charged for perks and even normal services that we once took for granted, like drinking water and checking luggage. But in 1908 the aviation industry, just like the auto industry, was just getting off the ground, so to speak. That year the Wright Brothers successfully completed a sustained flight, as opposed to the quick jaunt of fifty-nine seconds in 1903, making true commercial aviation possible. Wilbur in France and Orville at Fort Myer, Virginia, just outside Washington, D.C., made repeated demonstration flights to awed civilian and military spectators. On a somber note, Lieutenant Thomas Selfridge joined Orville for a flight at Fort Myer on September 17, 1908. After several minutes, a propeller blade fractured and severed a key cable. The plane crashed, killing Selfridge, the first passenger fatality in aviation history. Orville was seriously injured, but survived. Wilbur refused to let the tragedy discourage him. Four days later he flew over Le Mans, France, for over ninety minutes, far surpassing all previous in-flight records and securing once and for all the future of aviation.

The world had not changed this profoundly since our nomad ancestors first settled down, began to grow crops and brought them to the new market towns thousands of years ago. And 1908 arguably marked the beginning of the dominance of the United States in all things economic and industrial. All this, "Take Me Out to the Ballgame" and a Cubs World Series, too.

At the risk of sounding unpatriotic let's contemplate what's staring us in the face: 2008 could mark the true end of America's one hundred year run of world economic supremacy. China leads the world in both manufacturing and pollution, which seems to be a perverted indicator of success: the black soot gloom of London, England, in the nineteenth century; the dark gray steel mill fog that seemed a permanent condition in Pittsburgh during that insane 1908 season; and the emissions-induced smog over Los Angeles for the last half century. Today, as they prepare for the 2008 Summer Olympics, China plans radical strategies, including seeding the air with artillery fire, to keep the air clean enough for the athletes to breathe. A strong sign of industrial might, as if we needed it. Check your clothes, right now. I'll bet you're wearing something from China, if not everything.

The first All-Star Game was played on July 6, 1933, at Comiskey Park on Chicago's South Side, so there was no All-Star break in 1908. The Cubs played straight through July with no real letup, thirty-two games in 31 days, including five double headers. At the end of play on July 13, their record stood at 45–30–1, a .592 winning percentage. In 1908 if a game was called because of rain or darkness (there were no lights—the first night game was played in 1935) with the score tied, it was ruled a tie and would be made up only if the results affected the final standings.

The 2008 Cubs go into the break on July 13 winning fifty-seven and losing thirty-eight for an even .600 winning percentage. Concerns? Leading the list is the Cubs' terrible road record. They are 20–26 away from Wrigley Field. In fairness I must point out that among the first place teams, Boston, the White Sox and Arizona also have losing road records, with only the Angels and Phillies playing over .500 as visitors. The Cardinals, in second place behind the Cubs, are more balanced with winning records both home and away. For Cub fans this is a reason to worry, even more than usual, because even if they do break the sixty-three-year jinx and make it to the World Series, they will play four road games to only three home games because of the National League loss in the All-Star Game.

Once Soriano returns from the Disabled List, the Cubs should be pretty healthy. It's often assumed that player injuries are a somewhat recent development, and that players during the bygone era, or eras, never got hurt, or if they did, they played through it. Not true. Players suffered as much, or more, a hundred years ago as today. The difference today is the comparatively higher level of medical technology and more sophisticated training regimens.

In July of 1908, for instance, Cub second baseman Johnny Evers spent some time out of the lineup due to a leg injury—a lot like Soriano earlier this year. Evers was not only a key element of the Cubs defense, but also a good hitter. He would bat an even .300 in 1908. He turned twenty-seven that July, and so his youthful energy, skill at the plate and with the glove contributed day in and day out to the Cubs' success. Because of his range and his style of extending his arms wide and seeming to crawl around the infield scooping up grounders and liners anywhere and everywhere, he acquired the nickname "The Crab." The description also fit his personality. He didn't get along with anyone on the team, including player-manager Frank Chance, and especially his famous shortstop partner Joe Tinker of Tinker-to-Evers-to-Chance double play notoriety. It seems that in 1905 Evers hopped into a cab (in 1905 it would have been some variety of horse-drawn conveyance) alone, leaving Tinker and other Cubs behind at the team hotel, and took it to an Indiana ball field where the Cubs were to play an exhibition game. Upon arriving later, Tinker berated Evers over the slight and they got into a bloody fist fight right on the field. The legend goes that they didn't speak to each other for three decades, even during the pennant-winning years of 1906, 1907, 1908 and 1910, and apparently fought more than once again.

CHAPTER SIX

Dog Days

The Cubs resume play on the road in Houston and Phoenix and either score a ton or hardly any runs at all. Unfortunately for four out of the six games it's the latter. By the time they return to Wrigley Field on July 24, 2008, they are only one game ahead of the Brewers and two ahead of St. Louis. The Angels are now ten games up in the AL West, but the rest of the races are as tight or tighter than before the break. The Phillies and Mets are tied with identical records in the NL East. The Diamondbacks are only one game up in first place, in spite of the Cubs' valiant effort to get them over .500 and open up some breathing room between them and the second place Dodgers.

Soriano's back from his injury and as the Cubs head home, they are able to field their normal starting lineup again, except that they still don't have an everyday centerfielder. Johnson and Edmonds continue to platoon, although Edmonds can only pinch hit because of an ailing left knee. But it looks like Fukudome will remain in right instead of bouncing around the outfield as he did when Soriano was out. DeRosa will return to second base.

In high-scoring games, the Cubs dominate. But if it's 1–0, 2–1 or 3–2, forget it. Even if they're up by a run, they can't hold the lead. The starting pitching is steady and good. The bullpen is suspect with Kerry Wood on the DL, Marmol giving up a lot of runs and Howry completely unreliable, especially with a slim lead. The starters have been handed some pretty painful no-decisions and even losses when they have pitched good enough to win.

Rich Harden has been on the short end of this dubious streak in both of his starts with the Cubs. His third outing on Saturday, July 26, 2008, against the Florida Marlins will be the third game of the four game series, each team winning one. It's the middle of this long, hot summer, the kind

105

of day thirty years ago we might have taken the el to Wrigley Field to watch a meaningless game, the Cubs well below .500 and already out of it. But not this year. The Cubs remain in first place by a game.

We sit and watch WGN. I will type this section as we watch the game, going back only to correct typos and other blatant errors and sins of grammar.

Harden walks the lead-off man on four pitches, but then strikes out the side, looking sharp. Bob and Len talk about his changeup, and how he alters his grip and his delivery so it looks different to batters each time he throws it. But the last batter of the first inning is blown away by high inside heat.

Will the Cubs support him with any run production? This is the question that weighs heavily on our minds, and the minds of the 41,000 plus that sit in the sunshine under a blue Chicago sky. By the way, we ask ourselves, why aren't we there?

With two out in the bottom of the first, Derrek Lee doubles. Aramis Ramirez follows him and singles into somewhat shallow left field. We don't feel good about the way the play develops because third base coach Mike Quade is waving Lee home as Marlin left fielder Josh Willingham cocks his arm to throw to the plate. We remember yesterday's game when Alphonso Soriano tried to score from second only to be thrown out by a mile, dumping a large bucket of cold water on what might have been a big inning. The Cubs went on to lose 3–2.

Lee lumbers around third. On deck hitter Mike Fontenot, moving into Lee's line of vision behind home, pushes both of his arms and the palms of his hands down, down, down, urging Lee to slide, which he does. Marlins catcher John Baker straddles the plate, but the throw arrives a little high, allowing Lee to slip his hand onto the plate between Baker's feet for a run. Nice.

Harden walks another Marlin in the top of the second, but strikes out two more and gets out of the inning with no runs scored.

In the bottom of the second, Cubs catcher Geovany Soto leads off with a double that bounces high off the ivy in the left field well. Kosuke Fukudome, who's been struggling, starting the day at .275, follows with an infield single to short, but Soto can't advance. Fukudome is playing center field today. Yesterday he made a spectacular catch high against the ivy in right field, so, as the boys in the booth are wont to say, even when he's not hitting as well as he is able, he helps the team each and every day with his glove. Harden comes to the plate and shows bunt, but on a freak play, Baker misses a high fast ball that hits home plate umpire Gerry Davis flush on his mask's chin guard. The ball bounces off to the left and both runners advance, but the ump is not doing well. He looks stunned. The Cubs' trainer comes out and after a few minutes it is obvious that Davis cannot continue. He heads to the Cubs dugout and the umpires' dressing room beyond, and after a break, the game resumes with a three-man crew—Rob Drake at first, Bruce Dreckman taking Davis' place at home and Brian Gorman on the left side of the infield.

Harden, who no longer needs to bunt with first base empty, strikes out and Soriano follows with a ground out. Two men in scoring position with one out and they score nobody. Not good. One run is not going to be enough. And as if to prove how costly lost opportunities can be Jeremy Hermida ties it with a homer with two out in the top of the third, the Marlins' first hit of the game. Harden ends the inning with another strikeout, his sixth, but the Cubs are going to have to get their bats cracking.

As Derrek Lee hits in the bottom of the fourth, beyond him in the lower boxes behind the on deck circle we see a familiar figure, the slightly hunched form of a beer vendor we remember from the 1970s. His scraggly dark hair, which always seems to be the exact same not-quite-shoulder-length, sticking straight out from under his Cub hat like a mop turned upside down, has signs of gray, and it should. He must be at least my age and my hair is rapidly approaching white. About ten years ago we had seats in the upper tier of third base boxes, the vendor's traditional territory. We bought a couple of beers from him and commented then that we remembered him from twenty years before. He and a huge, muscular body builder were there every game working those third base aisles. He shrugged as if to say, well here I am and so what? And a decade later, he's still there. He could become the Pat Piper or Yosh Kiwano of beer vendors if he can stick with it another quarter century. Pat Piper was the longtime Cub field announcer who wore the white shirt and blue pants of the Andy Frain usher uniform as he sat behind the backstop to the right of home plate. A microphone had been wired in where his chair was tucked behind the screen's support pole. He sat on the field instead of in the press box because his other duty was to manage the supply of game balls for the home plate umpire. He had a clipped, grizzly, Walter Winchell kind of voice. From our seats in the center field bleachers we could see him lift the microphone as he checked his scorecard, and then over the big speakers above us we'd hear: "'tention. 'tention please. Now hitting. For the Cubs. Number twenty-six. Billy. Williams." Piper began working for the Cubs when they were still at West Side Park. He was sitting in his spot during the 1932 World Series when Babe Ruth hit the home run that became known as the called shot. He must have been the only Cub employee who later claimed that Ruth did indeed point to the seats in right center just before he sent the ball into the stratosphere.

Yosh Kiwano is the Cubs clubhouse manager who first worked for the

Cubs in 1943. He was there for the last Cub World Series in 1945, and just retired this past April. We ran into Yosh last year, about this time. I entered the contest to sing the seventh inning stretch "Take Me Out to the Ball-game." We drove to Chicago for the audition and entered Wrigley Field through the Waveland Avenue gate. We passed a familiar, elderly Japanese gentleman wearing a floppy fishing hat, and turned. A Cub employee nearby noticed us gawking and said simply, "Yeah, that's Yosh." Yosh looked crabby so we left him alone.

Aramis goes deep to left with two out to give the Cubs back the lead 2–1. But even this bothers us. Home runs are great, but when the Cubs are too dependent on them for run production, it's a bad sign. It feels that way now. And Ramirez's dinger was a solo shot, which seems way too frequent these days.

Nothing much happens in the fourth, except that Rich Harden strikes out two more Marlins, bringing his total K's to eight, all of them swinging. And then in the top of the fifth he strikes out two more making this the third game in a row, his first three games as a Cub, that he has struck out ten. But the Cub lead remains at one, which is making our stomachs boil and turn. Not enough to win this game. With all those strikeouts and three walks, Harden's pitch count is building. There is no way he will finish this game, which means that the Cubs will depend at some point on their shaky bullpen. They need more runs.

And sure enough, Sean Marshall takes the mound in the top of the sixth. Harden threw only 87 pitches, but, as Len and Bob explain it, the Cubs are going to be very, very careful with a pitcher who has a history of injuries. They want him healthy come September. Marshall gets three up and three down in the top of the sixth, looking good. We hope that his big, slow curve will be difficult for the Marlin hitters to time after the steady diet of Harden changeups and heaters.

In the bottom of the sixth, Fontenot leads off with a single, but they can't move him around, Soto ending the inning by hitting into a double play. The crowd is subdued in spite of the Cubs' lead. They know. For the new bandwagon fans and all the fans who have known the Cubs only since the 1980s when they began to appear regularly (for the Cubs) in the playoffs, the evil spirit still haunts the friendly confines. You can feel the loss coming, even when the Cubs are in front. Maybe not today, we all hope. Not again. This year the race is for real, so far.

The seventh inning begins with WGN's Fan Cam, a feature that supposedly shows a cross section of fans in the stands. We have long since renamed it Bimbo Cam because the red-blooded WGN camera operators must spend the first six innings searching out the most voluptuous young women wearing the tightest Cub T-shirts. They throw in a token shot or two of an overweight male beer-guzzler, but the sequence is definitely a flimsy excuse to celebrate the impressive physical attributes of young female Chicagoans.

Notre Dame football coach Charlie Weis sings the seventh inning stretch. He's a big guy who sings badly, but most seventh inning guests do. There's some banter about a former player of his, Jeff Samardzija, who made his major league debut as a Cub reliever yesterday. The only thing of note in the Cubs' half is that once again they get a man on—Marshall, who punches a single through the left side—but can't get him around. Soriano hits into a double play to end the inning. The ominous feeling of doom grows deeper and more profound.

Hermida proves that we had reason to worry. He leads off the top of the eighth against Marshall by putting one into the basket in right to tie the game, his second home run of the day. For Harden, it means three impressive starts as a Cub with only three no-decisions to show for it all.

Marshall has otherwise looked great, and indeed he proceeds to strike out the side. But now the Cubs, who can't hit worth beans in these situations, and who haven't touched up the Marlins' bullpen at all this series, have to get some runs. The fans are quiet. Bob and Len sound subdued at best, almost defeated already.

Willingham leads off the Marlins' ninth with a base hit to left off new pitcher Neal Cotts. A sacrifice bunt moves him to second, and out comes Lou Piniella to make a pitching change. Carlos Marmol comes in from the bullpen. At the beginning of the year we would have cheered. But now, as the dog days wear on, we groan. Every Marmol outing seems to turn into an adventure, like this past Thursday night when he walked three, but also struck out three and gave up no runs. He starts out with a wild fastball but follows with a slider over. He finally buckles the hitter, whose name I missed because I'm typing too much, with a 94 mile-an-hour fast ball, knee high and over the outside corner. That's the Carlos Marmol we once knew. Luis Gonzalez pinch-hits. Marmol pitches three straight balls, and then puts two fast balls over. Full count. The crowd finally comes alive, jumping to their feet and screaming for that last strike. But Marmol walks him. Two on, two out with Ramirez coming up. He sends a hard-hit ball deep to right center, toward the gap between DeRosa and Fukudome. Time seems to stop as we, and the packed house at Wrigley Field, hold our breath and follow the ball's trajectory, trying to judge if either fielder can get to it. A kind of instantaneous geometry problem. And then we know, at the last instant, that it's okay because DeRosa looks confident as he runs it down in right to end the inning. But it was tense. On to the bottom of the ninth. As Jack Brickhouse used to say: "As we go into the bottom of the ninth, any old kind of a run will do it!" The score—the Cubs two; the Marlins two.

Pinto pitches the ninth for the Marlins. Patricia points out that we have his autograph. He was on the Cubs spring training roster when we went to Arizona in 2004.

With one out Mark DeRosa hits a slow grounder deep to short. He slides into first (oh, no!) head first. There is a cloud of dust as Ramirez's throw arrives. DeRosa is called out. Cubs first base coach Matt Sinatro slams his helmet to the ground in protest and is immediately thrown out of the game. The crowd is on its feet howling and cheering and laughing as Piniella races out of the dugout, if you can call Piniella's waddle racing, to pick up the argument with first base umpire Rob Drake, and he is thrown out, which really gets him going. He has his nose in Drake's face, and then Brian Gorman's face, screaming, and we can easily read his lips, "What the fuck's the matter with this guy?" gesturing at Drake. He stays on the field for several minutes and appears to bump an ump! This could cost him money and maybe a suspension. He finally retreats to the dugout, still screaming, but then comes back out to let home plate umpire Bruce Dreckman know what he thinks, too. So even if the Cubs lose, the fans have been entertained and, as the rhubarb is replayed ad nauseum on WGN, ESPN, Fox and mlb.com, they will be able to say, as we love to say whenever we can, "I was at that game."

Len points out that this is the second ejection of the year for Sweet Lou, the previous incident also at the discretion of Rob Drake during the series with the Sox at the Cell. Derrek Lee had words with Drake today, too, after a dubious called strike three on a checked swing.

The Cubs do not score in the ninth, so the game goes into extra innings. Marmol stays in to pitch the tenth. He gives up a single, and then, with two out, a long fly to the warning track in left, which gives us, who witnessed the dropped fly in Pittsburgh, minor heart palpitations as we watch Soriano back up almost to the wall. But he reaches up and squeezes it with his glove (why does hardly anybody catch with two hands anymore?) and that's it for the Marlins in the top of the tenth.

Fukudome leads off the Cubs' half with a single. Man on, nobody out. Can the Cubs get him around? It seems like miles between first base and home when the Cubs are up, but a mere hop, skip and jump when their opponents get the leadoff man on in late innings. Hank White (Henry Blanco) lays down a perfect sacrifice, so the Cubs have the winning run on second with one out and the top of the batting order coming up. The Marlins change pitchers, bringing in Justin Miller. Soriano pops it up to right, and it looks like it might drop, it has a prayer, but second baseman Uggla races over between first base and right field and makes a nice over-the-shoulder catch. Two out. Theriot hits a tailing fly down the right field line. We, and the crowd and the Cub bench as shown in the replay, try to will it to drop. But it doesn't. Fukudome is stranded.

The Cubs bring in Chad Gaudin, the relief pitcher who came over from the A's in the Harden deal, to pitch the top of the eleventh. The Cubs need to shut down the Marlins and win it soon, if they're going to, because there ain't too many guys left in the bullpen. Gaudin gets them in order, so maybe he'll be good for another inning if needed.

Heart of the batting order coming up for the Cubs. Miller stays on the mound for the Marlins. Lee, Aramis and Reed Johnson, who pinch-hit in the ninth and stayed in during a switch that sent Fukudome to right, DeRosa to second base and Fontenot to the bench, all hit weak ground ball outs.

Gaudin stays in for the Cubs. Andino greets him with a base hit to the right-center gap. Johnson runs it down before it can go to the wall and wheels to throw to second. Andino hesitates for just the shortest moment rounding first, but then turns on the jets and heads for second. Johnson's throw is perfect, straight in to Theriot on one hop. Andino's hesitation at first was enough. He is dead at second.

Ramirez fans. Hermida comes up and doubles down the left field line. The play at second on Andino looms large. But then Jorge Cantu hits the second double of the inning, scoring Hermida, his third time across the plate today counting for all of the Marlins' runs, and giving them a 3–2 lead. Cantu must feel justified and relieved because he was robbed twice today, once on a line drive that Aramis Ramirez jumped and stretched high to pull out of the air before it could find left field, and the second on an acrobatic, diving catch by Johnson in right center field. For us, it feels like the inevitable has occurred, and the Cubs only need to make their quick three outs in the bottom of the twelfth inning to seal the deal. We sit quietly, until Lucy finally says it for all three of us. "This doesn't feel too good." We're bummed and now I'm pissed that we have to watch that stinking Justin Timberlake Pepsi commercial where a bikini-clad babe pulls on a straw and sucks Timberlake into her back yard, for the twentieth time today, and probably the thousandth time this year.

Marlins closer Kevin Gregg comes in. DeRosa hits a smash grounder behind Gregg that off the bat looks like a base hit through the box. But Gregg swings his mitt behind his back and snags the ball in what looks like a trick catch, a showoff play, for the easy out at first. Soto then grounds to short. Fukudome is the Cubs' last hope. He takes a ball, then looks sick swinging and missing and stumbling out of the batter's box. Then a called strike, a foul ball and fast ball that just misses outside. We've seen that pitch called a strike often. Then another ball so the count is full. The crowd stands and somewhat half-heartedly cheers Kosuke on, but he, surprise surprise, fans. Lucy expresses it again for us. "It's so brutal, these losses."

Cub pitching struck out twenty Marlin batters. As I type this, Patricia comments from the kitchen that this was the perfect game for me to follow, typing as it unfolded, as it was so typical of how the Cubs have been playing lately.

I discover on the Internet that they'll be on TV again tomorrow, Sunday, but not on WGN. TBS is picking up the game. It's a pleasant surprise! We thought it would be Internet radio for us. After Saturday's game, though, why should this be good news? Another opportunity to be frustrated and led to slaughter while watching Justin Timberlake get sucked into a sun-bathing girl's back yard a dozen times, or maybe happy middle-aged couples in twin tubs experiencing post–Cialis bliss set against a ridiculous sunset. Oh, but it is good news. It's flippin' great news. Beautiful news. Patricia, who missed a lot of Saturday's game because she was working, is especially pleased. We'll be watching, and we still have half a bag of pistachios.

Marquis takes the mound on Sunday, July 27, and he's typically rocky. The Marlins take a 5–0 lead going into the bottom of the third. The Cubs show some life by tying it with two in the third and three in the fourth, but then Florida takes a 6–5 lead to the seventh, by which time Marquis is gone. He can only get the loss today. Then D-Lee leads off the seventh with a homer to tie (taking Marquis off the hook, although the six earned runs over six innings won't help his ERA at all), the Cubs load the bases and "Little Mikey" Fontenot (our nickname, I think, only. Sorry Mike. But he is short, which we've noted in person. For their pre-game pep routine, Zambrano mimes pounding Fontenot into the floor of the dugout. He then pops up and jumps on Zambrano's back for a piggy-back ride! He looks like a little kid on "Big Z's" back.) pinch hits and drives the ball to the opposite field, over Willingham's head in the left field well for a bases clearing double. The Cubs lead 9–6, and that's how the game ends.

Does this give us any degree of optimism going into the big four-game series in Milwaukee? Why should it? I know we're being somewhat irrational here, and not at all analytic, but, God bless America, the Cubs' history over the years isn't exactly....

We're very happy that the Cubs got at least a split with the Marlins, with whom they have that dreadful 2003 playoff history. There is no need to review the details of the big collapse with five outs to go, etc. If you're interested in reliving it, Google "Steve Bartman." Today there are about 129,000 links.

As already stated, we drove to Miami once. On or about Wednesday,

October 8, 2003, we got a call from Lucy's brother Paul who lives in Coral Gables, Florida, a suburb of Miami. His message was simple. "I have three for Sunday if you can get here. You can stay with us."

Lucy, echoing my response to Frenchy all those years ago, said simply, "We're there." We would somehow figure out how to do this.

The high cost of flying three of us from Baltimore to Miami made that option impossible. We knew that the drive would be about eighteen hours. Ordinarily, we would cannonball it and make it in one day. However, there was a problem. The Cubs and Marlins were scheduled to play night games both Friday, October 10, and Saturday, October 11. Could we do it using up only one vacation day, as I was just about out of them for the year? Of course we could!

We would leave York at about 5:00 Friday and drive as far as we could, hopefully to Richmond, Virginia, check into a hotel in time for the game, watch the game, drive Saturday as far as we could—well into Florida, we figured, but probably not all the way to Coral Gables because there would not be enough time—check into another hotel, watch the game, and then proceed on to Coral Gables Sunday morning to pick up the tickets and then backtrack to Pro Player Stadium for the game, scheduled to start at 4:40 P.M. so the NFL can get their network games in before the first pitch.

The only thing that could sabotage the plans was a Marlins sweep. They had won the first game 9–8 at Wrigley Field Tuesday night. If they swept the series it would be over on Saturday, making our drive a waste. But we had to commit one way or another, and so we packed our bags. If worse came to worst, we would continue down to Coral Gables and have a nice visit with Paul and Bunny.

But the Cubs won Game Two, handling the Marlins 12–3 at Wrigley Field, sealing our fate. One way or another there would be a Game Five Sunday afternoon, and we would be there.

Hoping to hit Baltimore before rush hour, and maybe avoid the worst of Washington's rush hour, too, we headed south on I83 out of York, Pennsylvania, at about 3:30 Friday, October 10, as soon as Patricia got out of school. We figured it should take three to four hours to get to Richmond where we would stay for the night and watch the game, scheduled to start at 8:15. And we were mostly right. We slowed a bit on I695, the Baltimore Beltway, and then did pretty well on crowded, but moving, I95 South. The inner ring of the D.C. Beltway was okay, too, but things started going real bad as we approached Springfield, Virginia, the D.C. suburb where the Beltway rejoins I95. Slow, slower, slowest, dead stop. We watched the October light slowly fade from its golden glow to a dull blue haze that melded the individual cars, SUV's, trucks and vans into one long ribbon of dreary, monochromatic, colorless metal, punctuated by the bright red pinpricks of brake lights permanently illuminated. We longed for them to fade into the steady, subdued red of vehicles in full motion—averaging a civilized 75 MPH instead of inching along at less than five. But in spite of the existence of reversible express lanes, traffic crawled, and crawled, and crawled even when we were so far south of D.C. that we were technically no longer in its metropolitan area. It was as if everybody on the eastern seaboard was heading to Miami, or at least points south of Washington.

Okay, we thought, we need to get out of this mess and into a hotel. But then we hit a stretch where there seemed to be either no exits or no hotels at the exits. Maybe it was our imaginations but in the middle of traffic that would do the Kennedy Expressway at 5:30 proud, we seemed to be a million miles from anything resembling civilization.

It grew dark, with nothing at all visible except those relentless brake lights ahead of us, and the stream of headlights heading north, moving quite nicely, of course. There seemed to be no other vehicles on our side of the highway except SUVs and semis whose blinding headlights reflected off our rear view mirror so intensely that I had to cower toward the car door just to be able to see the traffic jam ahead of me. Seven-thirty ... 7:40. How long will it take to check in? And will we find food? A Marriott, or some other chain that has a restaurant, and hopefully a bar, would be best so we could order room service during the game, but we were rapidly running out of options. 7:45, half an hour until first pitch. Nothing suitable. Approaching 8:00, after over four hours on the road, we desperately searched the signs for a hotel and finally saw a Hampton Inn advertised at an exit somewhere just north of Fredericksburg. We pulled off with less than a quarter of an hour to go until the first pitch. The hotel was, luckily, right next to I95, and, even luckier, there was a strip mall with a fast food joint adjacent to the hotel! So we were checked in and had bad food spread over the beds when the game began.

It was excruciating to watch. The box score and play-by-play are a matter of record, but at the time, the series was tied and the Cubs and Marlins were playing the first of three in Miami. The Cubs took a 2–0 lead. Then, by the seventh inning, the Marlins were ahead 3–2. The Cubs took the lead again, up 4–3 in the eighth, but the Marlins tied it at 4 heading into the ninth. The Cubs didn't score in the ninth so the Marlins could win it with a run. But they didn't. And then no one scored in the tenth. In the Cubs half of the eleventh, Lofton reached with a single and was tripled home by Doug Granville, pinch hitting for pitcher Joe Borowski. YES! Cubs led by one, but could they hold it? Mike Remlinger came in to pitch and looked good. Pierre grounded to short, and then Castillo struck out swinging, but oh, no! He reached first safely because the third strike got away, ruled a wild pitch. We're dying inside. This is it! They're gonna blow it and be down two games to one with two to play in Miami.

If my brother Steve was with us, he would either turn off the television right now, or go out to look for a bar that wasn't broadcasting the game. In 1984, he and his three-year-old son, Nathaniel, joined us, along with Frenchy and his wife, Peggy, to watch the Cubs win, we prayed, Game Five of the playoff series with San Diego, and thus move on to the World Series for the first time in thirty-nine years. In fact, this was already the first playoff series of any kind for the Cubs since 1945.

We moved into our two-flat apartment on the 4700 block of North Drake Street in 1977, and had always gotten by with a small, twelve-inch black and white television. For such a momentous occasion, however, Jeanne, age six, and I walked up to Lawrence Avenue to a small, storefront electronics retailer and purchased our first color television. When the Cubs eventually choked, Lucy suggested that it was perhaps my purchase of the color TV that sealed their fate. They had, after all, done just fine all season as we watched on our little black and white. But to have the pretense to want to watch the playoffs in color? Yet another kiss of death.

Again, the game is a matter of history, the pain relived often by Cub fans. The replay of Leon Durham letting a routine ground ball to first scoot between his legs into right field is *still* broadcast in 2008 as part of Cubs futility montages that include the black cat in 1969, Bartman, etc. That error spawned the post-season joke: "What do Leon Durham and Michael Jackson have in common? They both wear one glove for no apparent reason."

Going into the bottom of the seventh, the Cubs held a 3–2 lead, needing only nine more outs to head to the 1984 World Series. Rick Sutcliffe was on the mound. You would think that giving up only two runs over six innings signaled a strong game from the 20 and 6 "Red Baron" who would win the Cy Young Award that year. But then Sutcliffe walked the leadoff man on four pitches. That was enough for my brother! He *knew* it was over. He stood and said, "Come on, Nathaniel. We're not gonna watch this." And they left. Nothing more was said. We didn't even protest that the Cubs were still winning and try to talk him into staying, because for all of us, the feeling of impending doom had turned our celebratory afternoon into a death watch. Steve and Nathaniel didn't even see Durham's error!

Steve's a Sox fan, and I don't think that game did much to improve his opinion of the Cubs.

In 1984 we believed that the Cubs had a legitimate shot, even more than in 1969 when the sensation of hope was so new and difficult to understand. The season started fast with the Cubs winning ballgames while

General Manager Dallas Green made deals to strengthen their very dubious rotation. Green was a high profile GM for the Cubs, very publicly put in place by Tribune Company, who had bought the team and the ballpark in 1981, to build a winner. He was visible everywhere you looked in the newspapers and on the radio and television, to the extent that of all the GMs in all the seasons since I was a kid, he's the one I remember best.

The Cubs had finished at or near the bottom of their division every year since 1979, including the previous two Tribune years, and although they had acquired some promising hitting and fielding talent, like Ryne Sandberg and Leon Durham, their pitching was woeful. So when Green brought in Scott Sanderson and Dennis Eckersley and then Rick Sutcliffe to join Steve Trout, they had a solid rotation, one to rival the 1969 lineup of Jenkins, Holtzman, Hands and Selma. The promise of a great season took full hold on us the week Sutcliffe came to the team in mid–June. Earlier that month, the June 11, 1984, cover of *Sports Illustrated* featured a full page photograph of Leon Durham confidently tossing his bat away after an apparent walk. The captions read "HOW 'BOUT THEM CUBBIES!"; "Budding Superstar Bull Durham." When we first saw it our question was, does this curse the Cubs or just Leon Durham? It turned out that the SI Cover Jinx would infect both.

On June 23, 1984, the Saturday following Sutcliffe's first start as a Cub, we watched the Cubs play the Cardinals at Wrigley Field on *Game of the Week*. It was a raucous, high-scoring contest that found the Cubs down 9–8 in the bottom of the ninth inning. The rest, as they say, is history and has come to be known as "The Sandberg Game" as the young (only twenty-four) second baseman hit home runs off ex–Cub and future Hall of Famer Bruce Sutter in both the ninth, to tie the game, and again in the tenth with a man on to tie it up again, setting the stage for a dramatic Cub come-from-behind win in the eleventh. By the end of the game we were standing and cheering in our living room. And it felt like poetic justice because Sutter had won the Cy Young Award while on a strictly mediocre Cub team in 1979 and was a perennial All-Star. We were still smarting from the 1981 trade that sent him to the Cardinals for ... did the Cubs get Ernie Broglio back again? But Cub fans would get used to the idea that a Cy Young award could only mean that Cub management now saw a brilliant pitcher as expendable—Greg Maddux, need we say more? The next day Sutcliffe pitched a complete game shutout against the dreaded Cardinals in front of an SRO crowd of over 39,000 (1984 Wrigley Field capacity was 36,755). The Cubs were rolling and anything was possible.

By mid–September it looked to be all but over with the Cubs in first place, sporting a 7½ game lead over the hated Mets as the two teams began a three game weekend series at Wrigley Field on September 14. Jane McCon-

ville, a co-worker at the small ad agency where I was employed, told me that
her friend Chuck had three tickets for Friday's game. We cut work and met
Chuck at the gate on the corner of Sheffield and Addison. He had a small
portable TV, which I thought was odd. He explained that he liked to watch
the replays.

Jane wasn't a Cub fan, or even a sports fan, but it seemed like everyone
on the North Side was caught up in the frenzy as the end of the 1984 season approached with the Cubs making national news for closing in on their
first post-season action since 1945. One might accuse her of being a fair
weather fan, but that wasn't the case. The Cubs had electrified the city. You
had to be dead not to notice the craziness that was swirling all around you.
Jane was just getting in on the fun.

The promotion of the day was a small white Cubs towel. We presented
our tickets and accepted our towels and headed for our seats—first row of
the grandstand, right field side, halfway between first base and the visitors'
bullpen. Chuck set up his little gray television set. It must have had about
a seven-inch screen. Wrigley Field looked packed, but it wasn't quite a sellout. Nonetheless, the crowd was charged up, the air buzzing with excitement as Rick Sutcliffe took the mound. He was 18–6 for the year, had lost
only one game as a Cub since the June trade, and was 12–0 for the months
of July, August and September to this point. And he had just pitched a complete game shutout against the Mets less than a week before.

The Cubs scored first in the third inning on a double by Bob Dernier
with Larry Bowa on first. And then it began. Someone, I think it was a fan
along the third base line, started waving a promotional towel in the air. It
caught on and soon the entire ballpark became a sea of twirling white terry
cloth. Variations of the rally towel had existed before this game and are common in sports today. The Minnesota Homer Hanky and the Pittsburgh Steelers' Terrible Towel are two famous examples. But back then it was a unique
experience for me, and I haven't seen the phenomenon at Wrigley Field since
that afternoon.

Jody Davis was one of the most popular Cubs that year on a team
loaded with popular players. In the bottom of the sixth the Cubs scored a
run when Keith Moreland grounded out with the bases loaded and one gone.
With first base open, the Mets elected to walk third baseman Ron Cey to
load them up again. I didn't quite understand why they chose this strategy
because the next batter was Davis, who was hitting better than Cey. The
righty vs. lefty percentages didn't come into play because Cey, Davis and
Mets relief pitcher Brent Gaff were all righties. But as the second intentional ball sailed wide of the plate and the fans realized who stood in the on
deck circle, the chanting started and increased in volume and intensity until

the ballpark seemed to shake with the resonance of over 32,000 screaming "JoDEE! JoDEE! JoDEE!" in unison. We felt in our collective gut that if Davis could connect, clinching first place might actually be within the Cubs' grasp; that there was almost no way the Mets could catch them, as they did in 1969. There wasn't time enough left in the season for another Cub collapse.

Ball four. As Cey trotted down to first and Davis approached the plate, the chanting escalated to a deafening roar. The crowd came to its feet and those little towels began to fly. And then, when we heard the sharp, satisfying sound of the bat meeting the ball at the sweet spot, Cub fans began to jump and hug and laugh and shout and scream and wave those towels with a manic joy as the ball took off on its no-doubt-about-it flight to the left center field bleachers.

The Mets scored one in the eighth, but Sutcliffe went on to finish the game and notch his nineteenth win. The Cubs were 8½ games ahead of the Mets with only fifteen left to play. They would clinch it exactly ten days later at Three Rivers Stadium in Pittsburgh, Cub manager Jim Frey stuffing his hat under his shirt as he charged the mound after yet another Sutcliffe complete game victory.

Sutcliffe looked brilliant in Game One of the best-of-five National League Championship Series against the San Diego Padres, pitching seven shutout innings and giving up only two hits as the Cubs won easily 13–0 at Wrigley Field. The Cubs won Game Two behind starter Steve Trout and had three games to win one more to clinch the pennant. The rest of the series moved from Chicago to San Diego. San Diego won Game Three easily, but it seemed almost inevitable that the Cubs would win at least one.

Game Four went back and forth and ended in disaster with a Steve Garvey walk-off two-run home run in the bottom of the ninth off Cub closer Lee Smith. The momentum pendulum had swung decidedly in the Padres' favor. The mood in Chicago was dark; 1984 began to feel like 1969. But Sutcliffe was scheduled to take the mound in Game Five, the deciding game, so we had some justifiable hope, mixed with the usual dread of the inevitable, of the Cubs going to the World Series. After all, he had lost only one game as a Cub all year!

Leon Durham homered in the first with Gary Matthews on base to give the Cubs a 2–0 lead. Jody Davis hit a solo shot in the second and all seemed right in the Cubs' world: 3–0 with Sutcliffe on the mound. The impossible seemed plausible. But then Durham booted Flannery's easy ground ball in the bottom of the seventh and Sutcliffe, and the Cubs came unraveled like the yarn of a baseball that's lost its cowhide cover.

Lucy and Peggy looked on as Frenchy and I slowly walked to the kitchen and downed a mourning shot of whiskey. We then decided to go to Wrigley Field and walk around the park. Strolling morosely along Waveland, the booze told us that it would be a good idea to climb over the huge metal doors at the Waveland Avenue entrance, across from the fire station, and get some dirt from the mound. If Cooney had some, why shouldn't we scoop some up for ourselves? One of us, I'll not say who and don't remember exactly how, scrambled to the top of the door but the drop onto the concourse floor looked more harrowing than the climb so we gave up and continued our funereal march around the ballpark.

Somewhere along Sheffield a police car pulled up. The cop on the passenger side rolled down his window and said, "We heard that there were a couple of guys trying to break into the ballpark. Know anything about it?"

The firemen had ratted us out! "No, sir. Haven't seen a thing."

The cops laughed and drove off toward Addison.

The feeling in that Hampton Inn room near Fredericksburg, in the bottom of the eleventh of Game Three of the 2003 NLCS, brought us back to 1984's Game Five. The inevitability of the coming horror.

But the horror would be put off for a few days. A ground out followed by our future favorite D-Lee, then on the Marlins, hitting into a fielder's choice gave the Cubs a two games to one lead in the series. So it was with happier, but not exactly light, hearts that we slept a few hours (the game ended sometime around 12:30 A.M.) and got up for the long haul south to Florida.

Saturday morning traffic on I95 was light so we made good time. There was nothing remarkable about the weather or traffic conditions as we drove through Richmond and the Carolinas. I remember that the dozens of repeating "South of the Border" billboards intrigued us, each with a different message featuring their mascot, Pedro. A lot of bad puns, like "Chile Today, Hot Tamale," so when we finally passed the joint, just "South" of the North Carolina–South Carolina line, we were amazed by its size, but not its tackiness. The billboards had warned us about that. It looked like it included an amusement park, restaurants and shops. We kept driving.

Through Atlanta and Georgia and down into Florida, the dry autumn cool of the North now warm and becoming muggy. Past Jacksonville and St. Augustine, where Anne Lise went to Flagler College for a year, Daytona Beach and Vero Beach. Time again was running out.

We had a cell phone so we had the brilliant thought that maybe we should call and find a hotel near I95 and near us, wherever the heck we were at 7:15 P.M. First pitch was scheduled for 8:00. Once again, we hoped for a Marriott because they often have restaurants and bars. So I called and gave

Wrigley Field's Waveland Avenue gates. After the Cubs lost Game Five of the 1984 NLCS in San Diego, someone tried to climb into the ballpark over these imposing doors (photograph by the author).

the customer service person our approximate location. They assured us there was a Marriott in Port St. Lucie (appropriately named!) and made a reservation for us. We exited at St. Lucie West Boulevard and drove east looking for access to what looked like a mixed use subdivision to our left. Darkness had fallen. It was about 7:30. We found the road into the subdivision and followed the directions given us, but found no Marriott. Well, crap. What's up with this? I called Marriott again. Well, I was told, it's there, on Courtyard Circle.

Is it a Courtyard?

No.

It's a Marriott?

No.

No?

No, it's a SpringHill Suites by Marriott.

Well, *crap*. But Lucy remembered passing the SpringHill Suites, so at least we had our bearings now.

Time was wasting. We had noticed a sub shop on the south side of West St. Lucie so we pulled in there and bought sandwiches before checking in. Once again, we were in our room and sitting in front of the TV just in time for the first pitch.

Game Four was blissfully unexciting, the Cubs scoring four in the first inning and never looking back, finally winning 8–3. The implications of this win descended upon us and enveloped us in an aura of impossible hope. The Cubs were not only up three games to one but could actually clinch their first trip to the World Series since 1945 with us in attendance. We might, just might, *be there for it*! Life was good, although we would never vocalize our hopes. That would be yet another kiss of death.

We arrived at Paul and Bunny's house midday. They were very gracious, understanding our anxiety, and didn't expect us to visit very long. They gave us our three tickets and told us that their son-in-law John had the fourth and would meet us at our seats. And so we were off to the stadium early afternoon, Sunday, October 12, 2003.

The parking lot and landscaped outer concourse around Pro Player Stadium, which used to be Joe Robbe Stadium and is now, in 2008, Dolphin Stadium, looked like a Cubs convention. Ninety percent of the early arrivals were Cub fans, jaunty and guardedly enthusiastic. We all felt the possibility that we would be present for baseball history. The muggy South Florida air was heavy with our hopes and fears.

We found our seats and John was already there, high in the upper deck almost all the way down the right field line. We didn't care. We're used to these seats, especially when we lived in Cincinnati and would take advantage of the Reds' "Top Six" prices. John cared, though, and had bought a scalped seat behind the Cub dugout. We told him we understood, and promised that we'd join him there in the late innings if things went the Cubs' way.

The stadium filled, and Cub fans no longer dominated, although there were a lot of us. A group of big, meaning large, male Marlin fans in their twenties sat in front of us. They wore tight T-shirts that bulged with scary muscles. One of them eyeballed us in our Cub hats and shirts and scowled. "Cub fans, huh?" We smiled meekly. These guys were big indeed, and they were drinking and probably had been drinking before entering the stadium. The same guy turned again and asked, "You come in just for this game?" We smiled again and nodded. He turned back to the field for a moment, and then looking back at us asked, "All the way from Chicago?"

"No," I said. "We live in York, Pennsylvania."

"You fly in?"

"No."

He nodded. "How long a drive is that?"

"About eighteen hours."

"When you goin' back?"

"Tomorrow."

"Eighteen hours you say?"

I nodded.

He nodded. "I can respect that." He held out his hand and we shook.

Josh Beckett started for the Marlins. He went the distance, pitching a two-hit shutout. We could tell early that it was going to be tough for the Cubs to score many runs, so it was like watching a game that was already long over. A Josh Beckett highlight reel. It was, I believe, the first game during the playoffs that really made his name, which he followed up on with a brilliant World Series against the Yankees. Now he makes about $10 million a year with the Red Sox. He won twenty games in 2007. Why didn't the Cubs go after him when they traded for Derrek Lee? What a package that would have been! Maybe they wouldn't have gotten swept by the D-Backs in the playoffs last year. But we can't think about it. Maybe this, maybe that, what if, why didn't, why won't, why don't ... forever and ever amen.

We said little during the ride home. We weren't entirely discouraged, knowing that the Cubs were still up 3–2 with two games to play at Wrigley Field, Prior followed by Wood, if necessary, scheduled to start, but that old feeling of swimming through mud had returned.

Almost five years later as we sit on our back deck waiting for a Cub game to start on TV after they eke out a split with Florida, and since the All-Star break not winning a single series against anyone, Lucy says, "The

Marlins always seem to have the Cubs' number, no matter what." Whether or not it's true, it sure feels that way.

On August 10, 2008, we are on vacation on Honeoye Lake in the Finger Lakes district of Upstate New York. The whole family is there. Jeanne's husband, Brian, arranged everything. His parents own a picturesque property complete with both a cottage and a cabin, with a private pier on the lake.

Anne Lise and her boyfriend, Jeff, drove up from Bloomington, Indiana; Steve left Chicago on Friday, picked up his girlfriend, Tara, at her family home in Maumee, Ohio, and continued on to New York; and Lucy, Patricia and I came up Friday night, joining Jeanne, Brian, and their children (our grandchildren!), twins Willa and Lucy, who turn five at the end of the month, and Jasper, all of eight months old, who arrived from Brooklyn on Thursday.

Amid all the swimming and kayaking and Pétanque and eating, we debate whether, in a do-or-die situation, we would pitch Zambrano or Dempster. Steve insists on Zambrano, stating emphatically, "He's the ace! Ya gotta go with him."

I reply, "Yeah, but he goes psycho. When he loses it, the Cubs are dead." I am speaking specifically about Saturday's game when Zambrano gave up nine earned runs against the Cardinals, including four home runs, in four and one-third innings. The Cubs had won 3–2 on Friday, so the three game series stands at one apiece, the rubber game scheduled for tonight's ESPN *Sunday Night Baseball*. "I think Dempster is much more consistent."

"Zambrano is one of the top pitchers in the majors," says Steve.

"Yeah, but, I feel way less nervous with Dempster on the mound."

"Dempster," says Brian, "who we used to call 'Dumpster' as a closer."

"Love him now, though. Fan's prerogative."

The term "fan's prerogative" was first expressed to me by my brother Steve. We'd be in the bleachers during some meaningless Cub game thirty years ago and let's say Ivan DeJesus made an error. "DeJesus, that jerk," my brother would claim. "DeJesus, you BUM!" he would stand and scream, careful not to spill his beer, as if the Cub shortstop could hear him all the way from under the scoreboard. The next inning, DeJesus would come to the plate and deliver with a clutch, run-producing hit, which was unusual. He hit .278 in 1978, but drove in a paltry 35 runs. Steve would stand again and yell, "Atta baby, Ivan!" Then he would sit and say, "Best Cub shortstop since Ernie." We would stare at him as if to protest that not ten minutes before he was ready to send DeJesus to Iowa. Steve would shrug and smile and say, "Fan's prerogative."

So, right now, in August of 2008, we *love* Dempster. Okay, not like we *love* Kerry Wood and Derrek Lee, but we really like him a lot and feel almost optimistic when he's scheduled to take the mound, as he is tonight. We are confident that the Cubs have a great shot at winning the series with the Cardinals. And they have been winning all of their series since the end of July, and the end of that abysmal return from the All-Star Break. Not only winning, but sweeping the four game series against Milwaukee July 28 through 31. The atmosphere in Milwaukee was, as expressed by everyone covering the series for the Cubs on TV and radio, "playoff-like." It looked and sounded like Cub fans at least equaled Brewers fans at what many hand-made signs in the crowd called "Wrigley North."

Lucy and I listened to the first game via WGN on the Internet. The final three games were broadcast on television that was available in York, Pennsylvania. The Cubs dominated, outscoring the Brewers 31–11 for the four games. Cubs pitching was excellent, three of the four starters notching wins—Zambrano, Dempster and Harden, his first victory since coming to the Cubs although he had pitched well enough to win every outing.

They were five games ahead of the Brewers at that point and went on to win three-game series against the Pirates and the Astros at Wrigley Field. But it felt like they should have swept at least one of those two struggling teams.

Now they're about to face the Cardinals in the rubber game of their weekend series at Wrigley Field. We speculate that the atmosphere around the ballpark is crazy. Steve verifies that it would be insane, as it is every day and night the Cubs play at home this year. He reports, however, that they've been told to stop their Waveland Avenue street parties. It seems a group of "Iowa college boys," as Steve describes them, moved into the first floor apartment across from Steve and have gone beyond the limits of both neighborly and legal toleration.

"They face their speakers out the window and blast hip-hop loud enough to be heard at home plate," says Steve. "We didn't complain, but someone talked to our alderman who talked to our landlord who talked to us."

"That's awful," we all agree. It was a friendly and mostly harmless scene before, with even paddywagons full of cops stopping to watch the game on Steve's TV.

"Yeah," replied Steve. "I put a sign on their door that says 'Way to blow it for everyone, Iowa boys.'" He shrugs. "We're going to go out there again anyway and see what happens."

The Honeoye cottage television is a tiny 13-inch. It reminds us of our old Drake Street TV. When Brian tunes in ESPN the static and snow break up the color so badly that the screen becomes essentially black and white, just like thirty years ago. "Looks perfect to me," says Lucy. And indeed, the whole experience makes us feel even more like we're roughing it. The sound doesn't work at all, but we don't mind. In fact, Cub-hater Joe Morgan is doing the game so we prefer the sound off.

Steve cooks thick New York strip steaks on the grill while I sauté three batches of homegrown green beans. A storm blows in, dumping buckets of rain on us, but Steve grills on. I, being old, move into the kitchen and peer across the family room at the tiny, snowy TV and it's like looking at an Impressionist painting—the farther back you stand the more the dots come together and the clearer the picture gets.

Dempster pitches two-hit ball through six and two-thirds innings, but the offense and both defenses help. The Cardinals look sloppy in the infield during the Cubs half of the sixth, contributing to a five-run inning that could have scored even more. Two runners, Edmonds and Cedeno, get a little too aggressive and get thrown out at third. Edmonds and Fukudome rob Cardinals hitters of base hits, Edmonds' diving catch preventing two runs. Cedeno bare-hands a Molina grounder to short. He fires to Lee who summersaults off first to catch the throw and just tag the runner. The Cubs keep the Cardinals at bay and win 6–2, number thirteen for Dempster. A great night of great food, great wine, great fun and great Cubs baseball. We switch to the Olympics to see the USA Men's swimming team just edge out the French in an amazing comeback in the 400-meter freestyle relay, the anchor Jason Lezak catching up and out-touching the French swimmer Alain Bernard for the Gold Medal. No way! He was half a body length behind with half a length to go! Holy cow, indeed. One website, Associated Content, is already dubbing it "the Best Race in History."

The Cubs are off Monday. Brian fashions Cubs pancakes out of batter (ha ha), blueberries and red raspberries. We eat, pack up, say our bittersweet goodbyes at about eleven-thirty and head south for York.

Being back at work after a three-day weekend of much hilarity can strain the spirit to say the least. Tuesday night brings further disappointment. All day long we call each other and remind ourselves that the Cubs play Atlanta at 7:00 P.M. on WGN. So we have our evening planned, and look forward to it with guarded excitement. Then, at the end of a particularly miserable day on the job, we settle in with a delicious pasta tossed with tomato, onion and zucchini, along with a nice Côtes de Rhone, and tune in to see Len and Bob standing above an empty Turner Field, the tarp covering the infield. The game has been postponed because of rain, only the twelfth time in the history of that ballpark. Crap. No Cubs baseball at all is even worse than watching them lose.

Instead of baseball we watch three episodes of *The Wire* season five, which is fresh out on DVD today. Then we watch the Michael Phelps show from Beijing. He wins two more gold medals, bringing his total to five at the games and eleven for his career. World swimming records are being drowned every day. Can he be the greatest athlete *ever*?

No. Michael Jordan still reigns supreme.

They'll make up the Cubs–Braves game tomorrow, Wednesday, playing a doubleheader of sorts, the first game starting at 1:10. Then they'll clear the stadium and charge again for game two, which starts at 7:10. The first game is on WGN TV, but not on WGN Radio, so I'll be on Gameday while "at work." Lucy and Patricia will be watching at home.

The Cubs sweep the double header and then the Atlanta series, outscoring the Braves 29–9. I listen to the Atlanta radio team (never caught their names because I was distracted by my job, but neither announcer was Chip Caray whose voice I would recognize from his years on WGN TV with Steve Stone) for the first game of the double header and they are clearly impressed by all of the Cub fans in attendance. The color commentator echoes Lee Elia's tirade of April 1983 by claiming that there aren't more Braves fans at the weekday afternoon game because, unlike Cub fans, they work for a living. He actually repeated the lame crack late in the game assuring the Braves' listening audience that there would be more Braves fans at the night game because they would be off work.

One incident of note that was much remarked upon: Before the fifth inning, as the skies darken, the umpires rule that the lights must be turned on before the inning can begin in order to give both teams equal time under artificial illumination. Braves manager Bobby Cox protests, claiming that the time it takes to turn on the lights fully can disrupt the flow of the game, especially the pitchers' routines. This complaint might be reasonable (Lou Piniella made the same complaint to the same umpire, Joe West, nicknamed "The Cowboy," at Wrigley Field, stating, "The Cowboy thought he was an electrician today."), but apparently Cox's language is a bit too colorful and he gets tossed for the 142nd time, extending his Major League all-time ejection record over long-time holder of the dubious distinction John McGraw, manager of the Cubs' 1908 archrival New York Giants. McGraw's record of 131 was broken by Cox in 2007. It had been one of those records, like Babe Ruth's home runs and then Henry Aaron's home runs and now Barry Bonds' alleged steroid-fueled record, Ty Cobb's stolen bases and then Maury Wills' stolen bases and then Lou Brock's stolen bases and now Rickey Henderson's stolen bases, that pundits and fans alike thought would never be broken. Or how about Mark Spitz's Olympic record seven gold medals? This year, during the *greatest sports year ever(!)*, Michael Phelps earns eight gold medals.

There aren't many unbreakable records left. DiMaggio's 56-game hitting streak looks safe, but you never know.

There doesn't seem to be any more Braves fans at the night game, or maybe the Cub fans are just louder having quaffed an afternoon's worth of beer while the Braves fans toiled nobly at their appointed tasks. In fairness, attendance at the afternoon game: 27,220. Night game: 33,714. So at least 6,494 Braves fans hold down day jobs.

And let's not neglect Reds broadcaster Marty Brennaman while we're complaining about other teams' announcers. In April he took off on Cub fans in a way surpassed only by Elia, calling them (us) "by far and away the most obnoxious fans in this league." The bad behavior of these (us) awful Cub supporters is what "makes you want to see this Chicago Cubs team lose." And lose they will, according to Marty, because "at the end of the day they are still the Chicago Cubs, and they'll find a way to screw it up." Wow! Marty, Marty, Marty. Chill a little, dude.

At this point it's a little confusing, though. Was he trashing the Cubs themselves, their fans or both? Both it would seem! Quite a professional piece of broadcast journalism.

Cub fans drove Brennaman to this level of frenzy because they threw a bunch of baseballs on the field after an Adam Dunn home run. The number of balls differs depending on whom you read or listen to. Brennaman said fifteen or eighteen at the time, although that number sometimes balloons to forty on some blogs and Web sites. I guess Marty thought the fans were somehow dissing Adam Dunn, or showing their frustration over the home run. But then I learned that the score at the time was 11–2 in favor of the Cubs, which leads me to believe that Cub fans couldn't have cared less and were lampooning their own tradition of throwing visitors' home runs back onto the field. It's a well-known secret that the actual ball is rarely thrown back anymore. Bleacherites and ballhawks on the street bring a supply of beat-up Little League balls (or worse) to toss onto the field while keeping any homers they're lucky enough to grab. Throwing all those balls on the field in that situation was nothing more than an impromptu satire of the practice.

Listening to Brennaman's tirade now, in August after four months of cooling down, it sounds to me like he flipped out over something minor. Frustration and jealousy of the Cubs' fan support, among other things, were getting the better of him.

One of the blogs had an interesting observation, which I quote below. It's titled "Fuck Marty Brennaman" which is unfortunate because some of the points made are good ones. Posted by "Hick Flicks" on a blog called Rumors and Rants, April 22, 2008. Here's the link: http://sportsyenta.blog spot.com/2008/04/fuck-marty-brennaman.html.

It seems that some 20 years ago, then–Reds manager Pete Rose was tossed from a game by ump Dave Pallone. Enraged by the call, it seems Brennaman encouraged those listening to the game on their headphones at Riverfront to join in the fun and continue tossing garbage, lighters, etc. onto the field at the umps.

This led to the rather rare occurrence of a broadcaster being criticized by the commissioner's office. As then-commish Bart Giamatti told the *New York Times*:

"Inciting the unacceptable behavior of some of the fans were the inflammatory and completely irresponsible remarks of local radio broadcasters Marty Brennaman and Joe Nuxhall.... There is no excuse for encouraging a situation where the physical safety and well-being of any individual is put significantly at risk. Nothing justifies such unprofessional behavior."

As the late, great Mel Allen used to say, "Well how about that!"

But we sympathize with Marty and all Reds fans to some extent. No one can take their World Series championships away, but Major League Baseball did take their biggest hero from them. Pete Rose actually did it to himself, but the result is the same. One year you think that your city is the home of the greatest hitter in the history of the game, and a year later you find out that not only will he never be admitted into the Hall of Fame, but he is banned from the game itself for life. This has to make a fan bitter, and so when one does make the effort to go out to the Great American Ballpark only to see that more Cub fans have traveled five or six hours than Reds fans have driven less than one hour from just about anywhere in metro Cincinnati (we know this because we used to live on the outskirts, miles beyond I275, almost as close to Dayton as Cincinnati), it could easily turn a Reds fan into a Cub hater. And think of poor Marty who has to see this happen every Cubs–Reds game in Cinci, and then travel to Chicago to see that virtually no Reds fans have made the trip.

Anne Lise and I have a special place in our hearts for Pete Rose. On Sunday, September 8, 1985, I had two tickets to the Cub game at Wrigley Field. They were scheduled to play the Reds. That morning Lucy and I sat in our kitchen chatting about who would go to the game. We had no chance of getting a babysitter for our three kids. Jeanne was seven, Steve four and Anne Lise had just turned six years old the day before. Lucy would not hear of going with one of the kids and leaving me at home with the other two, but somehow it was okay for me to leave her behind! Okay okay, I was born a Cub fan and she only became one upon moving to the Chicago area from New York during high school, but still....

The door to the girls' room opened and Anne Lise stumbled out, rubbing her eyes, still sleepy. The decision was made. She was the first one up, so she would have first dibs at going to the game.

"Anne Lise," I said. "I have two tickets to the Cub game today. Want to go?"

Her eyes lit up and she was instantly wide awake. She gobbled down some cereal, quietly got dressed so as not to disturb her sister Jeanne, and off we went, walking to the el station at Lawrence and Kimball, the end of the Ravenswood line.

Riding the train as it rattled along the surface tracks, then climbed to become a true "el" as it approached Western, and then made the turns around Damen and then down and around to Southport, I explained that we were going to a very important game, maybe. The star of the Cincinnati Reds was Pete Rose and he needed only two base hits of any kind today to tie Ty Cobb's record of 4,191 career hits. He could break the record if he got three hits. Anne Lise had been going to Cub games all of her six years and so knew the game and certainly understood that this could be a day at Wrigley Field to remember. The number 4,191 impressed her as being very big in terms of hits.

It was overcast and rain had been predicted, and our tickets were for the upper deck along the third base line which meant we'd be right in the path of winds out of the north or off Lake Michigan. So we were bundled up and ready for any weather. We arrived at the ballpark, bought our score-cards and pencils, and made our way to our seats.

The upper deck was well populated, but we sat down the line above the bullpen where the crowd was a bit thin. Later we learned that over 28,000 watched the game, a good crowd by my standards (back then I was still pleased anytime the upper deck was open), and by Cub standards that year which had been disappointing after the National League East Division–winning 1984 season. They would finish the year 77–84, which adds up to only 161 games. The 162nd game was a tie—the game Anne Lise and I attended that Sunday.

A sense of anticipation vibrated through the stands. The fans knew that the game could be historic and most around us were animated as they talked about the possibilities. You could feel the tension in the air when Rose came to the plate in the first inning. And he delivered on the first pitch with a single to left. Cub fans cheered loudly! Only one more hit to go to tie the record with almost a whole ballgame left to play. Anne Lise and I were excited. She had entered the players' numbers on her scorecard. I reviewed the basics of keeping score with her, as I did with all of the kids every time we went to a game. She gamely made her entries for the first few innings, but then the excitement of the day overwhelmed her and her scoring became a little spotty.

Looking to my right, I noticed some empty seats, so throughout the game we kept moving closer to the plate. By the fifth inning we were directly over third base when Rose came up to bat again and worked the count full.

CHICAGO CUBS vs CINCINNATI REDS

CINCINNATI

CHICAGO CUBS vs CINCINNATI REDS

9-8-85

(#4191)

CINCINNATI

		1	2	3	4	5	6	7	8	9	10	11	AB	R	H	RBI	E
20	Milner CF	4-3	E	18		F6	8			18							
14	Rose 1st	1B	4-3				6-3			K							
39	Parker RF	5B	4-3			1B	1-3			K							

Anne Lise, age 6, keeps score (top), September 8, 1985, when Pete Rose tied Ty Cobb's record for the most hits. The author keeps score, too (bottom).

And then it happened. A clean line drive single to right. Number 4,191. The record was tied and we were there to see it! The partisan Cubs crowd stood and roared, clapping and screaming and stomping their feet for Pete Rose of the Cincinnati Reds. The ovation lasted a long time. The *Tribune* later said it went on for three and half minutes, but it seemed much longer than that. Rose, standing on first base, was visibly moved. I think I remember him wiping his eyes with his sleeve and waving to the fans. But it was twenty-three years ago so forgive me if I miss a couple of details.

It was a stirring moment. Rose was quoted as saying, "Any day is a special day when you get a couple hits and ... get a reception like I got here."

And there were still four innings to go. He could break the record today. What would the crowd do then?

But it was not to be. The rain started and delayed the game for over two hours. At six years old Anne Lise was already a fierce follower of the family law of never leaving a game early, so we stayed, as did most fans hoping to see another Rose hit. But Dunston threw him out 6 to 3 in the seventh and Lee Smith struck him out in the ninth with a runner in scoring position. Cub fans booed Smith loudly for not giving up what could have been the game-winning hit—the Reds had already tied the score that inning.

That's how it ended. Smith struck out the side and then the game was called because of darkness after the Cubs failed to score in the bottom of the ninth. It remains a tie in the record book.

Ironically, Rose wasn't going to play that day. Steve Trout, a lefty, was scheduled to pitch but fell off a bike and had gravel imbedded in his pitching hand. Player-manager Rose would only put himself in the lineup if a right-hander was scheduled, and so when he heard that Trout was to be replaced by righty Reggie Patterson, he wrote his name on the lineup card.

In a second irony, perhaps we actually did see Rose break the record because in a review of the record books it was subsequently discovered that two of Ty Cobb's hits were counted twice, so he only hit 4,189 and Rose's first inning single to left was indeed the record-breaker, but nobody knew it. I must point out, however, that if you go to Ty Cobb's stats at mlb.com, they still list his hit total as 4,191.

But we had a great time. Anne Lise was so thrilled by the experience that she made a point of getting up early every weekend or holiday morning until the season ended in the hope that she would be taken to another historic game. And from that day on, Pete Rose was a special player for the two of us. His gambling problems and subsequent banishment made us sad. It reminded many of the 1919 Black Sox gambling scandal that resulted in the banning of several Sox players including "Shoeless" Joe Jackson, another tragic figure considered by many to be one of the best of all time.

On Wednesday, August 27, 2008, we will drive Patricia to Temple University in Philadelphia to begin her freshman year. We think it a suitable sendoff to go to Pittsburgh the night before to watch the Cubs play Game Two of their last series against the Pirates for the season. How can we not? Pittsburgh has been the scene of more memorable, or infamous, Cub capers for us than any city outside Chicago. Also, although we're sure there will be more trips to more Cub games, dropping Patricia off at her dorm will be poignant to say the least. We have four children: Jeanne, Anne Lise, Steve and Patricia. Patricia was born eight years after Steve and so for years it has been just the three of us, two and a half years in Cincinnati, and six and a half years in York. Whenever we've hopped in the car to go anywhere—for a wedding in Florida, a family gathering in the Finger Lakes, a visit to a museum in Baltimore or Philadelphia, a birthday party in Brooklyn, a meaningless Cub game in D.C., a National League Central Championship-clinching series in Cincinnati, an NLCS playoff game in Miami, or another horror in Pittsburgh, it's been Lucy and me in the front and Patricia in the back, listening to CDs or NPR or an audiobook or just complaining about the Cubs or the Pennsylvania Turnpike or both. With Patricia heading off to dorm life, it will be just Lucy and me for the first time since Jeanne was born almost thirty-one years ago. We are sad.

Patricia and Lucy meet me in Lebanon, Pennsylvania, where I'm working, so we can start our drive west at 3:00 to make it to PNC Park in time for a 7:05 first pitch. Lebanon sits several miles north of the Turnpike and east of Harrisburg, but we figure it's about the same amount of driving time from there to Pittsburgh as it is from York. It's a beautiful night for baseball—sunny, clear and in the low seventies. Pennsylvania looks lush and idyllic in the warm late afternoon, late summer sunlight, the first hint of the leaves, cornstalks and soybeans fading to their harvest gold colors. The dog days are fading, too.

Traffic is clear for the most part so we walk into PNC as the national anthem rings over the sound system. We sit in the tenth row of the second tier of lower deck seats, just beyond first base, among the best seats we've ever had in Pittsburgh. Cub fans surround us and make up probably a third of the crowd. But this is nothing new.

We're excited because Zambrano is scheduled to start and he is due for a good outing. But which "Z" will it be tonight: "Big Z" the Cub ace, or "Psycho Z"? It's distressing because Zambrano stated early in the year that he was going to work hard on controlling his emotions. Sometimes he wins the battle, sometimes not. And lately, he has not looked sharp, even when winning.

But he looks sharp against Pirates' leadoff man Nyjer Morgan, striking him out with a pitch in the dirt. But wait! The ball gets away from Soto and rolls all the way to the screen. Morgan runs to first and makes it easily. No no no no no no no no. This is exactly the kind of thing that can trigger the metamorphosis from "Big Z" to "Psycho Z." And it does. Morgan steals second. Next batter walks. Next batter flies to left, but the next batter doubles. Next batter singles. After one more single in the inning, the Pirates plate three on three hits.

The Cubs, however, do their best to keep Z in the game, scoring one in the third, four in the fourth and one in the fifth to take a 6–4 lead. But Z can't hold it and gets the hook in the bottom of the inning with the game tied at six. He will not be the pitcher of record.

It's one of those nights at the old ballyard. The lead changes hands three times. The Cubs then explode in the eighth inning, bringing eleven batters to the plate and scoring seven, putting the game out of reach and sending most Pirate fans to the exits. Cub fans now comprise most of the crowd. Soto is the man of the night, clearing loaded bases with a double not once but twice and hitting a solo home run in between the doubles, strangely the only homer of this high-scoring game.

Kerry Wood comes in to pitch the ninth, even though the Cubs have a 14–8 lead. We figure he needs the work. He strikes out the side, but in the meantime gives up a run on back-to-back doubles, and then a single. Not a good outing. Maybe it's one of those games when a closer comes in with such a big lead that the pressure is off, and so there is not the same level of adrenalin that gives him the edge he needs to be effective. Nonetheless, we leave Pittsburgh, after four hours, a little bummed instead of elated. Zambrano looked psycho. Wood looked schizophrenic. The Cubs got fewer hits than runs, which isn't always a good indicator. They drew eight walks and one hit batsman. They committed three errors. But it was a wacky game in general. We commented on the way home that we saw about everything but a balk, a triple play and a squeeze. Wild pitches, a passed ball, Morgan caught off second base after he overslid on a stolen base attempt, lots of bunts, nine doubles (five by the Cubs), lots and lots of pitchers (fourteen), stolen bases, a triple, a homer, errors, defensive indifference, ten Pirate strike-outs by a variety of Cub pitchers, a Pirates pitcher (Grabow) who walked three consecutive Cubs after giving up two consecutive singles, a run-down between short and third, Fukudome gunning a rope to Ramirez to cut down a runner going from first to third on a single ... a real "Pier Six brawl," as Brickhouse used to say.

We arrive back in York at about 2:30 A.M.

The next day we drive Patricia to Temple. Checking in and moving her in take all of twenty minutes, so the three of us quickly leave campus and look for a sports bar that is broadcasting the early afternoon game from Pittsburgh. I had done some research on the Internet and located a joint on 3rd in North Philadelphia, but when we arrive we learn that they neither get the Pittsburgh station nor WGN, so we're out of luck. Not enough research. I should have made some phone calls. But in this era of the World Wide Web, one almost feels dated relying on any other medium for any kind of information. The bar has maybe eight wide screen TVs, but it's all sports highlights, NFL previews and the Little League World Series. Our waiter tells us, however, that the Cubs are winning 2–0 in the eighth. The eighth inning? Already? They go on to sweep the Pirates, winning the third game, which lasts only about two and a quarter hours, and even pull off the squeeze we didn't get to see the night before.

We eat some burgers and take Patricia back to campus. The three of us are misty-eyed, but we make it quick. She's ready to move on and walks determinedly into the dorm. Lucy and I quietly get back in the car and drive home to York. Our granddaughter Willa, who turns five tomorrow, had predicted that we'd cry so much that we'd "fill up Pennsylvania" with tears. It's not quite that bad, but she wasn't entirely wrong either.

Lou Piniella has repeatedly emphasized that the key to success in 2008 is to win series. As August comes to an end, the Cubs either split or win every series since they lost two out of three to the Diamondbacks in Phoenix, July 21 to 23. That's eleven series producing a won-loss record of 26–10. They come out of the dog days with the second best record in baseball (and the best record in the National League) at 82–52, four and a half games ahead of Milwaukee, who wins three in a row while the Cubs lose the last two games of August to the Phillies. For such a good record, the race is just too darn close. C.C. Sabathia, traded to the Brewers mid-season, doesn't lose and has sparked a fire under an already good team.

If we think the race is still close, however, we need only take a look at the National League at the end of August 1908, to find a race that was really close. The New York Giants sat atop the league only 3 percentage points ahead of the Cubs and a half game ahead of the Pirates. But the Cubs had major momentum going for them in 1908. They didn't just win series; they won nine games straight to finish the month, including a three-game sweep of the Giants at West Side Park. The stage was set for one of the wildest Septembers in baseball history.

The 2008 version of the Cubs finish August losing two to the Phillies at Wrigley Field. We're worried about their pitching. Z has looked awful. Dempster begins to look vulnerable. But perhaps worst of all, their hitting cools off. No more clutch hits. No more extra base hits at all since Soriano's home run in the 7th inning of their last win on Friday, August 29.

September looms on the horizon and the Cubs seem to be crawling, instead of charging, to get to postseason play.

Saturday, August 30, we drive to Brooklyn for the twins' fifth birthday party. It's a costume party. Lucy goes as a chef, complete with toq atop her head, Patricia as Dorothy from *The Wizard of Oz*, and I go as Ernie Banks. We have a ball, wolfing down Brooklyn pizza in Carroll Park with the girls and their friends. On the way back to their apartment, all along Smith Street Mets fans, noting my costume, ask why the Cubs lost to the Phillies and can't they help them out a little more?

That night, Jeanne's husband, Brian, disappears into their bedroom where their computer resides. He emerges half an hour later with a huge smile on his face saying, "I got 'em. A whole bunch of seats in nosebleed for the September 22nd game at Shea Stadium. Fourteen bucks each."

Fourteen bucks? Imagine paying fourteen bucks for a seat in Wrigley Field! Impossible.

"We're there," we say.

CHAPTER SEVEN

Stretch Run

September 4, 2008. I receive an e-mail from Patricia, now at college, that reads:

Poor Ron (Santo). You can feel his pain over the radio transmission.
Five, five, five in a row, six in a row let's go.
I told Mom, I'm looking into living in the Galapagos. Or maybe Europe.
Wherever I can be as far away from baseball as possible.
I feel sick.

The five in a row to which Patricia refers is the five straight games the Cubs have lost at Wrigley Field. Last night the Houston Astros, who are hot and about to catch the third place Cardinals, completed a three-game sweep of the Cubs, including two shutouts.

This stinks. The Cubs stink. They cannot score any kind of runs at all, let alone in the clutch. Okay, Tuesday's game went into extra innings, so the Cubs did come back and tie the game at seven. But then they put the lead-off man, and potentially game-winning run, on in the eighth, ninth and tenth innings but could not get him around. And in the eighth they had the bases loaded with one out. D-Lee hit into a double play. He also struck out with two on to end the Cubs' half of the tenth inning. Oh D-Lee, D-Lee, D-Lee! What's the deal?

But Lee's not the only one. We hear that Z has a bum arm. Details to come. He apparently took himself out of the game during the fifth inning of the 9–7 mess on Tuesday. What next?

On this date, September 4, the 1908 Cubs played the Pirates at Exposition Park in Pittsburgh. In the bottom of the tenth inning Honus Wagner

135

stepped up to the plate for the Pirates. The score was tied at zero. The Cubs wished that "The Flying Dutchman" had retired, as he had threatened before the start of the 1908 season. Now he was hitting around .350 and was bound to put the ball in play.

The steep hills to the west of the junction of the Monongahela and Allegheny rivers threw broad, long shadows over the playing field. The light, already dimmed by clouds of black smoke pouring out of the steel mills across the river, was going fast. Everyone knew that the game would be suspended for darkness before many more innings could be played. And the outcome of any single game could mean the difference between going to the World Series and going home for the winter. The Cubs, Giants and Pirates were all within reach of each other at the top of the National League with a month to go in the season.

Pirate left fielder, and manager Fred Clarke stood on second base representing the winning run. There was one out. Clarke was as mean a bastard as Johnny Evers and would do anything, use any trick to gain an edge and win this game.

Sure enough, Wagner connected, driving a hard ground ball to Evers' left. He leaped for it and knocked it down, preventing it from rolling into right field. Clarke had to stop at third base, but Wagner stood safe at first. Still only one out.

Standing on the mound, Three Finger Mordecai "Miner" Brown looked at Wagner, looked at Clarke and looked at Evers. A Tinker to Evers to Chance double play was in order. Get the ground ball. Brown's hand of only three mangled fingers, the result of two accidents involving farm machinery, threw the sharpest curve in baseball. Lots of ground ball outs, if the hitter hit the ball at all. And against the next batter, rookie first baseman Warren Gill, the hook broke beautifully, but right into his leg. Gill was awarded first base and Wagner moved on to second.

The bases were loaded with one out. A ground ball could still end the inning. But then Brown, angry with himself for letting a youngster like Gill reach first in such a crucial game, got Ed Abbaticchio on strikes. That brought up Owen "Chief" Wilson, another rookie fresh up from the minor leagues.

Could this kid hit "Miner" Brown's curve? The Cubs were betting he could not, but hit the curve he did, on the line into center field for a single. Clarke trotted home with the winning run. Disgusted, Evers looked at Gill running from first to second. The rookie stopped halfway, jumped up and down once in celebration, and retreated to the Pirates' bench, a common occurrence back in the early twentieth century. Runners often didn't run out hits or advance to the next base if the hit drove in a walk-off winning run.

In addition to his skills on the field, Evers was a crabby student of the game, reading and rereading the rule book and not hesitating to get into an umpire's face and challenging any call if it helped the Cubs. On July 19, 1908, a small entry in the *Chicago Tribune* might have caught Evers' eye, according to speculation by G.H. Fleming in *The Unforgettable Season*, and seconded by David Anderson in *More Than Merkle*. Every Sunday the *Tribune* published a column titled "Inquisitive Fans," a question-and-answer feature covering fan inquiries about the rules of baseball. Each column printed a dozen or more questions from readers and the editor's terse answers, often pretty crabby themselves, as in the following:

> Chicago—[Editor of the *Tribune*]—A batter, after making an uncertain hit, slides for first base in order to beat the throw. Is there any rule prohibiting this? F.A.N. [*sic*]
> (Answer) No. Why not read them (the rules)?

The questions came from around the Midwest, as far away as Nebraska this particular Sunday, demonstrating that during this era of no broadcast media of any kind, unless you count the telegraph, the syndication of newspaper features had already made the country a little smaller. It also demonstrated the countrywide fascination with big league baseball at a time when there were only eight teams in each league, and only two west of the Mississippi, both in St. Louis.

The following entry lay buried near the bottom of July 19's "Inquisitive Fans" column:

> Chicago—[Editor of the *Tribune*.]—In the last half of the ninth, with the score tied, two men out and a runner on third, the batter hits to left and the runner scores. The batter, seeing the runner score, stops between home and first. The ball is thrown to first baseman, who touches his base before the runner reaches it. Can runner score on this? JOSEPH RUPP
> (Answer) No. Run cannot score when the third out is made before reaching first base.

The rule involved, Rule 59 in the rule book that was active in 1908, states in part:

> If (the runner) reach(es) home on or during a play in which the third man be forced out ... a run shall not count.

Very simply, if there's a runner on third with two out and a ball is hit on the ground resulting in a force play for the third out, the runner on third cannot score. The ball is live until every runner reaches base safely. If the hitter, or a man on first, for example, fails to touch the base to which he is forced to run by the hit, even if the ball is in the gap and bouncing around the outfield, the defensive team can throw the ball into the infield and force the runner. The run from third won't count even if the runner had crossed the plate minutes before the force play.

Whether or not Evers actually thought of Rule 59, Joseph Rupp and "Inquisitive Fans" we'll never know for sure. One thing we can be certain of, he knew the rule and chose this moment to try to enforce it for the first time. Evers ran to second, and screamed at Jimmy Slagle in center field to throw him the ball. Slagle threw the ball. Evers caught it and stepped on second base forcing Gill out, as far as he and the Cubs were concerned, and nullifying the run from third. But he made his protest to no one but other Cubs. Umpire Hank O'Day was on his way off the field and didn't see the play. When pressed by Evers, he refused to nullify the winning run.

Cubs owner and president Charlie Murphy was convinced, however. After the game he sent a telegram to Harry Pulliam, National League president, at the National League offices on the fourteenth floor of the St. James Building, 26th and Broadway, New York City. The building still stands on the southwest corner of the intersection.

The telegram read in part:

> Chicago claims Gill should have touched second base before he ran to the clubhouse, and will prove by affidavits ... that he failed to do so.

One of the league president's duties in 1908 was to supervise the umpires. Most games had only one umpire who stood behind home plate calling balls and strikes, but who was also responsible for every other play and call. If a hitter reached first base, the umpire would move out behind the pitcher so he could call balls and strikes and also have a better view of the bases. When available, a second umpire would cover the infield. On September 4, Hank O'Day was the only umpire working the game in Pittsburgh. Pulliam called O'Day, who gave him his version of what happened, or rather what he didn't see happen. Pulliam considered the situation carefully and, as he usually did, sided with his umpire. He replied as follows: "The umpire in this case, by allowing the winning run, ruled that there was no force at second, because if there had been the run could not have been scored. The protest is denied."

In essence, he agreed with both O'Day and Evers. He reinforced that Rule 59 applied in this case, as Evers claimed, but he was also clear that O'Day did not see Evers force Gill out at second. The umpire's decision was therefore final. But Evers, O'Day and Pulliam would all remember this day and the Gill play should a similar situation ever arise. They could have had no idea just how soon an almost exact repeat of the play would occur, and how critical that play would be to Cub history, and to the game of baseball.

And all of them, Pulliam, Evers and O'Day, would be there when it happened.

On September 5, 2008, we sit up in our loft listening to the Cubs get destroyed by the Reds in Cincinnati. They have already lost five in a row, including a sweep by the Astros at Wrigley Field, and look poised to make it number six. Lilly doesn't have his good stuff at all, while Arroyo for the Reds sounds like Three Finger Brown.

In the news, McCain gives his speech at the Republican National Convention and Alaska governor Sarah Palin accepts the Republican nomination for vice president, so this election is guaranteed to be historic because either an African American will be our next president or a woman will be our next vice president.

But with history staring them in the face, the Cubs turn and run from destiny. They travel to Cincinnati to play the Reds in a three-game weekend series September 5 through 7. Piniella and first base coach Matt Sinatro decide to drive, which provides the weekend's humor because instead of taking the I75 exit off I80-90, they continue on toward Cleveland. The normal five to six hour trip takes them eight, with players and coaches wondering where on earth they might be. An accident? Did they forget about the time change from Central to Eastern? They end up driving diagonally back across the state of Ohio to make it with two hours to spare before the first pitch.

Lots of laughs, until the game starts. The Cubs lose 10–2.

Several times we have driven to Cincinnati for two of the three games played over a September weekend. Not possible this year, but our daughter Anne Lise and her boyfriend, Jeff, represent the family at the Saturday night game. We have guests for dinner. Periodically Anne Lise calls to tell us that Alphonso Soriano has just hit another home run. Three in one game! She's sitting in the tenth row along the left field line and says it's crazy with Cub fans as the Cubs put on a monster display of hitting.

Later that night, we check Cubs.com to find that they did indeed win, but gave up eight runs in the last two innings just to make sure that all the Cub fans who made the trip left pissed off in spite of winning 14–9.

They are on WGN on Sunday, so, in spite of the fact that it is a beautiful day, we hunker down in front of the tube for the rubber game of the three-game series. They squander a lot of opportunities, leaving ten men on base, but go into the bottom of the ninth leading 3–1. Wood trots in from the bullpen. We feel sick. Please, please, please make it a quick one-two-three inning.

But it's not to be. Encarnacion singles to center and takes second when

Edmonds misses the bounce and lets the ball dribble out of reach behind him. Soriano races over from left field and runs it down. It wasn't hard hit at all, but crap! There's a runner on second with nobody out. In short order, Wood loads the bases, but there is one out because Lee fields a bunt by Ryan Hanigan and forces Encarnacion at third.

Just like the Gill game of a hundred years ago, the Cubs need a ground ball. A double play will end it, the Cubs gaining a game on Milwaukee because the Padres have already handled them 10–1. (Chris Young had a perfect game going with two outs in the eighth when the Brewers scored their only run on a homer by Gabe Kapler.) Wood hasn't really gotten anyone out, if you don't count the failed bunt, but he hasn't been hit hard either. Bloop single and a couple of walks—not that walks aren't bad enough in the bottom of the ninth.

Chris Dickerson steps to the plate, pinch-hitting for Cordero. OHMY-GOD! He's hitting .322! Why couldn't Wood get the damn ball over when he faced .246-hitting Javier Valentin? First pitch is a curveball low and inside to the left-hander. Dickerson fouls off a fastball, so Wood is even with him at 1–1. Wood throws another curve. This one hangs up there high and inside. 2–1. Another fastball high and in the zone. Dickerson whiffs on it. Okay, okay. Fan him with another heater and then get the next guy any old way. The Cubs don't absolutely need a double play here.

And here it comes! Another fastball, but this time Dickerson tops it and sends it bouncing past the mound. From the TV camera angle we see Cedeno ranging easily and confidently to his left. This is it! The double play ball.

Ha, ha, ha, ha, ha! Joke's on us again. No double play ball, oh no, no, no. The ball bounces high. Cedeno, in for Theriot who felt sick and had himself taken out of the game, begins his move toward second and tries to force the runner before he has the ball! It never makes it into his mitt but bounces off the tips of its fingers and splits the outfielders so Dickerson is safe on an error and two runs score to tie the game. The grounder wasn't routine. Its hop was head-high. But Cedeno will tell you, I'll bet, that he should have gloved it, stepped on second and doubled Dickerson at first.

At this point there is absolutely no doubt in our minds that Wood will give up the winning run. Sure enough, Jolbert Cabrera hits the second pitch solidly down the line in left field. He tosses his bat in the air and waves his arms as the Reds' dugout clears to surround him in celebratory joy at first base. Wood, not happy about being shown up by the overt demonstration by Cabrera, points at him and calls him a "motherfucker" if we read his lips correctly, and there is little doubt that we did.

There have been ugly losses before, but few equal this one. Soriano's dropped fly ball in Pittsburgh perhaps, but that was early in the year. This is the end of the first week in September and the Cubs have now lost seven out of eight. Luckily, the Brewers have lost five out of seven so the Cubs remain four games in first place, but still, this one was the pits—right up there, or should I say down there, with Brant Brown's dropped fly ball in Milwaukee when the Cubs were vying for a spot in the 1998 playoffs just about exactly ten years ago.

Wood is now 4–4 with a 3.26 ERA and 28 saves. After a game like this we wonder, when did he get these saves? We don't recall any. And only four losses? It should be ten.

But Cedeno is the goat today, and it's too bad because he hit a run-scoring double to give the Cubs the lead in the seventh. On this day, however, he is Brant Brown, Leon Durham, Bill Buckner and Steve Bartman. Okay, maybe not that bad. And he's certainly no Fred Merkle, but at least for a few hours it's his error that we replay in our minds over and over and over and over. I don't think Cedeno will get over it too quickly.

Len Kasper announces that Cedeno's error has been changed to a double. That'll make Dickerson happy, but Cedeno knows he had the game bouncing to him and he let it get away. Having one error erased from his stats won't make up for that.

And that's it for the season in terms of playing teams with losing records. The rest of the year is Cardinals, Astros, Brewers, Cardinals, Mets, Brewers. It's not gonna be easy.

What do we now have to look forward to? The Bears play the Colts on *Sunday Night Football* tonight. There's a winning prospect for you!

Oh ye of little faith! The Bears handle the Colts 29–13 to start the season looking darn good. A safety, for heaven's sake!

Hurricane Ike hits southeastern Texas hard and devastates Galveston. Houston doesn't escape, windows blasted out of skyscrapers and thousands abandoning their homes. The Cubs and Astros, scheduled for a three-game weekend series September 12–14, are rescheduled for two games in Milwaukee, a supposed neutral site, Sunday and Monday. The third game will be played at the end of the year if necessary to decide playoff berths.

The scribes and blogs scream that the Cubs playing in Milwaukee is like a home game, and therefore it's not a fair solution to the problem. We're not sure what would have been fair because Cub fans go everywhere, but certainly Milwaukee is the last place the Astros want to play. Even though Chicagoland has been drenched with constant rain so that Cook County is declared a disaster area, it ain't no hurricane.

We have been visiting Anne Lise in Bloomington, Indiana, watching

Ike's progress. By Sunday morning the remains of the storm have pushed north and east, heading straight for us. We decide to leave a little earlier than planned to outrun the predicted wind and rain. Somewhere in Ohio we receive a text message from Anne Lise telling us that the power is out in Bloomington. It feels odd: with nature blasting so many parts of the country we drive through windy but clear weather with little traffic.

In spite of the rain, 23,000 Cub fans make the ninety minute drive up to Milwaukee to see Zambrano pitch. We naively think that this is a big enough game to televise nationally, but what do we know? Instead, the White Sox are the Sunday night game from the Cell. The Sox are in a tight race, too, so it's understandable except that the Cubs would have drawn a larger audience. The Sox draw 28,000 loyal fans willing to brave the Dan Ryan and Stevenson to their half-empty ballpark.

We listen to Pat and Ron. We ask ourselves, which Zambrano will show up, Big Z or Psycho Z? The first innings tell us it's decidedly Big Z, although we've seen this before only to have Z flake out in some middle inning. But so far, not this time. He gets through the critical third, fourth and fifth looking, excuse me, sounding solid. The Cubs are up 5–0.

And then it starts. Pat Hughes begins to end Astros' half innings with euphemisms such as, "Cubs five; Astros still looking for their first hit." Then by the seventh inning ESPN scrolls along the bottom of the screen, as we watch the Sox, sound muted: "Zambrano working on no-hitter" or something like that. The point is they articulated the word! They can't do that! They'll jinx him! Everybody knows that! Or maybe it doesn't jinx the pitcher when some unfeeling, sterile, digitized national network types it across the bottom of a TV screen. It's only a no-no when the home town folks mention the no-no word aloud. Right?

Shouldn't ESPN cut away from the Sox game? What will it take?

It takes the bottom of the ninth. ESPN picks up WGN's feed and we turn the sound back on to hear Len and Bob. Cub fans are standing and going nuts. Quintero leads off and grounds to Theriot at shortstop. One out.

The tension, coming through the TV and the radio, which we have not turned off, makes my nerves twinge like a fistful of broken guitar strings.

Lucy stands. She can't keep still. She hovers just off the left side of the television.

Pinch hitter Jose Castillo works Zambrano to a two-and-one count. Then, another ground ball to Theriot and another 6–3.

I move from my favorite chair to the ottoman and lean into the screen as Lucy stares speechless.

This is when it always happens! The bloop single. The monster home run. The no-doubt-about-it drive through the box. So many have come so close only to see it fall apart in the ninth, often with two out. And then they fall apart completely and blow the game. But the Cubs are ahead by five! So what?

Left fielder Darin Erstad steps in. Zambrano starts him out with a fastball that misses. Then another. Two and oh.

Zambrano looks confident, working quickly. He delivers a called fastball strike on the inside corner. Nothing but heaters. And yet another that Erstad gets wood on and fouls. Two and two.

More heat? Will Zambrano challenge him?

Here it comes! A breaking ball heading for the dirt outside. But Erstad lunges for it and has no chance and fans. It's over.

Zambrano drops to his knees on the first base side of the mound and gives thanks as the crowd and his teammates succumb to joyous delirium. Lucy and I shout "Yes!" almost simultaneously, exchange high fives and hug as we almost break into a victory dance. Sullivan texting is fast and fierce, a flurry of simple "Z!" messages.

Many have said that Zambrano is a top contender among today's pitchers for a no-hitter, if he could only hold himself together for nine innings. And he pulls it off. Under somewhat bizarre circumstances in Milwaukee, but in front of a home crowd nonetheless.

Now he needs to pitch like this for the rest of the season, and into October if the Cubs make it that far.

Saturday, September 20, 2008, and we are as mad as we can be. All week Comcast.com has listed the Cubs–Cardinals game as scheduled to be broadcast on Fox at 3:55 P.M. EDT. But when we turn on the TV and check it out, the Brewers–Reds game is on. I call and complain to Comcast. I call and complain to Fox, promising never to watch their stinking network again, which, I know, is a lie driven by irrational anger. Not that it will do any good. They no doubt changed to the Brewers game because the Phillies are in a wild card race with the Brewers—sort of. Most Phillies fans, I would bet, are much more concerned with the Mets, with whom they are trading first place off and on these last days of the season, and are watching college football waiting for the game tonight against the Marlins.

Oh why, why, why, why did they do this? And make no mistake, we feel like Fox did this to us personally, the East Coast–centric network boobs. Sure it's our Second City Complex–chip on the shoulder, but in our hearts, it's the truth. Since Zambrano's no-hitter, the Cubs have won three out of five bringing their magic number down to one. If they win, they clinch first place, and we won't be watching. A major pitfall of being Cub fans in exile. We have to move back to Chicago. Missing big moments in this centennial season is a painful matter.

I indeed lied to Fox because we tune in the Brewers game, being played in Cincinnati, put the sound on mute and listen to Pat and Ron on the Internet, assuming the idiots at Fox will show Cubs highlights. Which they do. In the bottom of the second the Cubs load the bases with one out. Pitcher Ted Lilly strikes out, which is better than hitting into a double play. Soriano steps up and drives a single to left, which eludes the left fielder, clearing the bases. We hear this on the radio, and then Fox cuts away from Cinci and shows the highlight. Cubs three, Cards nothing.

Fourth inning, DeRosa doubles high off the vines in left, driving Soto home, and ends up on third. Lilly squeezes DeRosa home! We love it! Lilly is THE MAN. He pitches, he bunts, he reigns. Cubs five, Cards nothing. Meanwhile in Cinci, the Brewers take the lead 2–1.

With two out in the top of the sixth, the Cardinals score four as Lilly seems to blow up. It ain't over yet. All can still go horribly wrong.

Meanwhile, in Cincinnati, C.C. Sabathia seems to have settled down.

Lilly pitches a strong seventh, but will leave for a pinch hitter in the bottom of the inning. The Cubs will go with Marmol in the eighth and Wood in the ninth, if they can hold the one-run lead. We are ill.

The Cubs fail to score in the seventh, Santo beside himself with every routine out.

Back at the Great American Ballpark, the Reds load the bases and score three to take the lead 4–2 in the sixth.

At Wrigley Field, Marmol comes in and gets the first out on a fly ball, which brings up Albert Puhols. He flies to right. Two out. Lopez up. He grounds to Lee. Three up, three down. The fans go beserk, but the Cubs could use some insurance runs in the bottom of the eighth. Santo moans and can hardly speak, not that he's ever very erudite! But we love Ron Santo. Cubs don't score.

Kerry Wood comes in to pitch the ninth. He walks the stinking lead-off man. Judas priest. Oh my God, not again. Not now. My guts are tied in knots. Why? The magic number is one, for crap's sake. They can blow this game and will no doubt still clinch, one way or another. But wouldn't it be great if they clinch by winning, instead of the Brewers losing, letting the Cubs back in as they did in 2007? No, it wouldn't be just great but vital to their spirit and attitude, and to ours.

Next batter, Adam Kennedy—fielder's choice. Man still on first, one out.

Why couldn't they turn the double play? An extra out!

Skip Schumaker at bat.

Ball one. Crap. Crap, crap, crap.

Fastball. Called strike.

Ball two.

Foul ball, foul ball, foul ball. Schumaker is hanging in there, getting wood (so to speak) on both curves and fastballs. The count stays at two and two.

Called strike three! The crowd goes nuts. Ron Santo goes nuts. Why doesn't Fox cut away from the Brewers–Reds game? We are one out away from the earliest Cubs clinch since 1932. We can see the game in our minds' eyes.

Closeup on Kerry Wood. Cut to the center field camera, the fans behind the screen and the low red brick wall all standing and clapping and screaming. Miles steps up to the plate.

Ball one. The crowd grows a bit subdued, but then the ear-splitting volume returns as Wood sets for the second pitch.

We hear it in Pat's voice, and Ron Santo yelling "Yes!" Miles lifts a routine fly ball to center. We know it's routine because the noise reaches a new high, although we also know that apparently routine catches can become fielding challenges for Cubs. But Jim Edmonds makes the catch as Santo repeats, his voice hoarse, high and cracking, "Yes! Yes! YES!" Cubs win! Cubs *clinch*!

But on our TV screen, we watch the Brewers and the Reds, not really seeing anything. In a few minutes, we turn to Channel 9 (actually, channel 14 for us). The story is already being covered by WGN News.

Pandemonium rules at Clark and Addison as the Cubs will go to the postseason for consecutive years for the first time in ... you betcha ... 100 years. 1907 and 1908. 2007 and 2008. The big difference is they won the 1907 World Series.

The intersection below the famous red marquee sign fills with celebrating fans. Our son, Steve, watched on TV in his apartment on Waveland (he's poor and can't afford a ticket), but he is on his way out the door to celebrate in the streets around the ballpark. He tells us SWAT teams are everywhere, but the mood is crazed.

But we've seen too many clinching celebrations since 1984 end in disaster. It is just beginning. No champagne for us yet. Although our daughter Anne Lise, watching in Bloomington, Indiana, texts us: "Celebrate while u can ... could b it!" She's no pessimist. She's a realist.

The Cubs themselves understand that although it's a happy, glorious day, it's nothing compared to what's ahead. The celebrations of September 20, 2008, will be forgotten if they lose the last game they play this year. Although they break out the bubbly and spray and douse each other in the clubhouse, on the field and in the stands, the interviews reveal a team with their eyes on the seriousness of October baseball. Fontenot at first resists Zambrano's attempt to pour champagne into his mouth. DeRosa speaks with a noticeably subdued tone. The language is the same; the usual "We have a lot of work to do still," and "We need to celebrate three more times," and "There's more baseball to be played." The mood is decidedly guarded.

Nonetheless, it will be a hot time in Wrigleyville tonight.

Monday, September 22, rolls around. Lucy picks me up at my York, Pennsylvania, office at around 2:00 and we head for Shea Stadium. Patricia catches the Chinatown Bus from downtown Philadelphia to Chinatown, NYC, and Steve and his roommate Chris fly into LaGuardia from Chicago. It is symptomatic of the current ticket situation in Wrigleyville that Steve, who lives across the street from the left field bleachers, has to fly to New York to see the Cubs in person. Brian bought us all tickets, and Chris's girl-friend, who works for United Airlines, was able to get them free airfare. Only Anne Lise can't make it because of her demanding ER work schedule.

Somewhere in eastern Pennsylvania, as we tool along on Route 78, we get a call from Jeanne. Little Lucy has an ear infection so Jeanne, Jasper and Lucy will watch at home while Brian brings Willa to the game. We are crushed. A major disappointment that we won't all be together for the last game of the year that we will see at a ballpark.

We make great time, driving past the site of the old Polo Grounds, now several high rise New York City Public Housing buildings, on Harlem River Drive with over ninety minutes to go before the first pitch, and are the first to arrive. We park and walk around the stadium to the subway-elevated station to wait for the rest of the crew. We lean against a dark blue concrete traffic barrier. Arriving Cub fans see us in our Cub gear and nod, smile, wave, and give us high fives as they exit the station and approach the gates. And there are plenty of Cub fans. Not the percentages we see in Cincinnati or Pittsburgh, but a significant number. A young woman from Humboldt Park walks right up to us and asks if we think the Cubs will do it tonight. Not that it's the biggest game of the year, the Cubs having long since clinched. We mention that if the Cubs win they'd also clinch home field advantage through the National League playoffs, so the game has some meaning. It's a much more important game for the Mets, still fighting the Phillies for the NL East title, and short of that, the Brewers for the wild card. We talk a bit about the old neighborhood, mentioning that we used to live in Albany Park due north of Humboldt Park. She tells us that Albany Park is experiencing a boom, which we're glad to hear. It was a tad iffy when we lived there. Some punk took a shot at Anne Lise and me at the corner of Drake and Lawrence when she was nine months old. But that's another story.

Finally, my cell phone rings. It's Brian telling me that they've just arrived

The site of the Polo Grounds, New York City, as it looks today (photograph by author).

at the station and will be down momentarily. We watch the hordes of fans descend the stairs and turn toward the park. We see Brian. Then Steve and Patricia and ... Jeanne! And Jasper and both girls! What the heck? They've come to say hi to us and then will take the subway back to Brooklyn. Both girls are "Cubbed up," as Steve describes it, in Cub shirts with their names, "Willa" and "Lucy," stitched on their backs, gifts of Steve himself. Jeanne wears a Cub jacket and when Jasper comes out of his Baby Bjorn Carrier we see he is wearing Cub overalls. Little Lucy is determined to join us for the game, earache or no earache, so we head around to Gate C. On our way, a Cub fan with a camera sees the twins and is so taken by them that he asks if he can take their picture. They comply and pose beautifully, which, as gorgeous twin girls, is nothing new for them. Nor is going to a Cub game, even at Shea Stadium.

Twins Willa and Lucy Meissner "all Cubbed up" at Shea Stadium, September 22, 2008 (photograph by Jeanne Meissner).

The twins' mother, our daughter Jeanne, brought the girls to Wrigley Field as soon as she could, during a visit to Chicago in the summer of 2005 just before they turned two years old. She tells the story about how when they climbed the steps and came out into the grandstands to first see the grass, the bricks, the vines and the scoreboard, the girls audibly gasped in wonder at the beauty of it all.

This is how Jeanne was raised, too. We recently waded through a large stack of old scorecards and found one dated June 8, 1985. On the front, above a photograph of Ryne Sandberg leaving the batter's box on his way to first, it reads "Jeanne & Dad go to the game 6/8/85" in Lucy's handwriting. Jeanne was seven years old and already keeping score. The Cubs beat the Pirates 7–3. Sandberg didn't play that day, according to Jeanne's records. I don't remember why.

When Lucy and Willa's brother, Jasper, was born, November 27, 2007, we were in Brooklyn babysitting. Their dad, Brian, came home briefly to check in with the girls and tell them about their new brother. While there he downloaded pictures of the newborn onto their computer and then hurried back to the hospital. Willa and Lucy, all of four years old, promptly

took over and put together a slide show for their computer-challenged grand-
parents. As they went through the shots of the adorable infant boy, one of
the girls (we don't remember which—sorry, they're identical twins!) said,
"Jasper is going to be a Cub fan. He's not gonna be no Mets fan!"

The other added firmly, "Or a Yankee fan either!"

Brooklyn friends Willie, Stacia, Dan and Vince join us at Shea Stadium so we take up most of a very long row waaaay up in nosebleed seats
directly above home plate. The kids, including ten-month-old Jasper, are fascinated by the spectacle of a big league ballgame but can last only a few
innings because of Lucy's ear, although she never complains, and the chill
that begins to settle over Shea Stadium. So Jeanne saddles them up and we
all say goodbye promising to get together again in October around my birthday for pumpkin patch and apple orchard outings in York, as well as hopefully watching some Cubs playoff action.

Marquis starts and doesn't look bad at all. The Cubs take a 1–0 lead in
the second, but then the Mets tie it on a wild pitch and take the lead in the
third 2–1, but we're having fun watching the game and visiting. In the top
of the fourth the Cubs string together a bunch of hits, tie the game and load
the bases. Marquis steps up to the plate. I check the scoreboard and see that
he's hitting in the mid–.190's—not exactly Zambrano numbers, but respectable for a pitcher. I mention this to Steve who confirms that Marquis hit a
home run the last time he pitched, and at that exact moment we hear the
crack of the bat and watch the arc of a deep fly to right field.

"Oh my God!" says Steve.

"What the...!"

It's gone. A grand slam by Cubs pitcher Jason Marquis. Cub fans go
nuts, standing and screaming and clapping and high-fiving any other Cub
fan in near proximity, of which there are many. A beautiful moment during
our last game at Shea Stadium, and the last regular season game Lucy, Patricia and I will attend this year. The Cubs score six in the inning. They score
again in the fifth and top of the ninth. As the Mets come up for hopefully
the last time, the score is 9–4. Marmol comes in and gets in trouble, giving
up a run and walking a couple of guys while securing only two outs. The
Cubs bring in Wood. The lead is four, but of course we are nervous. A group
of Mets fans directly behind me deride the Cubs for bringing in Wood to
face Luis Castillo whom they label "the worst hitter in baseball." As far as
they're concerned, it's over. As far as we're concerned, we'll believe it when
we see it. But sure enough, Wood makes Castillo look bad, throwing three
fastball strikes. Castillo never takes the bat off his shoulder. Bye bye, Shea.
You deserve your fate.

We give Patricia a lift back to her dorm in Philadelphia but take a couple of wrong turns attempting to get back on the Grand Central Parkway toward the Triborough Bridge. I miss the exit off Northern Boulevard and end up on Astoria Boulevard, a mistake I make almost every time. I hook an illegal U-turn and double back, only to miss the turn again. Feeling like the dope I am, I resign myself to Astoria Boulevard which, as I well know, hooks up with the Grand Central Parkway not far along. I could have saved fifteen minutes by doing this the first time around.

We take the bridge to Harlem River Drive and again pass the site of the old Polo Grounds where a hundred years ago tomorrow, Fred Merkle pulled up short before reaching second base, touching off the wildest controversy in baseball history. By the time we get back to York, Pennsylvania, it is 3:30 A.M., September 23, 2008.

Accounts of the ninth inning of the Merkle Game have been told and retold dozens of times, in almost as many versions, since the day it happened, September 23, 1908. The confusion began the very next day, if not that evening, with the coverage of the play in the Chicago and New York newspapers, heavily influenced by the team loyalty of the sportswriters and the paper for which each wrote.

We first heard the story while watching Ken Burns' documentary film *Baseball* on Channel 11, PBS Chicago, during the fall of 1994. We couldn't believe that we had never before been exposed to a Cubs story as crazy as this one, especially since the incident led directly to the Cubs' last World Series championship. Several days later I recounted the tale, to the best of my ability, to a group of friends whiling away a warm autumn afternoon on the front porch of Mike Tobin's house on North Magnolia Street. They couldn't believe the story either and howled in mock protest of its authenticity. Since then, I've told it to whoever will listen, often in bars, but also at work and just about anywhere the subject of the Cubs and their dubious centennial comes up.

The account of Merkle's Boner detailed by Charles Dryden in the September 24, 1908, edition of the *Chicago Tribune* is close to most versions one reads or hears today. In fact, the term Merkle's Boner was probably coined by Dryden, who wrote in the first paragraph of his account: "In the ninth round Merkle did a bone-head base running stunt identical with the recent exhibition which Mr. Gill ... gave at Pittsburg [*sic*] three weeks ago." The colorful writing of the era helps immerse us in the spirit of the times, and the insanity of the Merkle play itself. I will use Dryden as our base, although Giants fans would protest that he was biased, which he no doubt was. But this memoir is written by a Cub fan, so tough luck. We pick up the account in the bottom of the ninth. Score tied, Cubs one Giants one. The Giants come up to bat at the Polo Grounds in New York. The parentheticals are mine, added to make the article easier to follow a hundred years later.

Round 9 for the Giants opened with the out of Seymour. Then Devlin singled and [next batter] McCormick forced him [two out]. [Fred] Merkle's safety to right put McCormick on third [men on first and third]. On the first ball pitched Bridwell pasted a neat but not gaudy single to center. McCormick crossed the plate [with the apparent winning run], but Merkle, who was at first base, ran half way down to second, then turned and hot hoofed for the clubhouse.

Unless the said Merkle planted a hoof on second base, Bridwell could not be credited with a hit, and McCormick could not score. The Cubs and Hank O'Day were primed for the situation, having been through it once before, in Pittsburg [*sic*]. With one voice the Cubs set up a yelp like a cage of hungry hyenas and O'Day, working behind the plate, ran to the pitching slab [rubber] to see what came off at second base. Capt. Donlin realized the danger about to overtake the Giants, so he set off after the fat headed Merkle while McGinnity, who was coaching at third base [for the Giants], butted into the fracas coming off at the middle cushion.

Facts Gleaned from Survivors

The facts in the case gleaned from active participants and survivors are these: [Cub center fielder] Hofman fielded Bridwell's knock and threw to Evers for a force play on the absent Merkle. But McGinnity, who was not in the game, cut in ahead and grabbed the ball before it reached the eager Trojan [Evers, who came from Troy, NY]. Three Cubs landed on the iron man [McGinnity's nickname was "Iron Man"] from as many directions at the same time and jolted the ball from his cruel grasp. It rolled among the spectators, who had swarmed upon the diamond like an army of starving potato bugs.

At this thrilling juncture "Kid" Kroh [of the Cubs—a pitcher and not in the game either!], the demon southpaw, swarmed upon the human potato bugs and knocked six of them galley-west. The triumphant Kroh passed the ball to [Cub third baseman] Steinfeldt after cleaning up the gang that had it. [Cub shortstop] Tinker wedged in, and the ball was conveyed to Evers for the force out of Merkle, while Capt. Donlin was still some distance off towing that brilliant young gent by the neck.

Some say Merkle eventually touched second base, but not until he had been forced out by Hofman, to McGinnity, to six potato bugs, to "Kid" Kroh, to some more Cubs, and the shrieking, triumphant Mr. Evers, the well known Troy shoe dealer. There have been some complicated plays in baseball, but we do not recall one just like this in a career of years of monkeying with the national pastime.

In my favorite version, based on Evers' own account given years later to John Carmichael for his book *My Greatest Day in Baseball* (1945) and the one I relate often, the fan who caught the ball tossed by McGinnity was a tall gentleman wearing a brown bowler. Cub Harry Steinfeldt and Floyd Kroh chased him down and fought him for the ball. But he was a tenacious Giant fan and wouldn't let go until one of the Cubs pounded the bowler over his eyes. While attempting to regain his vision, he dropped the ball. It rolled among the storming feet of the celebrating fans followed by and groped at by a crawling Floyd Kroh, who eventually grabbed it, stood and relayed it to Tinker who then threw it to Evers.

The *New York Herald* reported, after describing the essence of the play as Dryden did:

> Chance ran to O'Day, claiming the run did not count.... A riotous mob at once surrounded the couple, and ... everyone recognized a good opportunity to get a shot at the umpire. Those within reach began pounding him on all available exposed parts not covered by the protector, while ... attackers on the outskirts began sending messages by way of cushions, newspapers and other missiles.
>
> A flying squadron of real police ... rushed O'Day to McGraw's coop under the grandstand and Chance was escorted off the field....
>
> O'Day, under the press of circumstances, did not render a decision on the field, but after he had dressed he told a reporter of the *Herald* that Merkle had not gone to second and the run did not count....
>
> Merkle said after the game that he had touched second en route for the clubhouse, and McGraw refused to say any more than that the game had been won fairly.
>
> All our boys [the Giants] did rather well if Fred Merkle could gather the idea into his noodle that baseball custom does not permit a runner to take a shower and some light lunch in the clubhouse on the way to second.
>
> Then again ... an enormous baseball custom has had it from time immemorial that as soon as the winning run has crossed the plate everyone adjourns as hastily and yet nicely as possible to the clubhouse and exits.

This last observation is agreed to by just about every baseball historian who has since written about the incident. It was common practice since baseball's earliest days that runners in force play situations need not continue to the next base on a game-winning, walk-off hit.

However, few agree, to this day, on what actually happened. This version appeared in the *New York World*:

> Umpires O'Day and Emslie admitted to newspaper men that they had not seen the play. O'Day was back of the catcher when the riot started and endeavored to reach first base, where Chance was struggling in the clutch of a mob. Emslie was trying to save himself and his wig from being trampled.

The *New York Evening Mail* quoted Giants pitcher Christy Mathewson:

> If this game goes to Chicago by any trick ... [and] we lose the pennant thereby, I will never play professional baseball again.

I had started for the clubhouse when I heard Chance call to Hofman to throw the ball to second. I remembered the trick they had tried to play on Pittsburgh [the Gill play] and caught Merkle by the arm and told him to go to second. Merkle touched the bag. I saw him do it.

Sam Crane of the *New York Evening Journal* backed up this version:

Merkle did make a run for the clubhouse to escape the onrushing fans ... but he turned after going only a few feet and broke for second. Hofman did return the ball, but it went far over Evers' head, hit Tinker in the back and went on to [Cub catcher Johnny] Kling. Merkle was then on second with Mathewson, and as Evers, Tinker and [Cubs' pitcher Jack] Pfiester all rushed toward second, Matty [Matthewson], according to his own story, to which he will take an affidavit if such a ridiculous act is necessary, took Merkle by the arm and said: "Come on to the clubhouse; we don't want to mix up in this," and both Matty and Merkle left the base together.

In her book *Crazy '08*, published in 2008, Cait Murphy describes the play as follows:

Now Hofman is tossing the ball toward Evers, and here comes ... McGinnity, who rushes in from the first base coach's box to intercept the ball. He gets it, shakes off a few Cubs and throws the ball into the stands. *Another ball* [my emphasis] appears from somewhere, and there is Evers, standing in triumph, his hand clutching *a* [my emphasis] ball raised above his head.

Note that she moved McGinnity across the diamond from the third base line as described by Dryden who was at the game. But she's not the only one. *Time* magazine, among others, in a March 1956, article also had McGinnity coaching first. Frank Deford in his 2005 book *The Old Ball Game* states, "Three different pitchers—McGinnity, Wiltse, and Mathewson—all seemed to have later remembered that they were coaching first."

But Murphy must be from New York! Although she admits that there are multiple versions of the story, she leads with the one that says that the ball relayed to Evers wasn't the game ball, giving that version an added air of authenticity. This interpretation echoes a 1961 description of the play by Lee Allen in his book *The National League Story*: "Joe McGinnity raced over from the Giant coacher's [*sic*] box, wrestled [Cub Floyd Kroh] for it, and is believed to have thrown it into the stands. Somehow Evers obtained another ball, stepped on second, and raced over to the plate umpire, Hank O'Day." Allen was from Cincinnati, long a bastion of Cub-haters like Marty Brennaman and Joe Morgan.

John Lund in his brief review of the season, *1908: A Look at the World Champion 1908 Chicago Cubs*, describes it this way: "Johnny Evers ... called for the ball to be thrown to second to force Merkle ... Frank Chance ran to cover second but before the throw could reach him the ball was intercepted by Giant pitcher Joe McGinnity, who threw it into the crowd in *celebration* [my emphasis] before Chance could complete the force." Nowhere does Lund mention that any ball at all made it to second base for a force play. And he's an admitted lifelong Cub fan! His little book is not dated nor is a publisher identified, but the point is that even a Cub fan relates yet another version, not necessarily in support of the Cubs' claim that they forced Merkle out.

National League president Harry C. Pulliam attended the game and saw the play. From what seat, I admit, I don't know and have not been able to find out. What's clear is that he made his way to the umpires' dressing room, called the coop, and spoke to O'Day and Emslie. O'Day confirmed his decision that Merkle was out, and that the game was tied and could not be resumed. Pulliam asked that the two umpires meet him at his residence in the New York Athletic Club to discuss the matter. That evening, O'Day scribbled a hand-written note, addressed to Pulliam, confirming that Merkle was out (original in the archives of the National Baseball Hall of Fame and reproduced in Allen's *The National League Story*). But he as much as said that Merkle was out because McGinnity interfered with the play, not mentioning that the Cubs had forced him at second. So whether or not the ball that ended up in Evers' mitt was the game ball became a moot point.

Pulliam backed the decision of the umpires, saying that if necessary the game would be replayed in the unlikely event that the Giants and Cubs ended the season tied for first place. Both teams protested—the Giants claiming they won the game outright, and the Cubs demanding that the game be declared a Giants forfeit because they could not make their field playable after the incident, nor did they show up to play a makeup game (as dictated by the rules) before the scheduled September 24 contest between the Cubs and Giants. Ironically, the Giants agreed that the game should either be declared theirs or forfeited. The protests would be reviewed by the National League board of directors, a group of owners who had final say concerning disputes. The appeal process would go on into the first week of October, up to the very end of the season.

But first, one of the most incredible performances in the history of major league pitching took place on September 26, 1908. According to the September 24 *Tribune*, since neither team won the Merkle game, the Cubs remained 6 percentage points behind the Giants, with the Pirates only another 7 points behind. The Cubs lost to the Giants on the 24th, 5–4, and then crossed the East River for a three-game series against the Brooklyn Superbas (they would become the Trolley Dodgers in 1911 and then just the Dodgers in 1913 but change their name to the Robins in 1914 and keep that name until they changed it back to the Dodgers in 1932). In spite of their name, Brooklyn was anything but superb in 1908 and would go on to lose

101 games. The Cubs needed to take advantage of the struggling Superbas to stay close to the Giants and won the first game 5–1. A doubleheader was scheduled for the 26th. Cubs manager Frank Chance slated pitcher Ed Reulbach to start the first game. He shut out the Superbas 5–0. He still felt strong so Chance started him in the second game of the twin bill. He shut out the Superbas again 3–0 in a game that lasted just over an hour and ten minutes. He gave up a total of eight hits the entire day. Back in the Deadball Era the same pitcher winning both ends of a doubleheader happened now and then. In fact, two other pitchers, Ed Walsh of the White Sox and Detroit Tiger Ed Summers, accomplished the same thing *that same week*. But to pitch two shutouts? Few believed that Ty Cobb's stolen base and hit records, Babe Ruth's and then Henry Aaron's career home run records, etc., etc., would ever be bettered. "Records are made to be broken," but I think Reulbach can rest in peace in the knowledge that no pitcher will ever again pitch two complete game shutouts in one day.

The last game of the 2008 regular season is played September 28 in Milwaukee and Steve is there, again because he has to travel to see the Cubs in person. Free tickets courtesy of his roommate. They are sitting in Row 16 directly behind the Cubs dugout. He texts us that the scene is a bit ugly, Brewers fans trash talking and not appreciative of the thousands of Cub fans traveling to their fair city and spending untold dollars in support of the eastern Wisconsin economy.

All National League division races are settled, but the wild card is a dead heat between the Brewers and the Mets, who play Florida at Shea Stadium. If one team wins and the other loses, the winner goes to the postseason. If they both win or both lose, there will be a playoff game. Also, if the Mets win the wild card, they play the Cubs. If the Brewers win it, the Cubs play the Dodgers.

Milwaukee pitches C.C. Sabathia on a short, three-day rest for the third time. The Cubs start Angel Guzman, but then parade almost their entire bullpen to the mound. By the eighth inning it's 1–1, while the Mets are also tied in New York. But wait ... the Marlins have taken the lead 4–2 in the top of the eighth. Then the Brewers take the lead 3–1 on a Braun two-run homer off Howry in the bottom of the eighth. The atmosphere at Miller Park is electric, like a playoff game. It ends with a Derrek Lee double play. C.C. Sabathia goes the distance. Milwaukee fans have to wait for the results from New York as they remain in the stands celebrating their clutch win.

The Cubs end the regular season 97 and 64, one of their best years ever. Bob and Len sign off for 2008 with Bob claiming that this Cub team is their best shot at the World Series in memory. And as they say their farewells, no one leaves Miller Park. They watch the action in New York on the big scoreboard. But not Steve. He's on the way back to Chicago. Not a great way to end the season, but what a great season it has been.

No, no, no, no. What a simplistic, insipid thing to write. In truth, from Soriano's dropped fly ball in Pittsburgh, to Ramirez's game-winning homer against the Sox at Wrigley Field, to Zambrano's blowup in Philadelphia, to his no-hitter in Milwaukee, to the Cubs winning the last game we'll ever see at Shea Stadium, it has been a typically chaotic ride, in spite of the Cubs' National League best record. We have too many things to worry about. Zambrano is number one. Which Z will show up for the playoffs, Big Z or Psycho Z? Lee's propensity to hit into rally-killing or game-ending double plays. Fukudome's fadeout, which has been very upsetting because we love Kosuke! Soriano's strictly mediocre last week of the season. And the ninth inning adventures of Kerry Wood.

But on the bright side: Lilly! Dempster! Ramirez! DeRosa! Theriot! Soto! The contributions of Edmonds and Johnson! Enough to take it all for the first time in a century? Maybe. But the negatives need only rear their hideous heads for an inning, a single batter, a brief excruciating moment to bring the whole trembling edifice down in ignominious flames.

We need to escape and maybe not think about the Cubs until Wednesday night. Monday and Tuesday? We'll watch the Sox tomorrow. They've played only 161 games, but won today to remain a half game behind the Twins. So they will have to make up a postponed game against the Tigers. If they win they will be in a dead heat with the Twins and there will be a playoff game on Tuesday. We'll watch that, too.

As nuts as 1908? Not quite. One hundred years ago the National League standings as of the end of September had the Giants only 4 percentage points ahead of the Pirates, a virtual tie, and Pittsburg only 2 percentage points ahead of the Cubs. And there was still about a week to go, with the Cubs scheduled to end the year against the Pirates in Chicago on October 4, and the Giants to finish with a three-game series against the Boston Doves (later the Boston Braves, then the Milwaukee Braves and now the Atlanta Braves) October 5 through 7.

Meanwhile, in the American league the Tigers were a half game ahead of Cleveland and only a game and a half in front of the White Sox.

We find the Marlins–Mets game on TBS with Chip Caray announcing, bringing back Cub broadcast booth memories of recent history. New York gets a man on in the ninth, but can't score and is eliminated, the last game ever at Shea Stadium, a loss that boots the Mets out of the playoffs. There will be no New York team playing postseason baseball in 2008, a prospect so refreshing that it gives a light and cheery air to October. Mets fans stand stunned and unwilling to leave the ballpark, the first true Mets home. As for us, as Ron Santo said, we'd be happy to take a sledgehammer and help rip the dump down.

The Cubs will play the Dodgers.

In 1908, the controversies just kept on coming. In the last game of the Cubs' and the Pirates' season on October 4 at West Side Park, the two teams battled in front of a record crowd of over thirty thousand for a chance to tie and perhaps win the pennant, depending on the Giants' series against Boston. A loss for either would mean the end of the line. Again, umpire Hank O'Day called the game from behind the plate with the help of one field ump, Cy Rigler. In the top of the ninth with a man on first, and the Cubs winning 5–2, Pirate Ed Abbaticchio drove one high and deep down the first base line. When it landed in the crowd O'Day called it a foul ball. But the Pirates claimed it was fair and protested vehemently. If fair, two runs would have scored and the lead would have been cut to a run. O'Day consulted Rigler who backed him up, and that was that. The nascent rally was killed as Cub pitcher Three Finger Brown shut down the Pirates and kept the Cubs' hopes alive for playing in the World's Series for the third year in a row.

Actually, the Pirates still had one hope. If the Giants won only two of the three games against the Doves, but then beat the Cubs in the replay of the Merkle game, if played, there would be a three-way tie for first with each team ending the year with 98 wins and 56 losses.

Legend has it that sometime after the end of the season a woman tried to sue the Cubs because she was hurt by Abbaticchio's hit. To prove she was at the game and in the area where the ball landed, she produced her ticket stub. Her seat had been in fair territory! Cait Murphy in *Crazy '08* details how decades later a sportswriter named Herbert Simons worked with *Baseball Digest* to prove or disprove the legend. They searched Chicago court records for two years after the game and found nothing. However, what if the woman filed suit in a neutral venue to avoid bias—like in Pittsburgh?

The other event of note that allegedly happened at the ballpark that day was detailed by the *Tribune* as follows:

"BASEBALL BABY" BORN IN PARK
AS CUBS TROUNCE PIRATES

Stork Arrives with Child at Dramatic Moment of
Chicago Team's Battle for Championship

Just as Brown swatted the ball bringing Tinker in in the last half of the sixth inning, killing the immediate possibility of a tie game between Chicago and

Pittsburg [*sic*], and as the host in the grand stand rose to cheer, a baby was born far up on the stand, in the midst of the dense crowd.

There is considerable mystery attached to the birth of the "baseball baby." The mother fell forward in her seat and the crowd, thinking she had fainted, fell back to give her air. To a woman who raised her head she told the happening and immediately mother and child were carried to the club house, where medical attention was summoned.

Then an ambulance was summoned and both were taken away.

The woman refused to give her name, and the west side hospitals last night denied that any such case had been brought to their attention.

Maybe the woman just took the baby home. In 1908 home births were still very common.

With the Cubs' win over the Pirates, it was now up to the Giants. They needed to sweep the Doves to tie the Cubs for the pennant, forcing a replay of the Merkle game if the National League board of directors backed up Pulliam's ruling. The board sat in Cincinnati, no doubt cheering for either the Pirates or the Doves to win their games making whatever decision they came to irrelevant. The Pirates had failed them, so it was now up to the Doves.

Rumor had it that the fix was in.

CHAPTER EIGHT

Postseason

This could be the shortest chapter of all, and not just because it can potentially cover only three series, but because the Cubs have not gone far into October in recent years. Again, pessimism? Perhaps. Realism? Let's just say caution in the face of history: 2007, 2003, 1998, 1989, 1984.

I attended my first postseason game on October 4, 1989, Cubs vs. Giants, NLCS Game 1, the first night postseason game at Wrigley Field. Skeptical about night baseball when the lights were first installed the previous year, Lucy and I were charmed by the warm ambience of the ballpark when we went to our first night game on August 23, 1988, two weeks after the first official night game on August 9, 1988 (the much publicized "8-8-88" first night game had been rained out in the fourth inning). The Cubs beat the Astros 9–3. Jamie Moyer went the distance.

The neighborhood fight to keep lights out of the ballpark had been vigorous. Yellow signs with bold orange type reading "NO LIGHTS! IN WRIGLEY FIELD" and signed "Citizens United for Baseball in Sunshine," or C.U.B.S. appeared in house and apartment windows throughout Lakeview and beyond. Meetings were held. The complaint was not so much the loss of a treasured tradition (day baseball), as the window signs suggested, but the threat of street parking chaos and late night rowdiness. But Major League Baseball had threatened to forbid the playing of any playoff games at Wrigley Field unless lights were installed so it was a choice of night baseball or no baseball as the Cubs would certainly have moved. Many neighbors would have preferred no baseball. During the late 1970s and throughout the 1980s Wrigleyville had changed from a mostly blue collar neighborhood to an up-and-coming area populated more and more by the young and upwardly mobile. Many seemed to have moved there not understanding that

159

the ballpark had stood there since 1914 and that 81 times a year 35,000 or more people would invade their streets, drink lots of beer and make lots of noise. Some were vocal about their desire to see the Cubs move away and Wrigley Field torn down. Why did they move there in the first place? we wondered. The ballpark is hard to miss when you drive along Addison or Clark, or ride past on the Howard el.

Compromises were made. City Hall limited the number of night games and created permit parking for residents which resulted in the aggressive and expensive towing of fans' cars during night games. The late night rowdiness could not be stopped, however, as Clark Street became a burgeoning night life strip that today includes dozens of bars, restaurants of every kind, souvenir shops, night clubs and theaters extending roughly from Grace Street a block north of the ballpark to Newport on the south where it blends in with the greater Clark Street commercial and entertainment thoroughfare that continues all the way to the Loop over four miles south and east. But beyond Clark it is still a neighborhood. An expensive neighborhood to be sure, but drive or walk along any of the tree-lined streets that border Wrigley Field, except Clark, or run perpendicular to it like Kenmore, Seminary and Patterson and you'll see block after block of houses, two-flats and apartment buildings just like the ones visible beyond left and right fields, without the billboards and grandstands on the rooftops. Even busy Addison is a residential street as soon as you get beyond the Cubby Bear Lounge and Taco Bell. Today it seems that the blocks immediately adjacent to the ballpark are populated by the very young, like our son, Steve, who moved there precisely because of the Cubs, the ballpark and the night life, in that order of importance.

NO LIGHTS!
IN WRIGLEY FIELD

Citizens United for Baseball in Sunshine

No Lights! sign seen in house and apartment windows throughout Wrigleyville leading up to the first scheduled night game, 8-8-88.

My seat that October 1989 night was in the upper deck, tenth row above third base. I went alone because my ticket source could get me only one seat. From that vantage point the park and the city looked beautiful, the light from the graceful white fixtures above the roof softly spilling beyond the bleachers and gently illuminating the facades of the buildings along Waveland and Sheffield Avenues.

Maddux started and didn't look good, getting roughed up in

the first inning. But the Cubs came back and kept it close, down 4–3 until the fourth, Maddux's last inning on the mound, when the Giants exploded for four runs and never looked back, scoring three more in the eighth to win it 11–3. Cub bats were anything but silent, with ten hits including home runs by Sandberg and Grace, who went three for four. The trouble was that Giant Will Clark went four for four that night, including two homers and a double. And that was just the beginning.

Grace and Clark would battle the entire five games of the playoffs in one of the most exciting and extraordinary hitting contests on record, Grace finishing the series hitting .647 and Clark .650. We were frustrated watching it unfold because no matter how good Grace played, Clark seemed just a little bit better. And that was pretty much how the series went, ending with insult piled on top of injury when Don Zimmer brought in Mitch

"No Parking" sign with permit number and tow zone warnings, put in place to relieve night parking congestion during Cub night games at Wrigley Field. The back of the scoreboard can be seen in the distance, corner of Waveland and Sheffield (photograph by the author).

Williams to face Clark in the eighth inning of Game Five in San Francisco. The Giants were up in the series three games to one. The game was tied at one. Cub starter Mike Bielecki, who'd had a great year finishing the regular season with a record of 18–7 and an ERA of .314, began the inning getting the first two batters but then walked the bases loaded with Clark due up next. Anyone would have pulled Bielecki, but to bring in a fastball pitcher to face a fastball hitting Clark who was all but impossible to retire? Scott Sanderson was available, and he was one of the few pitchers who had gotten Clark out. He pitched two innings in Game Four the day before, allow-

Wrigleyville is still a residential neighborhood. Patterson Street west of the ballpark, visible in background (photograph by the author).

ing no runs, Clark popping up to second base. As a career starter he was plenty strong enough to pitch again.

We sat watching the game on television, waiting for the inevitable and livid with anger. We liked Zimmer a lot, but in this case couldn't believe his decision.

You could feel it coming. The only surprise was that Clark hit only a single instead of a grand slam. The Cubs showed some life in the ninth when they combined three singles with two out to get back within one run, but then Sandberg grounded to second and it was all over.

A win wouldn't have clinched the 1989 NLCS, but it would have sent the series back to Chicago with the Cubs only one game behind the Giants. There would have been some momentum with the Cubs winning one in San Francisco, in essence taking back the Game One loss in Chicago.

Clark was named series MVP.

The 2008 Cubs wait two days after their last regular season game to begin their 2008 Division Series with the Dodgers. The White Sox, in the meantime, may play two more games, one a makeup game against the Detroit Tigers at Comiskey Park. They finished the season a half game behind the

Twins. If the Sox win the makeup game on Monday, September 29, they end the year tied for first and will then host the Twins for a playoff game, again at Comiskey Park—excuse me!—U.S. Cellular Field, aka the Cell.

The makeup game is delayed by rain and sparsely attended. The Sox win, beating Detroit handily 8–2. The next night fans mostly dressed in black Sox jackets and sweatshirts in response to the team's request that they "black out" the ballpark, pack the Cell and wave black rally towels. It's an eerie scene, reminiscent of photographs of ballparks of the Deadball Era when spectators wore dark suits during the chilly months of the season. The TV cameras often show Mayor Richard M. Daley cheering from his seat. The Daleys' ancestral homestead is within walking distance from the Cell, in neighboring Bridgeport, although I hear he now lives somewhere near McCormick Place in the burgeoning South Loop area. Although Daley is the mayor of both sides of Madison, I don't recall seeing him at Wrigley Field, but I could be wrong.

The game proves to be an exciting pitchers' duel, the lone run a monster center field jack by Jim Thome in the seventh inning. Earlier, the Twins' Michael Cuddyer tried to tag up at third and score on a shallow fly ball to Sox center fielder Ken Griffey, Jr. Griffey nailed him at the plate, but we sat wondering why anyone would run on a ball that shallow, even if the fielder is an old guy like Griffey. Seeing Griffey in a Sox uniform is an odd sensation for us. We lived in Cincinnati when he joined the Reds, hailed as the team's, and the city's, savior. Didn't quite work out that way, but we saw him often, if from a long distance in our top six seats at Cinergy Field.

With the Sox' 1–0 win, they and the Cubs are both in the playoffs for the first time since 1906. Chicago becomes the center of baseball mania, the entire city suffering acute playoff fever.

This did not happen in 1908 as the Detroit Tigers held off the Cleveland Naps (later the Indians) and the White Sox, although it came down to the final game of the year—the Tigers visiting and beating the Sox on October 6, 1908, to end their season.

In the wider world, the election and the economic meltdown dominate the news. As of October 1, 2008, Obama has rebounded in the polls and enjoys a slight lead over McCain. Many attribute this to the impending disaster, or ongoing disaster, of the freezing credit markets, the big wipeout of mortgages everywhere, a plunging stock market and a string of big, noisy, ugly bank failures. President George W. Bush, in addition to the flak he's been taking for Iraq, health care, global warming ... you name it! ... now finds himself bearing the brunt of the blame for the worst financial collapse since the Great Depression. Republican candidate John McCain tries pitifully to distance himself from the president, but voters don't seem to be buying it.

The two VP candidates will debate Thursday, October 2, 2008. Sarah Palin's shooting star seems to be burning out as she looks at best dazed and confused on a series of television interviews. The debate starts at 9:00 P.M. Game Two of the Cubs–Dodgers series starts at 9:30. We'll have to watch the debate on the Internet some other time.

Our family feels no sense of elation as game one approaches on Wednesday. There is no frantic texting, no calls, no e-mail. Grim reality. Time to face the music. The crowd at Wrigley Field seems to be of a similar spirit. Not a lot of noise. Few smiles. Hard faces staring out at the field. The scene looks and feels different from the festive atmosphere of regular season games—a feeling of hope and appreciation for being inside this great, beautiful ballpark to watch Cub baseball with all the other crazies. No evidence of crazies tonight, except one lady fan of late middle age who sports a Cubs Santa hat.

And then I think the fans look different because they *are* different. The lower boxes are populated more than usual by the fat cats, the rich guys and their clients who can expense the tickets, or pay the hundreds (thousands?) of dollars for the seats out of pocket change. It's the same as all the other playoff series since 1984, only more so. The rich, with the cooperation of the Cubs' owners and scalpers, have banished the regular fan from the ballpark. And these guys have no sense of fun. They are too dignified, too sophisticated, in their own view of themselves, or too wealthy to show much more emotion than a blasé sense of entitlement. They are there because it is the big event in Chicago, not necessarily because they are Cub fans.

Maybe the Cubs sense the difference.

Dempster looks horrible, but in spite of wildness gets out of jam after jam. DeRosa hits a long fly ball down the right field line which looks like it will either go foul or be caught in the deep well of the right field bleachers. But it goes out for two runs, scoring Edmonds who had singled ahead of DeRosa. A great beginning. Now if they can build on that....

But Dempster keeps walking people, loading the bases in the third, but gets out of it with a strikeout. In the fifth he walks the bases loaded again. Can he get out of it again? Dodger first baseman Jim Loney comes to the plate. He tags it. It was just a matter of time, we think as we watch it leave the park for a grand slam: 4–2 Dodgers. The fans are silent. We are silent. Our phones are silent.

That's all the Dodgers need, although they keep hitting home runs, off different pitchers because Dempster leaves in the fifth. They build their lead to 7–2. The Cubs look bad, like they don't belong in the playoffs at all.

There's no way they'll catch the Dodgers tonight, or maybe even in the play-off series at all. You can feel the game is long gone before the last out, which is Soriano (oh for five—continuing his stellar record as a playoff no-show at the plate) popping to first off ... Greg Maddux! The pitcher the Cubs never should have traded! Multiple Cy Young winner, future Hall of Famer and consensus best pitcher in the history of the game! Now, in his ongoing twi-light years, Maddux plays the role of a Dodger reliever used to mop up the Cubs, rubbing salt in the proverbial gaping, pus-filled and blood-spewing wound.

Big Z shows up for Game Two, but no one else does.

Lucy snoozes during the second inning. It's late for us old folks and I don't have the heart to wake her up to watch the grotesque promise of Game One fulfilled by the defensive ineptness of the Cub infield. Zambrano gets in a little trouble, but with one out, he gets his double play ball not once, but twice. First DeRosa bobbles a grounder from Blake DeWitt, and then Lee looks helpless as he loses a bouncer from Casey Blake. Both are charged with errors. I count a total of seven outs that the Cubs generously donate to the Dodgers' cause, allowing them to score five when Z should have been out of the inning.

There's no need to belabor this one. Five is all the Dodgers need, although they keep scoring in the late innings to double that total as the Cubs can muster no more than three. Before it's over all four infielders notch errors. Pineilla pulls Zambrano in the seventh. He'll get charged for the loss, but he really only gave up a solo shot to Manny Ramirez as far as we're con-cerned. He kept his cool and turned in an excellent performance. His field-ers and hitters let him down. The appreciative crowd understands this and gives him a nice ovation as he leaves the field, the only real Cub highlight of the night.

The next day I receive this e-mail from a co-worker in York, Pennsyl-vania: "Sorry about your Cubs, Floyd ... don't read what's next How 'bout them Phillies!!!!"

The emotions have not cleared my system by any means. Not even close. I respond:

> Thanks. It wouldn't be so bad if they would just lose like a normal team. But no. Their collapse has to be excruciatingly painful and historically humiliat-ing. Just when you think you've seen the worst, like on Wednesday, Thursday comes around to demonstrate that you haven't begun to taste the depths of the ring of hell reserved for idiots like those of us born Cub fans, who should know better.

But we'll be watching tomorrow!

I should have congratulated him on the success of the Phillies, but I'm too busy wallowing in my bitter soup of self-pity.

Game Three is more of a regular game. The Cubs just plain lose 3–1. But at least there are no tragicomic disasters as in Games One and Two, and Game Six in 2003, the three-game collapse of 1984 and Mitch Williams in 1989. The Dodgers score a couple in the bottom of the first. We all know that two runs will be enough.

We receive no phone calls, no e-mails, no text messages. It's over and we don't want to communicate anything about it.

To put this collapse in its proper perspective, the Cubs were first in the National League in the following regular season stats:

- Wins
- Runs scored
- Total bases
- RBI
- On base percentage
- Slugging
- OPS (on base plus slugging)
- Strikeouts (by Cub pitching, not hitting!)
- Opponents' Batting Average (lowest)

Yet they were the first team of either league to be eliminated from the play-offs, scoring a total of six runs in three games while giving up twenty to the Dodgers. Fukudome continued to disappoint, hitting only .100 for the series. But Soriano hit .071. Even Ramirez faded, hitting .182. But why dwell on the tragedy? It's over. The season ended, as all playoff seasons end for the Cubs, with a loss. The sports world is baffled that such a great team with so much depth, so many tools and such an amazing set of regular season stats could collapse so totally. Baffled, but not surprised. Neither are we.

On the way to work Monday NPR quotes a message posted on the *Tribune* website. The fan says he is giving up his season tickets because he can't take it anymore. I check the *Trib*'s site and find a similar posting:

> I've had enough. I've supported this team through thick and thin—mostly thin—for 40 years. Today I threw out my Cubs hats, t-shirts, and took the Cubs license plate frame off of my car. I no longer am a Cubs fan. Now I have all winter to decide what to do next summer now that I won't be wasting all those hours sitting on the couch watching guys get paid more than I'll make in 20 lifetimes, who don't seem to care enough to be respectable when the chips are down. Good riddance LOSERS!
>
> Posted by: Cub Fan No Longer | Oct 5, 2008 6:09:46 P.M.

Fair weather fans.

On October 7, 1908, the Giants faced the Doves at the Polo Grounds in the third game of their must-sweep series, having already won the first two. Oddly, attendance is extremely low—only about 5,000, perhaps in protest of the Merkle ruling. The National League board of directors had announced their decision and neither gave the game to the Giants, nor did they support Murphy in his demand that the game be forfeited to the Cubs. They supported Pulliam. There would be a replay of the September 23 game the very next day, October 8, 1908. Already, the Cubs were speeding across the country on a special express Twentieth Century Limited train from Chicago to New York.

There are two interesting stories regarding how the board of directors reached their decision. In *The Old Ball Game* Frank Deford details that Boston Doves owner George Dovey, who was on the board, told W.J. Macbeth of the *New York Tribune* that Christy Mathewson, in spite of how he had been quoted immediately after the game, signed an affidavit that supported O'Day. Matty apparently could bend the truth when interviewed by reporters—or was misquoted by those reporters—but could not lie when submitting a signed affidavit. He was apparently the only Giant with such a high standard of integrity. In his statement, as Macbeth quoted Dovey, "Matthewson swore that Merkle did not touch second base. He ... embraced Fred when Bridwell's hit was delivered and ran shouting to the clubhouse" after Merkle had gotten only halfway to second base.

As quoted in Deford's book, "Dovey then said: 'We took all the other affidavits and threw them into the waste basket. Matty's word was good enough for us.'"

Compare that to an article written by Sid Mercer in the January 4, 1944, edition of the *New York Journal-American*, excerpted below. In it Mercer, who covered the Merkle game for the *New York Globe*, claims credit for the board's decision.

Mercer Affidavit Clinched
League Ruling

O'DAY RETURNS

I stood up on a table in the old ground-level press box to see what was happening. O'Day had started for the umpires' dressing room ... but he turned and started back toward the diamond.... He saw Evers standing on second base holding a ball aloft.

Next day ... I was asked to make an affidavit as to what I saw. The directors finally upheld O'Day.

Afterward George Dovey told me:

"You were the only man in that press box who did not swear that O'Day disappeared under the stand—thus leaving the field—before he returned to be swallowed up in the crowd.

Since you were the only New York writer to see it as O'Day testified to us we threw out the rest of those affidavits as prejudiced."

For 35 years I have been trying to get Johnny Evers to admit that he fished up that ball from somewhere—maybe out of his blouse—and that the ball actually in play never was thrown back. But to this day [in 1944] Johnny sticks to his story.

Someone's affidavit impressed the board, whether Mathewson's, Mercer's, O'Day's, Emslie's or a combination of all of them. The replay of the Merkle game would be played on October 8. Its importance would be determined by the outcome of the last Giants–Doves game.

Whether the Doves series was really fixed, or whether the Doves, loaded with perhaps sympathetic ex–Giants and ex–Oriole teammates of McGraw's, just didn't bother to show up, metaphorically speaking, we'll never know, as detailed by David Anderson in his *More Than Merkle*. But the game was no contest, the Giants winning 7–2, completely eliminating the Pirates. The October 8 replay against the Cubs would be for all the National League marbles.

There's a heartrending story that members of the Giants led by Christy Mathewson visited team president John T. Brush on his sickbed at The Lambs Club in New York City to propose not playing the October 8 game in protest. Their honor was at stake. Brush supposedly sympathized with the concern they had over their besmirched pride, but felt the truly noble thing to do would be to show up and play the game to the best of their ability, as true Giants. He promised them a $10,000 bonus to split, win or lose.

What probably really happened was the Giants went to confront Brush because they would be playing an extra game and had no deal in the works that they would get paid for it. Brush was a notoriously hardnosed, some may say vicious, businessman who never missed a chance to make an extra buck. That he was on his sickbed there is little doubt as he had just returned from an exhausting trip to and from Cincinnati to petition the board of directors during the Merkle deliberations. And he suffered from locomotor ataxia, a painful disease that slowly eats away at the spine and nervous system, caused by syphilis. Brush stood to make a lot of money from the game's gate receipts. But $10,000 was a good chunk to be split by probably less than twenty players plus McGraw, so maybe Brush wasn't being so cheap. Or maybe the players made a strong case for themselves. The truth is probably somewhere in between.

Demand for tickets was already through the roof.

"The most bitterly contested championship race in the National League's history will reach a climax this afternoon."—*New York Sun*, Wednesday, October 8, 1908.

"That the game will be a struggle to the death is certain. The town is in the grip of the greatest excitement, fringed with nervous prostration. It is rumored that several sanitariums are constructing additions to take care of baseball 'bugs.'"—*New York Herald*

"The management, knowing the ardor of the enthusiasts, threw out a strong cordon of watchmen last night to prevent the bleachers from filling up overnight. About a dozen extra men were strung out about the fence..., and they spent most of the night digging small boys from under seats." —*New York Times.*

"More money will be bet on the game than has been wagered in the old town since the lid was put on horse racing."—W.J. Macbeth, *New York American.*

"If the Cubs don't win the pennant—tragedy! Despair, insanity, suicide, coroner's inquest, and a new chapter in baseball history."—*Chicago Tribune.*

"Police Commissioner Bingham has given orders that the crowd must be kept off the field for at least three minutes after the game.... This precaution has been taken on account of the riot that followed the famous game of Sept. 23."—*Chicago News.*

"The *Tribune* will show Cubs vs. Giants game on Electrical Baseball Board at Orchestra Hall today. For benefit Tribune Hospital Fund."—ad in *Chicago Tribune.*

That morning the two umpires scheduled for the game arrived at the National League offices on Broadway. They reported that representatives of the New York Giants had attempted to bribe them to call the game in the Giants' favor. League secretary John Heydler (Pulliam had gone from the Merkle deliberations in Cincinnati directly to Detroit to await Game One of the World Series) listened to their stories and determined that since there was no time to find replacements, the two umpires would work the game and, because they reported the incident, could not possibly be suspected of calling anything but an honest game. But the league had not heard the last of the attempted bribe.

If the game itself did not live up to the hype, the scene around the Polo Grounds more than outdid anyone's predictions. By one account 250,000 people tried to get in. By 12:45 the gates were locked for a scheduled 3:00 first pitch. Legitimate ticket holders were refused admission. Fights broke out everywhere as fans tried to get their money back from scalpers. Two men fell to their deaths. A mob tried to burn down an outfield wall and another

Lucky fans who made it into the Polo Grounds for the replay of the Merkle game, October 8, 1908. Perhaps 250,000 tried to get in (Chicago History Museum, SDN-054667).

tried to burrow beneath it to get in. According to Cait Murphy in her *Crazy '08*, presidential candidate Taft's brother Henry got in by crawling through the sewers, accompanied by a future attorney general. Fans walked planks laid between the el tracks and the outfield wall to sneak in.

"From the press box the skyline everywhere was human heads. They were located on grandstand, roofs, fences, 'el' structures, electric light poles and in the distance on smokestacks, chimneys, advertising signs and copings of apartment houses." —*New York Evening Telegram*.

Coogan's Bluff, rising high above the stands directly behind home plate, was black with throngs of "bugs" straining for a glimpse of the action. Dozens climbed out-of-service el cars in the train yard beyond the left field stands. Several trains took off downtown, frightened fans clinging to the roofs.

Jack Pfiester started the game, but it was soon evident that his arm, which was already hurt when he pitched the Merkle game, was still not right in spite of a trip to see the famous, or infamous, "Bonesetter" Reese in Ohio to correct the problem. Chance called on Three Finger Brown. He walked to the mound through the crowd of Giants fans that had spilled onto the field, eyes front, ignoring the torrent of abuse and threats delivered within inches of his face, and behind his back. "Unconscious of everything, careless in his bearing, the man who had faced and touched off many a death dealing blast in the depths of Indiana's coal mines walked to his position, hurled a few balls to Kling to assure himself of his accurate aim. Then he was ready!"—J.E. Sanborn, *Chicago Tribune*.

Wow! They don't write 'em like that any more! Except on some blogs maybe.

The Cubs won 4–2 but then had to "run for our lives," according to Brown. The mob descended on them, in spite of heavy police protection. A fan knifed Pfiester, although the wound proved superficial, and another punched Frank Chance in the neck from behind, breaking a cartilage in his throat. He lost his voice for a few days, but was otherwise able to play in the World Series. Other Cub players were attacked, and there were threats that a bomb or bombs had been placed on their train.

But on they went to Detroit, to a very anti-climactic World Series. They took it in five games, the only loss charged to Pfiester whose arm was still bum. The slashing in New York couldn't have helped.

Most notable about the series was the poor attendance. Nasty weather caused some of it, but a scalping scandal in Chicago seemed to keep fans away either in protest, or because they just couldn't afford street prices. Listed prices were reasonable: General admission $1; grand stand (sic), not reserved, $1.50; grand stand, reserved, $2; box seats, $2.50. It seems Cub president Murphy was not satisfied with that size take, so he presold large blocks of seats to scalpers. The fans stayed away in droves. Kind of makes me think about the morning of that Cubs–Sox game in June 2008, standing room sold out early, at supposedly one ticket per fan, but when I sought out scalped tickets not an hour later, the guy at the bar on Clark Street had a whole fistful of them. The more things change....

Much has been written about Fred Merkle's life. After the September 23, 1908, game he begged to be released or traded. He couldn't sleep. He lost fifteen pounds, and he was already very thin. John McGraw refused to blame him, as he refused to accept the loss of the pennant to the Cubs. Merkle came back and played for the Giants in 1909. He remained active until 1926, playing for a variety of teams including the Cubs for four years. But he never lost the nickname "Bonehead." Fans ridiculed him with, "Hey, Bonehead, did you touch second yet?" and other cruel taunts. Yet he played on and compiled good numbers, batting .273 for his career.

In his book *The National League Story*, Lee Allen relates this poignant personal story, which occurred during the 1950s:

> In the tawny dusk of a Florida evening a few years ago, the author of this volume sat in a barroom, the Ship Ahoy, in Daytona Beach, talking baseball with a rugged, ruddy man of middle age, a manufacturer of fishing boats named Fred Merkle. There was no point in asking the obvious question, and out of courtesy it was not asked, but Merkle, near tears and acting as if under compulsion, brought the subject up himself.
> "You want to know about the play, I guess," he said.
> "No," was the reply. "What is there to say about the play?"
> "It was a terrible thing to have happen," he said.
> Then he left, for that evening he wanted to see a Florida State League game....
> The years might have torn his heart, but they had not destroyed his love for baseball.

Merkle died in 1956 at age 67 and was buried in an unmarked grave.

National League president Harry C. Pulliam has been often blamed for the chaotic situation that followed the infamous September 23, 1908, game, both at the time and since by several baseball historians. I disagree in that his rulings were consistent with his policy of backing his umpires against the claims of biased players, managers and owners. Pulliam's decision to back umpire Hank O'Day after the Merkle game brought him untold pressure and abuse from Brush and McGraw of the Giants and Murphy of the Cubs, as well as the New York press and Giants fans.

In addition, there is a theory among some baseball historians that Pulliam was gay. He was handsome, thirty-nine and unmarried. It was noted at the time that his name was never associated in a romantic way with any woman. Newsmen often described his colorful clothes in a way that, taken together over the years, has been interpreted as code for labeling him as a homosexual. After the Merkle play, one theory has it that the Giants, and perhaps the Cubs, attempted to blackmail him.

During the winter meetings of 1909, held in Chicago at what is now the Congress Plaza Hotel at Michigan and Congress, Pulliam wanted to address both the alleged bribery of the October 8 umpires and the Chicago scalping scandal. None of the magnates wanted to look into either issue and put intense pressure on Pulliam, including, perhaps, blackmail—threats of outing him, to put it in twenty-first century language. He at first refused to cave in but was visibly shaken. The owners sent for his brother and a "Louisville intimate" to help them stop Pulliam from pursuing his controversial agenda.

Out of the blue, Pulliam announced that he was to be married to a woman from St. Louis. He said he was leaving the meetings to take a train there right away and would then honeymoon in Hawaii. He left the hotel and got into a cab, which then turned and sped off in the opposite direction from the train station. Pulliam, being very familiar with Chicago, protested to the driver, who turned out to be George Dovey, owner of the Boston Doves, put up to the kidnapping attempt in order to keep Pulliam from going to St. Louis. Why? It has been speculated that the magnates, knowing that Pulliam was gay and that there was no real wedding in the works, wanted to keep him close at hand and under their control. However, several of the owners including Dovey and Dreyfuss genuinely liked Pulliam. They could have been trying to save him from himself. His behavior had been erratic for months as the pressure from the Giants and Cubs ate away at him.

Pulliam bolted from the cab, leaving his coat, hat and luggage behind. He ran through the streets during a cold Chicago February to Dearborn Station, arriving just in time to jump aboard the departing train.

The owners arranged for him to be met at the station in St. Louis and then secluded him in hotels, first in St. Louis and then Cincinnati. He eventually went to Nashville to live with his sister Grace Pulliam Cain to begin treatment and to recuperate from the breakdown. He was given a leave of absence by the magnates.

He returned to his duties as president of the National League in late June 1909. On July 28 he arrived at his office and began going through a stack of letters. At some point he stopped, dropped the papers to the floor and sat staring out the window. He eventually told his stenographer, Lenore Caylor, that he was going home for the day because he didn't feel well. He returned to his rooms at the New York Athletic Club. At 10:00 that evening a club attendant noticed that Pulliam's phone was off the hook. When he couldn't get a response on the line, he went up to Pulliam's residence on the third floor and found him shot through the head but still alive.

Harry Pulliam died early the next morning, his death ruled a suicide. When told of the tragedy, Giants manager John McGraw commented, "I didn't think a bullet in the head could hurt him." Every team in the league sent a representative to Pulliam's funeral except the Giants.

We follow the rest of the 2008 playoffs and the World Series. The Sox are eliminated in the first round, too, but at least they win a game. We congratulate our Pennsylvania neighbors and fellow-workers on the Phillies' world championship. Now they've won two in their long history, same as the Cubs.

Epilogue

On October 17, 2008, as we are about to leave the house to pick up Patricia at the Lancaster, Pennsylvania, Amtrak station, I stare into the closet for an extra moment. Normally I would grab my green zip-up jacket on such a cool fall day. But at this moment, in spite of the Cubs' horrible playoff disgrace, I defiantly pull out my bright blue Cub V-neck pullover jacket (nylon exterior, 100 percent polyester lining) featuring a cubby bear climbing out of a huge Cub "C."

Anne Lise and her boyfriend, Jeff, are visiting and come along to pick up Patricia. Pulling up in front of the station we see that there are no parking spots so we stop at the curb in an illegal space and ask Anne Lise and Jeff to go inside and meet Patricia at the platform entrance while we wait in the car.

It's a glorious day. The late afternoon autumn light glows with a subtle golden cast that makes the 80-year-old station look positively monumental. The red brick and classical pillars of the two-story structure stand out in high contrast and detailed relief.

We wait.

"BLING!"

What's that?

It's Lucy's cell phone announcing the arrival of a text message. Surprised, she flips it open and presses the button: "It's from Patricia. 'Dempster. Look for him.'"

"What?"

"Here," she hands the phone to me.

"Dempster!!! look for him!"

"She can't mean Ryan Dempster." I say.

Lancaster, Pennsylvania, train station with the 200,000-mile Accord parked at a bus stop. Who's on the train from Philadelphia? (photograph by the author).

"No," says Lucy. "No way. What would Ryan Dempster be doing on a train from Philadelphia to Lancaster, Pennsylvania?"

"Isn't he from Canada or the Pacific Northwest somewhere?"

"Yes."

I open the car door and step out onto the station's semi-circle approach driveway. Looking past the station, I see the train pulling in on the sunken tracks below us.

Patricia's story

I was riding Amtrak's Keystone train from Philadelphia to Lancaster, en route to York to spend the weekend at home, a break from classes at Temple University. Between dozing off and looking out the window I heard the voice of a small child two seats in front of me talking about whether he preferred train or airplane travel. His parents sounded genuinely interested and nice in their responses, and they asked him more questions. I didn't think too much more about it until just before arriving in Lancaster I overheard a woman across the aisle and ahead of me striking up a conversation with the family. She asked if they had been to Lancaster before, and the mother said that she had grown up in the area but hadn't been back in many years. The father said he had never been to this part of Pennsylvania.

Then the woman asked where the family lived, and they responded "Chicago," which perked up my ears. The woman asked if they liked it and they said they loved it, which made me happy. But again, I didn't think anything of it.

The train stopped and the father stood to gather the family's belongings. I was looking forward, in his direction, because I myself was preparing to get off the train. I noticed he was tall and had red sideburns; then I noticed he looked a lot like Ryan Dempster. I kind of pieced together the info that I had just heard and realized that he *was* in fact Ryan Dempster. He moved into the corridor of the car and I lost sight of him.

Back to the curb in front of the station

"BLING!"

I lean down and look into the driver side window. Lucy hands me her phone. "Ryan dempster on my train."

"What the...?"

Passengers file out the three entrance doors, looking for loved ones or heading to the parking lot. But no Patricia, no Anne Lise, no Jeff and no Ryan Dempster.

Anne Lise's story

Jeff and I went into the train station to wait for Trish while Dad and Mom waited in the car. People started flowing out of the arrivals stairwell. Jeff and I moved back through the double doors to get out of the way.

We noticed a small, hunched figure carrying a backpack, weaving her way manically through the crowd.

I thought, I hope that's not Trish. The person seemed totally crazed, darting here and there, bouncing on her toes, looking for who knows who or what.

But she looked too familiar and as she got closer, to our dismay, it was Trish.

I remember thinking we can't send her back to Temple.

Patricia's story

By the time I made it onto the platform Dempster and his little family were nowhere to be seen so I raced past the slowly disembarking passengers, ran up the stairs, and speed-walked through the terminal, half-looking for Dempster and half-looking for a family member I could share the news with. I did not see Dempster, but I saw Anne Lise and Jeff off in the distance so I made a beeline for them and explained, without saying hello, who was on my train. They didn't want to disbelieve, but with Dempster nowhere to be seen, I think they thought I was crazy.

Anne Lise's story

First words out of her mouth: "I was sitting two rows behind Ryan Dempster!"

It seemed an obscure enough person that she must be telling the truth, so we waited, and waited and waited.

Finally, just as we were convinced of Trish's insanity, out of the elevator pops Dempster with his wife and son, carrying their luggage. They and a station attendant were the only ones around.

The three of us stood at the end of the corridor shamelessly staring. We let him walk by, all of us too shy to say anything. He and his family stopped at the top of the stairs leading down to the station exit.

Patricia's story

Sure enough, once all the other passengers had passed through the terminal, and the station was left almost empty, a group emerged from the elevator and we watched as the indistinguishable figures made their way towards us. As they came closer and closer, Anne Lise and I knew that it was indeed Ryan Dempster (not easily recognizable in his unremarkable long-sleeve T-shirt and blue jeans. No Cub hat!) The Dempster family passed us where we sat on one of the high-backed wooden benches in the ticketing lobby, too nervous to say anything. We stood up to exit the station and gawked from behind him. Jeff said something to us like, "You're really not going to say something to him?"

Anne Lise's story

Dempster left his wife, kid and luggage at the top of the stairs and headed down. Jeff finally asked: "Are you Ryan Dempster?"

He looked a little surprised, but smiled and said yes.

Jeff introduced himself and, pointing to me and Trish, said, "These are life-long Cub fans." Jeff held back the urge to say: "Tough way to end the season, eh?"

Dempster seemed pleased and asked us if we lived in Pennsylvania. We told him we grew up in Chicago but some of us lived here now. We told him Trish was at Temple. He thought that was great and asked Trish about school. Super nice guy. Chatty. Obviously Canadian.

Back on the curb

The front of the station is now deserted. But I know they're in there and at least our daughters and Jeff have to emerge. I stand watching and waiting.

The doors open again and they exit the building—the four of them, looking like they've known each other forever, or at least ten minutes. Dempster turns to his right and sees the pulsing blue of my windbreaker, lit up like a neon beacon by the brilliant late afternoon sun, and smiles broadly. I walk over and extend my hand. He speaks first.

"Ryan Dempster."

"I, uh, recognized you. Nice to meet you."

"Nice to meet you."

Anne Lise, Patricia and Jeff stand nearby, none of us knowing exactly what to do or say next. Dempster (or, now that we've been properly introduced, should I call him Ryan?) glances around as if looking for something or someone.

"Can I help you? Need a lift or something?"

"I'm supposed to pick up a rental car," he says. "At Avis."

Well this ain't O'Hare, I think. No Avis office attached to this small town station.

"Where is it?"

"Mannheim Road," he says, pulling out his Blackberry.

Mannheim Road? Melrose Park?

Then it dawns on me. "You probably mean Mannheim Pike."

"That's it. They said it was about two miles from the station."

And there are no cabs in sight. Again, this is Lancaster, Pennsylvania.

"Uh, we can give you a ride."

"You sure?"

Not really, I think. We already have five in a five-seater, so we'll be breaking some kind of law. But it's RYAN DEMPSTER for God's sake!

"No problem. We'll squeeze four in the back. Right over here." I gesture at our Accord. Lucy is standing at the passenger side front seat with the door open, watching the whole thing.

Lucy's story

Trish, Anne Lise and Jeff headed over to the car and I hopped out to give Trish a hug. As they piled into the back, Anne Lise and Trish giggled shamelessly, acting girly. I was excited to see Trish but also wondered if maybe Pops would bring Dempster over to the car—after all, I'm a Cubs fan too. Then they both headed over and Dempster reached out, shook my hand and said "Ryan Dempster." I was completely charmed. He was big. He was cute. And he was Ryan Dempster! There was some confusion now as he started to get into the car—the front seat of the car—and I realized that I had to stuff into the back seat or I would be left standing at the curb. Turned out we were giving him a ride to a rent-a-car office on Mannheim Pike.

There were four of us in the back seat and the Sullivan girls were acting like total dweebs, poking each other and laughing, and ogling Dempster. Anne Lise and Patricia texted furiously. Meantime Pops was conversing with Dempster, congratulating him on a great season and asking him why he was in Lancaster. He told us that he and his wife were expecting a second child. I thought to myself—we must be the first to know! At some point, he pulled out his Blackberry, put in our address and said he would send a souvenir ball. He seemed like a genuinely nice guy.

Back on the curb

I'm wondering, whom do we leave behind?

Patricia's story

I hugged Mom hello and got into the car, thinking we would soon depart (probably after Dad got Dempster's autograph). But before I knew it, Mom was getting out of the front seat and being stuffed into the backseat that was already filled with Jeff, Anne Lise and me. Ryan Dempster was getting into the front seat of our car.

In the car

"I really appreciate this," he says.
"No problem. It's actually on our way."
We spend the first few minutes figuring out the address of the Avis office and checking the numbers on the businesses that line Mannheim Pike so we have an idea of how far we have to go.
Then I ask, "What brings you to Lancaster?"

He explains that during the season he promised his wife that when it was all over they would visit anywhere she wanted. She grew up in the area, so she asked that they come here. And he tells us that she and their young son are waiting back at the station for him to get the car and go back to pick them up. He also gives us the happy news that his wife is expecting their second child.

OH MY GOD! WE MUST BE THE FIRST TO KNOW! MAYBE EVEN BEFORE *VINELINE*!

"Are you from Pennsylvania?" he asks.

"No. We're from Chicago."

"Why are you here?"

"Job."

He nods.

"But," I add, "it's actually pretty convenient for Cub games. We go to see you in Philadelphia, Washington, D.C., and Pittsburgh a lot."

"Really?" he says, genuinely interested.

"Yeah. We're part of that Cub nation you hear about, cheering for you guys no matter where we have to go. Cincinnati. Miami. We were at the game in Shea Stadium when Marquis hit his grand slam."

Dempster laughs. "Oh yeah. Before that game, me and DeRosa were standing outside the hotel."

DeRosa? I think. He knows Mark DeRosa!? Then reality sets in. Of course he knows Mark DeRosa. I am a dufus.

"And this guy recognizes us and tells us how he used to play with Marquis on Staten Island. And back then Marquis used to hit the long ball a lot."

I tell him about Steve and I chatting, sitting in our nosebleed Shea Stadium seats, discussing how Marquis had some pop in his bat and then there it goes, us watching the arc of his big blow to right field. Dempster enjoys the story.

I look back at Lucy, Anne Lise, Patricia and Jeff in the rear view mirror. They have four of the biggest

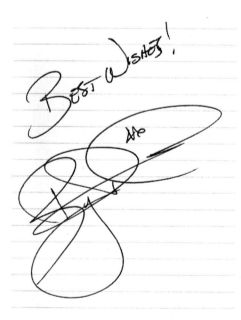

Ryan Dempster's autograph, Lancaster, Pennsylvania, October 17, 2008.

shit-eatin' grins in the world pasted across the entire width of the back seat. All giggly and jostling each other as if we had just picked up George Harrison, may he rest in peace.

"It was a great season," I say. The elephant in the car is Game One of the playoffs against the Dodgers. A bazillion walks. A grand slam. But I can't bring it up. "It was great to watch. As a fan. The way you went from being the closer to being the top starter in the rotation. One of the best in the league."

"I enjoyed being the closer," he says. "But I think of myself as a starter, so I liked getting back to that."

He pulls out his Blackberry again. "Let me get your address. I appreciate the help. I'll send you an autographed ball, or something like that."

I give him our address and then think, "WE ARE IN RYAN DEMPSTER'S BLACKBERRY!"

We arrive at the Avis office and as he steps out of the car he shakes hands with each of us.

"Good luck," we say. "And congratulations again on your second child."

"Thanks," he says.

"And we're ready for spring training."

He smiles. "The break is nice, though."

And he's gone. In the office. Signing papers or whatever. Lucy gets back into the front seat. We text Jeanne and Steve and tell our story.

Steve's reply: "You should have made him walk. Like he walked all those Dodgers."

Lucy's story

I was disgusted and bitter at the end of the 2008 Cubs season. Not that I was surprised—it was expected—but for the Cubs to humiliate themselves so profoundly after having the best record in baseball for most of the season—it was hard to take. The 2003 season had ended in disaster, too, but everything that happened up to the Bartman game had been pure gravy. We had no expectations for the Cubs and there they were in a pennant race. As horrible as it was, and even though I knew then that the curse was real, I also knew that we were going to spring training. After the playoffs of 2008 I just wanted to forget that the Cubs existed.

There's still the curse. The Cubs stink. Dempster was a bum in the playoffs. But after meeting him in Lancaster, everything changed. Or maybe became the same as ever again. We can't wait for spring training.

Resources and
Further Reading

Acocella, Nicholas, and Donald Dewey. *The Black Prince of Baseball: Hal Chase and the Mythology of the Game.* Toronto, Ontario, Canada: SPORTClassic Books, 2004.

Alexander, Charles C. *John McGraw.* Lincoln: University of Nebraska Press, Bison Books, 1995.

Allen, Lee. *The National League Story: The Official History.* New York: Hill and Wang, 1961.

Anderson, David W. *More Than Merkle: A History of the Best and Most Exciting Baseball Season in Human History.* Lincoln: University of Nebraska Press, 2000.

Bundy, Chris. *West Baden Springs: Legacy of Dreams.* 4th ed. Self-published: N.d.

Carmichael, John P. *My Greatest Day in Baseball.* Lincoln: University of Nebraska Press, 1945, 1973.

Cicotello, David, and Angelo J. Louisa, eds. *Forbes Field: Essays and Memories of the Pirates' Historic Ballpark, 1909–1971.* Jefferson, NC: McFarland, 2007.

Deford, Frank. *The Old Ball Game: How John McGraw, Christy Mathewson and the New York Giants Created Modern Baseball.* New York: Atlantic Monthly, 2005.

Evers, John J., and Hugh S. Fullerton. *Touching Second.* Jefferson, NC: McFarland, 2005.

Fleming, G.H. *The Unforgettable Season.* New York: Penguin, 1982.

Freedman, Lew. *Cubs Essential: Everything You Need to Know to Be a Real Fan.* Chicago: Triumph, 2006.

Golenbock, Peter. *Wrigleyville: A Magical History Tour of the Chicago Cubs.* New York: St. Martin's Griffin, 1999.

Green, David. *101 Reasons to Love the Cubs.* New York: Stewart, Tabori and Chang, 2006.

Kaduk, Kevin. *Wrigleyworld: A Season in Baseball's Best Neighborhood.* New York: New American Library, 2006.

Lindberg, Richard. *Total White Sox: The Definitive Encyclopedia of the World Champion Franchise.* Chicago: Triumph, 2006.

Lund, John. *1908: A Look at the World Champion 1908 Cubs.* Self-published: N.d.

Matthews, George R. *When the Cubs Won It All.* Jefferson, NC: McFarland, 2009.

Murphy, Cait. *Crazy '08: How a Cast of Cranks, Rogues, Boneheads, and Magnates Created the Greatest Year in Baseball History.* New York: Smithsonian Books, 2008.

Muskat, Carrie, comp. *Banks to Sandberg to Grace: Five Decades of Love and Frustration with the Chicago Cubs.* Chicago: Contemporary, 2001.

Myers, Doug. *Essential Cubs: Chicago Cubs Facts, Feats, and Firsts—From the Batter's Box to the Bullpen to the Bleachers.* Chicago: Contemporary, 1999.

Rasenberger, Jim. *America 1908: The Dawn of Flight, the Race to the Pole, the Invention of the Model T, and the Making of a Modern Nation.* New York: Scribner, 2007.

Seymour, Harold. *Baseball: The Golden Age.* New York: Oxford University Press, 1971.

Strasberg, Andy, Bob Thompson, and Tim Wiles. *Baseball's Greatest Hit: The Story of Take Me Out to the Ball Game.* New York: Hal Leonard Books, 2008.

Thomson, Cindy, and Scott Brown. *Three Finger: The Mordecai Brown Story.* Lincoln: University of Nebraska Press, 2006.

Weisberger, Bernard A. *When Chicago Ruled Baseball: The Cubs–White Sox World Series of 1906.* New York: William Morrow, 2006.

Websites

Google any subject, name or event described in this work and you will find thousands of links for each. I found the following sites helpful. Many are baseball sites, sports sites or media sites, and others are general interest sites or personal blogs. If I neglected to list a site that may prove useful to the reader, I apologize. The Web addresses give a pretty clear idea of the content of each site. Where I thought further explanation could help, I added such in parentheses.

answers.yahoo.com
associatedcontent.com
ballparks.com
baseball-almanac.com
baseballasamerica.org
baseball-fever.com
baseballisms.com
baseball-reference.com
baseball-statistics.com
baseball1.com (Baseball Archive)
bc3200.com (Way Out in Left Field Society)
bleedcubbieblue.com
blogs.chicagosports.chicagotribune.com
cbs2chicago.com
chicago.cubs.mlb.com
chicago.whitesox.mlb.com
chicagotribune.com
comcast.net
en.wikipedia.org
entertainment.howstuffworks.com
florida.marlins.mlb.com
flickr.com (photo sharing)
goatriders.org (Goat Riders of the Apocalypse—Cubs blog)

hardballtimes.com
justonebadcentury.com
lavieenrobe.typepad.com (entertainment blog)
losangeles.dodgers.mlb.com
mistupid.com ("The Online Knowledge Magazine")
mlb.com
msn.com
npr.org (National Public Radio)
sabr.org (The Society for American Baseball Research)
sports.espn.go.com
sportsecyclopedia.com
sportsillustrated.cnn.com
sportsyenta.blogspot.com
suntimes.com (*Chicago Sun Times*)
time.com
tnjn.com (University of Tennessee School of Journalism)
washingtonpost.com
waxpaperbeercup.com
youtube.com

Index

Numbers in *bold italics* indicate pages with photographs.

185